gettyimages

The French Millennium

1,000 Remarkable Years of Incident and Achievement

gettyimages

The French Millennium

1,000 Remarkable Years of Incident and Achievement

Nick Yapp

KÖNEMANN

Frontispiece: One of the many gargoyles adorning the Cathedral of Nôtre-Dame, a chimera imposes its timeless gaze upon the Ile de la Cité.

First published in 2001 by Könemann Verlagsgesellschaft mbH,
Bonner Strasse 126, D-50968 Köln

This book was produced by Getty Images
Unique House, 21–31 Woodfield Road, London W9 2BA

Design: Mick Hodson and Alan Price
Project manager and editor: Richard Collins
Picture editor: Jacquelene Connelly
Copy editor: Christine Collins
Proof reader and indexer: Liz Ihre
Editorial assistance: Tom Worsley, Gill Hodson, Joëlle Ferly
Scanning: Antonia Hille, Dave Roling, Mark Thompson
Special thanks: Michael Scuffil

Publishing director: Peter Feierabend

Typesetting by Mick Hodson Associates
Colour separation by AtColor srl
Printed and bound by Star Standard Industries Ltd
Printed in Singapore
ISBN 3-8290-6012-2
10 9 8 7 6 5 4 3 2 1

Based on an original idea and concept by Ludwig Könemann

CONTENTS

GENERAL INTRODUCTION

France, mother of arts, of arms, and of laws...
(*France, mère des arts, des armes, et des lois...*)
Joachim du Bellay, French poet, 1522–1560

Order and beauty have been the great gifts of France to the world. The first was the legacy of the Napoléonic age, sudden and overwhelming. The second was bestowed gradually – a series of gifts, each exquisitely fashioned, with the sum amounting to the richest treasure trove on earth. Napoléon harnessed the energy of the Revolution of 1789 and wrought structure from its chaos, laying the foundations of the modern state. Generations of men and women added their contributions to French grace and style to make life worth living.

There have been mistakes along the way. France has had more than the normal share of obsessions – with military glory, with religious conformity, with misplaced and misused opulence. And in each case France has paid a heavy penalty. But the madness has passed and the essential inspirational creativity of the French has triumphed. The rest of the world may know little of the carnage at Sedan on 1 September 1870, or the horrors of St Bartholomew's Eve in 1572, or the miseries endured within the walls of many a beautiful château. What the rest of the world does know, however, and delights in, is the part played by French books and paintings, dishes and wines, dresses and perfumes, music and films, to enrich the culture of the entire planet.

No other country has so perfected a national way of life. The images of France have more seductive power than a vision of heaven. There are the pavement cafés bathed in sunshine, graced by the smart and discerning; a thousand villages whose piecemeal growth has resulted in a charming hotchpotch of the grand and humble beyond the contrivance of any town-planner; menus to make the replete salivate; market-places bursting with colours that only the palette of a French artist could match.

Every country claims its golden ages. 'Now' has always been a contender in France, a parade of golden ages from Charlemagne to the present day. The dreamer may take his or her pick – chivalry in the 13th century; romance two hundred years later; the Court at Versailles in the 1700s; Voltaire and Rousseau and a dozen others in the 18th century; the *Belle Epoque*; wit and beauty in the 1920s; the excitement of the 1990s. You pay your franc and take your pick, but there is no need to hurry – there will undoubtedly be another French golden age very soon.

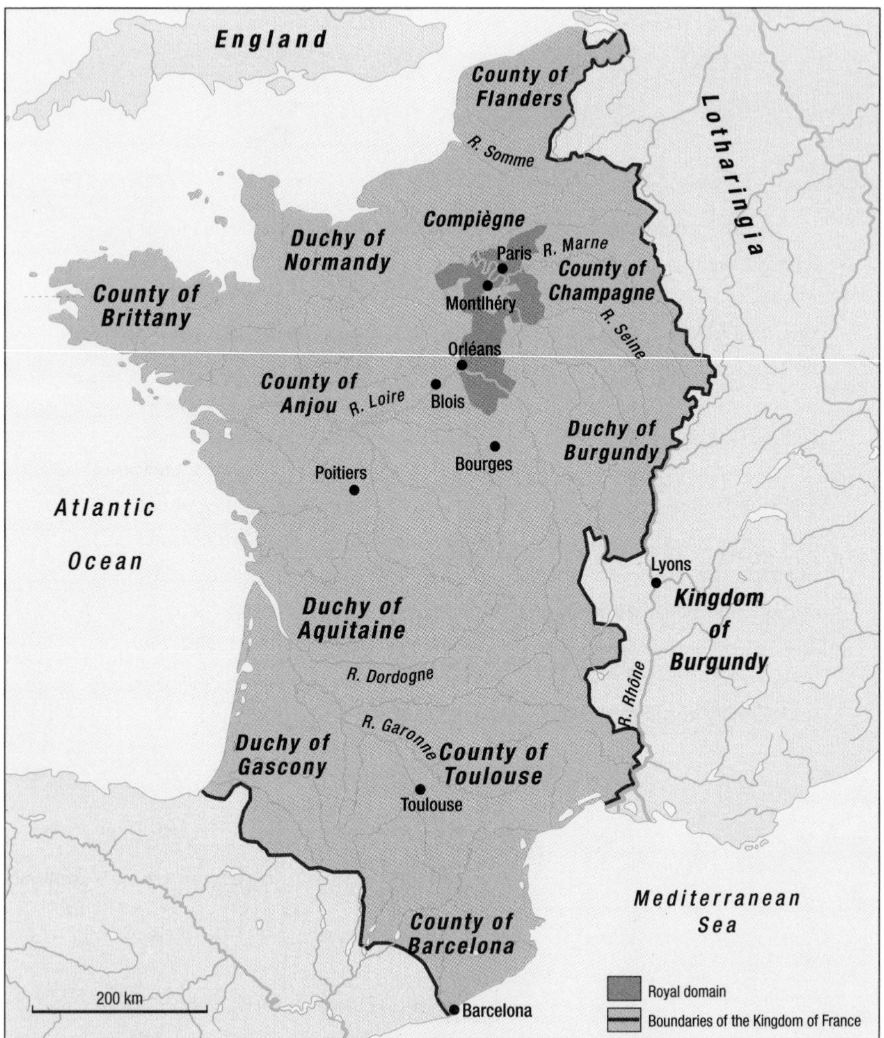

Map 1 France at the Beginning of the 11th Century

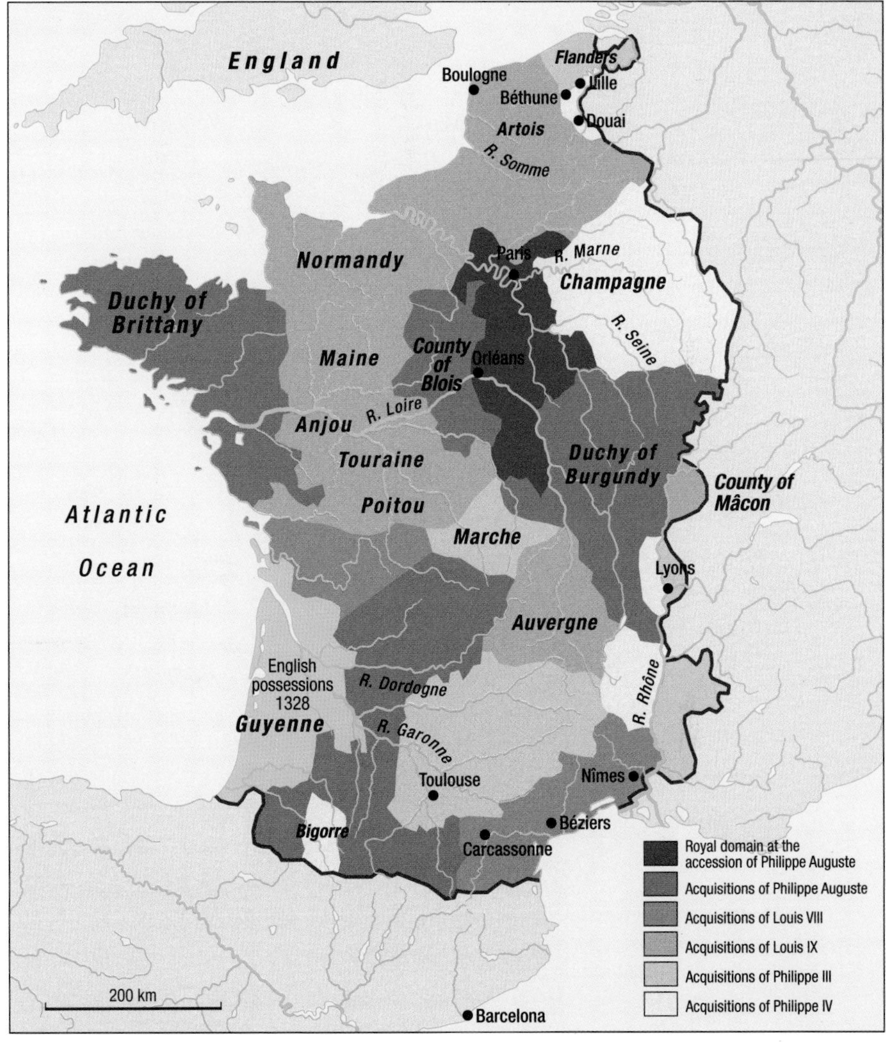

Map 2 Expansion of the Royal Domain under the Capetians, 1180–1314

Map 3 English Lands in France before 1327

Map 4 France in 1429

Map 5 France at the Death of Louis XI, 1483

Map 6 Regional Areas of Administration in 16th-Century France

Map 7 Pre-Revolutionary France

Map 8 Napoléon's Empire in 1812

Map 9 The Spread of Railways in France, 1848–1860

Map 10 The *Départements* of France, 2000

Introduction to Period 1 – 1000–1515

The Treaty of Verdun in 843 created the Kingdom of France, for the treaty established a territory known as Western Francia. To the east of this new land lay Lotharingia – an area that contained much of modern Belgium, north-west Italy and eastern France. To the west lay the Atlantic Ocean and the separate land of Brittany. To the south were the Pyrénées and the Mediterranean.

It was by no means an integrated country. Most of the population pledged allegiance and owed service to their local lord, and thought little and seldom of king or emperor, since neither was likely to defend them from attack by an aggressive neighbour. But the castles and keeps that were built by the lords to protect their local population could also be used as bases from which to control that same population. This pattern of social control in the early Middle Ages prepared the ground for the later suffering and subjugation that played its part in the Revolution of 1789.

Most people had other worries on their minds at the start of the 11th century. More than any other nation, France has always been concerned about birthrate and the rise and fall of population, and the Middle Ages was a time when this was literally a matter of life and death. Population growth meant there were more people to work the land, and this meant increased production. The population of France around the year 1000 was between 5 and 6 million. Three hundred years later, it had reached 18 million. Between the 9th and 13th centuries cereal yields doubled overall, though some areas were far more fertile than others. The wheat fields in the basin of the Seine, north of Paris, yielded over three times as much per unit area as those in eastern France.

More labour also meant that more forests were cut down, more marshes were drained, more terraces were cut out of the hillsides – more land was cultivated. The framework of modern France was erected between the years 1000 and 1250, with some 35,000 communities scattered across the countryside. It was a time of comparative peace. There were fewer Viking raids in the north, and fewer Saracen invasions in the south. Internal trade increased, with towns developing at the crossroads of the major trading routes along which trains of pack animals plodded with their cargoes of wine, wool and salt. The greatest of all was Paris, with 200,000 inhabitants, far and away the biggest city in all Europe, but this was also the period when Marseilles, Arras, Rouen, Orléans, Lille, La Rochelle, Bordeaux and Bayonne became rich and important.

But it was a stuttering advance. Three regular visitors ravaged any area they came to – war, famine and pestilence. War was often unexpected. Communication was poor, and an invading army could sweep down on an isolated community with little warning. Famine, on the other hand, was heralded by a wet summer (which destroyed many cereal harvests), a cold spring (which killed vines and restricted germination of seeds), or a drought (which reduced the yield of hay from pastures and led to subsequent loss of livestock). The years 1309 to 1311 and 1315 to 1317 were especially hard, for they amounted to a mini Ice Age in much of Western Europe. A poor harvest meant poor health, and a correspondingly high mortality rate the following winter.

A generation later, in the late 1340s, came the worst visitation of all – the Black Death. Over the next one hundred years, between 30 and 50 per cent of French men, women and children died of bubonic plague. Not until the very end of the 16th century did the population of France again reach 18 million. And the plague was not the only disease to destroy whole communities. Few parts of medieval France escaped regular outbreaks of typhus, dysentery, smallpox, and even malaria.

Little wonder that, for centuries, the French peasant tended to be guarded and inward-looking, hardly seeing beyond his own needs and those of the household, human and animal. At its best, this insularity manifested itself in pride in farm or village, a strong sense of community, and the development of 'neighbourliness'. At its worst, it appeared as bitter and hostile isolationism. The 12th-century *Geste de Garin de Lorrain* described a typical French peasant as a man with 'enormous arms, huge limbs, eyes a hand's breadth apart, broad shoulders, an enormous chest, bristling hair and a face as black as coal'. It was said such a man went six months without washing, and that the only water that ever touched his face was the rain.

The wonder is that medieval France produced such riches, so much talent, and such jewels of human creation. Architecturally this was the age of the great monasteries at Fontenay and Vézelay, Saint-Denis in Paris, and Clairvaux in Burgundy.

Even more spectacular were the cathedrals at Rouen, Orléans and Troyes. Chartres Cathedral was the broadest and tallest ever seen in western Christendom, and an inspiration to the entire continent, where a new Gothic cathedral was completed every year for the next one hundred and fifty years.

In literature, France produced the *Roman du Roi*, the *Chanson de Roland,* the *Sic et Non* of Peter Abélard, Andreas Capellanus's *Art of Love,* William the Breton's 10,000-line poem *Phillipside* and Jean de Meung's *Roman de la Rose.* French cartographers were responsible for the Mappa Mundi and the *Liber Floridus.* Early French technology developed the crossbow, the tidal mill, the broad-wheeled plough and the deep plough, the flying buttress, the water-powered saw, hand-warmers, the military catapult, and the first public clock.

French accountants invented a system of mechanical accounting that had no need for the abacus or the chequerboard. The citizens of Toulouse set up the *Société de Bazacle*, a mill-owning company reckoned to have been the oldest capitalist venture in the world – until nationalised by Electricité de France (EDF) in the mid-20th century. The first recorded strike took place in the 12th century, when French masons working on the church of a monastery at Obazine threw down their tools because the abbot (a vegetarian) had thrown away a pig they had killed and were looking forward to eating.

All in all, it was a lively time.

1
WORKERS, WARRIORS AND WORSHIPPERS 1000–1100

Early French castles were crude in design and constructed of earth and wood (*right*). They could be built with the simplest of tools, and at considerable speed. According to the *Chronicle* of the Counts of Angoulême, seven hundred labourers (the entire workforce at the counts' disposal) completed a castle in just three days. For all this, castles were strongholds against attack by bands of thieves, marauders and even errant knights. If a rival lord wished to destroy a castle in the 11th century, he would need to call on the services of local villagers who would use the same simple tools with which they built the castle to undermine it.

Introduction

For the first hundred years of the new millennium, the most powerful institutions in France were the monasteries. They were the repositories of holy relics, the final resting-places of saints, and the centres of healing and curing. Foremost among them at this time was Cluny Abbey, consecrated by Pope Urban II on 25 October 1095. It was the most ambitious piece of ecclesiastical architecture in the Western world, and had taken seven years to build since its inauguration by Saint-Hugues.

Less noble, but more practical, were the scores of motte-and-bailey castles that covered much of eastern and northern France. Each was a simple structure – a mound and a palisade – and could be built by fifty labourers within a single month. So rapid was their completion that in 1091 a law was passed in Normandy limiting their size and number: '... the digging of ditches with the aid of a ladder is prohibited, as is the construction of more than a single palisade... There must not be a circular walk around it, nor angles created along its course; the fortification of a rocky outcrop or island is forbidden in all circumstances.'

As the nation settled to less anarchic times, art and literature were served by William Wace's history of the Dukes of Normandy (*Le Roman du Roi*), by the Roda Bible of 1030 to 1060, the Mappa Mundi of 1050 to 1072, and by the love poetry of Philippe I, said to be the earliest that has survived in the French language.

Much of the century was taken up with attempts to codify the relationship between spiritual and temporal power, and in particular to place some religious embargo on warfare. The Truce of God movement of 1027 attempted to ban fighting during Lent and Advent, and on Sundays. This had little effect on William the Conqueror's rapid and successful invasion of England, or the First Crusade, summoned by Pope Urban in 1095. William's exploit established England as the power that was to be France's most persistent enemy over the next four hundred years, and was celebrated in the magnificent Bayeux Tapestry. There was little to celebrate in the First Crusade beyond the establishment of a perilous European presence in the Holy Land.

The attitude adopted when praying changed from one of superstitious amazement with the hands widespread to one of pious reverence with the hands placed together, and over half the knights of France went on Crusade, bringing back with them biscuits (a form of twice-baked bread), and an early forerunner of tennis.

Charlemagne (*opposite*), Emperor of the West, King of the Franks, lived from 742 to 814. He was the founder of France, though his vast empire stretched from the Ebro to the Elbe. In 800 he marched on Rome in support of Pope Leo III, and there he was crowned Emperor of the Romans. The Carolingian dynasty founded by Charlemagne lasted until the death of Louis V in 987. Louis was succeeded by Hugues Capet (*right*), whose own dynasty was to last another three hundred and fifty years.

Philippe I (*above*) had one of the longest and sorriest reigns in French history. He was only eight years old when his father died and he ascended the throne. Many historians have seen him as a wastrel and pleasure-seeker, 'wallowing in the pleasures of bed and table'. His reign did indeed mark a low point in the prestige of the Capetian monarchy, and he is chiefly remembered today for his elopement with Betrada, wife of Fulk Rechin, Comte d' Anjou. Although this move led to Philippe's excommunication, it was in some ways politically astute, for Betrada was related to the rich and powerful Dukes of Normandy – and, anyway, Fulk did not seem to mind.

A panorama in classical style, celebrating three kings of France (*above*). On the left is Robert II (Robert the Pious), King of Western Francia at the turn of the millennium. In the centre is Robert's son Henri I, who was told on his accession 'you are king and emperor by virtue of your ancestors' – for it was believed that the French royal line was descended from King Priam of Troy. On the right is Philippe I, Henri's son. When he died in 1108, Philippe left most of the territory he had gained to his eldest son, thus affirming the Capetian practice of primogeniture.

Henri I (*opposite*) unwisely gave the rich lands of Normandy and Burgundy to his brother Robert, thus creating a powerful rival to his authority in France. He spent most of his reign regretting what he had done. (*Left*) The many crowns of France. The oldest are in the top row (left and centre) and the small circlet (number 4), dating from the 6th century. Numbers 3, 6, 7, 9, 11 and 15 are from the 7th century. Numbers 5, 8, 10, 14 and 16 come from the 9th century. Numbers 12 and 13 are from the 10th and 11th centuries.

Lith de Delpech à Paris.

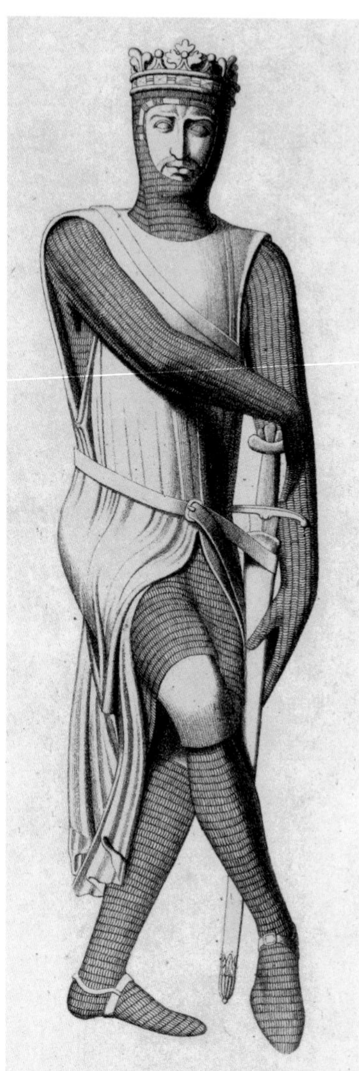

Robert of Normandy (*left*) was known as Robert the Magnificent. He was one of the sons of William the Conqueror, and brother to William Rufus and Henry I (both kings of England). Norman chroniclers, such as Robert Wace, portray Robert as a rich and generous man, though his gifts of widows, orphans and wealthy heiresses to his followers may seem heartless to modern minds. (*Opposite*) Robert of Normandy pays court to Lady Sibylla.

TIMELINES

MONARCHY		MUSIC, ART AND FILM	WAR AND POLITICS	TRANSPORT	SCIENCE AND TECHNOLOGY	LITERATURE	ARCHITECTURE	
CAPETIAN DYNASTY	1000	The making of the Bayeux Tapestry					Mont-Saint-Michel	1000
Robert II the Pious **996-1031**			The Truce of God movement				Saint-Hugues and Cluny Abbey	
						The Roda Bible	Church of Saint-Bénigne, Dijon	
					Quarrying and export of Caen stone		Monastery at Fontenay Saint-Père, Vézelay	
			City of Mons and self-government			Mappa Mundi	Notre-Dame and the Portal of Sainte-Anne	
			Peter the Hermit					
			First Crusade and Pope Urban's call to arms				Saint-Savin-sur Gartempe, Vienne	
	1025		Godefrey de Bouillon and the Kingdom of Jerusalem		Biscuits		Notre-Dame La-Grande	
		Renier of Huy			Wine making		Sainte-Radegonde, Talmont	1100
Henri I **1031-60**		*Chanson de Roland*	The feudal system		Tanning and rope making industries			
		Liber Floridus			The crossbow	Liber Floridus	Gisors Castle	
		Enamelled grave plate of Count Geoffrey of Anjou	Second Crusade		Mechanical accounting	Pierre Abélard and *Sic et Non*		
			Paris established as French capital		Land reclamation at Citeaux and the dike system		Abbé Suger and the rebuilding of the church of Saint-Denis, Paris	
			Henri of Anjou becomes Henry II of England		Tidal mills on Adour near Bayonne	Wace's history of the Dukes of Normandy - *Le Roman du Roi*		
					Windmills pioneered in Normandy		Laon Cathedral	
			Third Crusade			Chrétien de Troyes and *Lancelot*	Chartres Cathedral	
					Watermills in Picardy	*The Art of Love* by Andreas Capellanus	Philippe II builds wall around Paris	
			First Hundred Years' War				Château-Gaillard	12

1650 — 1700 — 1750 — 1789

1225 — 1250 — 1275

Louis VIII **1223-26**

Louis IX (Saint Louis) **1226-70**

Philippe III, the Bold **1270-85**

Claude Lorrain

Nicolas Poussin

Opening of Académie Royale de Peinture et de Sculpture

Pierre Mignard

Charles Le Brun

Philippe de Champaigne

Jean-Baptiste Lully

André Campra

Jean Jouvenet

Hyacinthe Rigaud

Antoine Watteau

Jean-Baptiste Siméon Chardin

Jean Philippe Rameau

François Boucher

Pierre-Alexandre Monsigny

Andre Grétry

---

and Normandy

Cardinal Richelieu, the power behind the throne

Va nu-pieds rising in Normandy

Canada becomes a province of New France

Colony founded in Louisiana

Protestant Camisard rebels

Massive increase in size of French navy

Invasion of Corsica

Corsica given to the French by Genoa

Alliance with Americans in the War of Independence

Political pamphlets and the end of censorship

LES VOYAGES DE LA NOUVELLE FRANCE OCCIDENTALE, DICTE CANADA, FAITS PAR LE Sr DE CHAMPLAIN

Montgolfier brothers and ballooning

Blaise Pascal

Academy of Science

Denis Papin

French surgery considered to be the finest in Europe

Harvesting and the rural economy

Bread, baguettes and baking

Rolling mills

The great wine producing châteaux

La Gazette

Pierre Corneille

Charles Sorel

Seigneur de Saint-Évremond

Jean-Baptiste Poquelin de Molière and *Tartuffe*

Jean Racine

La Rochefoucauld

La Bruyère

La Fontaine

Charles Parrault

Abbé Prévost

Claude-Adrien Helvétius

Jean-Jacques Rousseau and the *Social Contract*

Voltaire

Literary salons

Denis Diderot

Declaration of the Rights of Man

Fontainebleau

Le Pont Neuf

Place des Vosges, Paris

Vaux-le-Vicomte, Paris

Hôtel Lambert, Paris

Val-de-Grâce, Paris

Palais de Versailles

Academy of Architecture

Les Invalides

Canal du Midi

The Louvre rebuilt

Jules Hardouin-Mansart

Collège des Quatres Nations, Paris

The Bastille

Place Royale, Nancy

Grand Théâtre, Bordeaux

Queen's House, Versailles

Rebuilding of Rennes

Peter of Amiens (*left*), better known as Peter the Hermit, was a monk and a soldier who served as chief recruiting officer for Urban II's Crusade of 1095. Urban was a French pope – he had been born at Châtillon-sur-Marne. He became pope in 1088, and used his considerable powers of persuasion and eloquence to launch the First Crusade at Clermont in France (*opposite*). He was also the pope who excommunicated Philippe I.

Peter the Hermit's own powers as a preacher helped him raise an army of 20,000 peasants (*left*). He marched at their head to Asia Minor, where his ill-armed and untrained troops were annihilated by the Turks at the Battle of Nicaea. Peter then joined the 'army of princes' and took part in the siege of Antioch. He lost heart, however, and began the long journey home. He had not gone far before he was arrested, taken back to the army of princes and given a public reprimand. Peter lived for another eighteen years, devoting himself to less belligerent good works, among them the founding of the monastery of Neufmoutier, near Liège, Belgium.

Bohemond the Crusader, Prince of Antioch, was an impressive figure in the late 11th century. 'He was so tall in stature that he overtopped the tallest by nearly one cubit, narrow in the waist and loins, with broad shoulders and a deep chest and powerful arms...' – Anna Comena. '...by his nostrils, nature had given free passage for the high spirits which bubbled up from his heart...' Anna Comena was less happy with Bohemond's nature: '...in the whole of his body the entire man showed implacable and savage both in his size and glance, methinks, and even his laughter sounded like snorting...' (*Above*) The marriage of Bohemond and Constance of France, c. 1090.

Four contemporary scenes from the First Crusade – all to be found in the painted windows of the Abbey of Saint-Denis. (*Top, left*) Crusading knights charge the Turks early in the Crusade. 'Lords, and valiant soldiers of Christ,' roared Bohemond, 'here we are confronted on all sides by a difficult battle...' (*Above, left*) Crusaders storm the city of Antioch. (*Top, right*) A further battle scene between Turks and Crusaders. (*Above, right*) Siege engines are used in the final assault on Jerusalem.

(*Above*) The Battle of Antioch. The science of castle-building was considerably more advanced in the Holy Land. 'The next day [7 March 1098], at dawn, some Turks went forth from the city and collected all the fetid corpses of the Turkish dead...and buried them at the mosque beyond the bridge...Our men ordered the tombs to be dug up and broken...they threw all the corpses into a ditch and carried the severed heads to our tents...'– from the account of the siege of Antioch in an anonymous *Histoire de la première croisade.* (*Opposite*) Catapults are brought into action during the siege of Antioch.

(*Opposite*) Eudes I, Duc de Bourgogne, and one of the boldest fighters during the First Crusade. The French contribution was immense in terms of money and men. The flower of French nobility travelled to the Levant to 'free' the Holy Land from heathen rule. (*Above*) The 'prudent' Tancred leads his men in the capture of Bethlehem, 6 June 1099, after which they murdered almost every inhabitant. Tancred was Bohemond's nephew. After the Crusade, he stayed in the Levant as regent of Antioch.

By the end of the 11th century, towns were ceasing to be merely the focal point for the local rural community – places where goods were exchanged and administration was effected. The increasing wealth of towns gave them a life of their own. They became places of business – money-lending, the buying and selling of land, the organisation of trades. With the new wealth came new display, new grandeur. (*Left*) The splendid Hôtel de Ville (town hall) of Mons, then in the north-east of France.

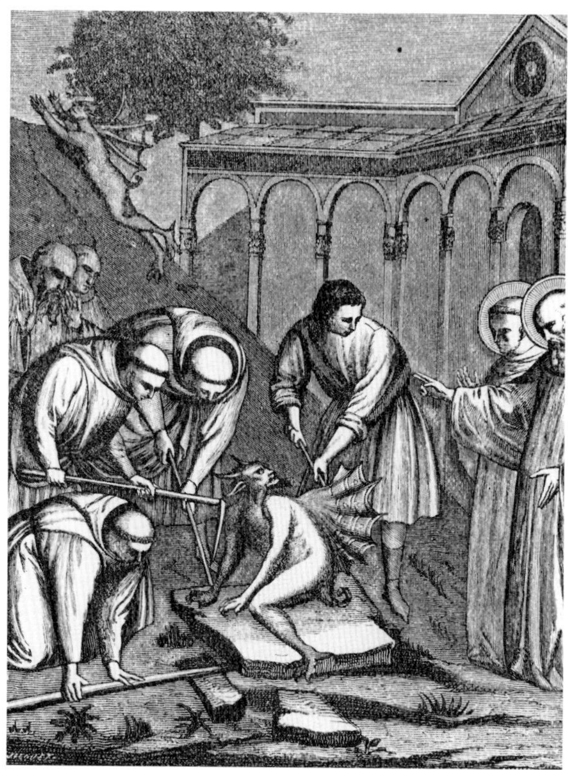

Benedict of Nursia, c. 480–547 (*above, right*), was the founder of the monastic order in Italy that bore his name. Considered to be the father of Western monasticism, he believed that only by seclusion and religious exercise could one escape evil. Later, however, he instructed his monks to add teaching to their tasks of manual and academic labour. (*Above, left*) Building work on Benedict's chapel at Nursia is interrupted by an obstinate devil who sits on the stone. Benedict is about to remove the devil by blessing the stone.

(*Above, left and right*) Two medieval images of Benedictine monks. In France reform of the Benedictine order had long been called for, and changes were accomplished in the late 11th century. Benedictines lived a purer life than other members of the clergy, and held themselves superior to the rest of mankind. Abbot Abbon of Fleury-sur-Loire placed monks at the summit of the earthly hierarchy in the treatise he wrote for the King of the Franks.

(*Opposite*) The magnificent nave of the church of Saint-Savin-sur-Gartempe, Vienne, constructed in the second half of the 11th century. (*Above*) Faces and scarlet leaves on the stained glass at Cluny Abbey. At a time when monasteries were the most powerful institutions in the whole of France, Cluny stood supreme in its magnificence and splendour.

The extraordinary achievement of William of Normandy in conquering England was celebrated in an extraordinary way. The Bayeux Tapestry is a 230-foot long pictorial representation of the events leading up to the Battle of Hastings, the battle itself, the death of Harold and William's triumph.

(*Opposite, above left*) A battle waggon of the late 11th century. (*Opposite, below left*) The death of the Saxon king, Edward the Confessor. Three scenes from the Bayeux Tapestry: (*left, from the top*), the Battle of Hastings – a group of Norman knights on horseback prepare to charge the hill occupied by the Saxons; William receives news of the death of Edward the Confessor and Harold's claim to the English throne; a hawking party sets out to hunt. The tapestry is more than a record of warfare. It is a portrait of the age, rich in its details of everyday life – how people dressed, farmed, built their boats and houses, and how they spent their leisure time.

Two 11th-century images showing a woman (*left*) and a man (*opposite*) carrying biscuits. The figures almost certainly celebrate the charitable natures of the pair, but are interesting for another reason. Biscuits first came to Western Europe at the very end of the 11th century. They were brought back by returning Crusaders, probably knights, but possibly the surviving remnants of Peter the Hermit's peasant army – those that escaped the slaughter at Nicaea.

The great advantage of biscuits was that, having been baked twice, they were hard and dry and, unlike ordinary bread, did not go mouldy. Biscuits were only one of a number of exotic imports from Asia Minor. The Crusaders also brought back with them leopards, parrots, bears and camels; cinnamon, saffron and sugar, cardamom, cloves and pepper; fine silks, damasks and thin cottons; the public bath-house; windmills; Greek fire; tennis; and the stern rudder on ships.

2
THE HEART OF FRANCE 1100–1150

The great age of cathedral building in France began with the reign of Louis VII in the 12th century. The new style of architecture, described as 'Gothic' today, was called by contemporaries *opus francigenum* – 'work in the French style'. An older, plainer church once stood on the site of Notre-Dame in Paris, but the new building (*left*) surpassed all that had gone before. It was a magnificent edifice, sumptuously decorated with stained glass, carvings, paintings and all the embellishments of the new Gothic style.

Introduction

No country in Europe could match France for industry and invention in the early 12th century. Peter Abélard led Europe along the path of formal and philosophical logic. Thierry de Chartres made the first bold attempt to explain the universe in terms of natural causes. Abbé Suger, Abbot of Saint-Denis in Paris from 1122, wrote his *Life of Louis VI* and presided over the building of the first cathedral in the Gothic style, a glorious creation coated with gold and jewels – but much derided by Bernard of Clairvaux from his newly-founded abbey some 250 miles away.

The vast forests of northern France fell to the axes of sweating woodsmen, supplying timber to make vats for brewing and casks for wine storage, for shipbuilding, for the frames of looms, and for fuel itself. Bark was stripped from the trees for the tanning and rope-making industries. And there was enough left for building purposes, though Abbé Suger had to ride some considerable distance to find the thirteen massive oaks he needed for the tie-beams of the roof of Saint-Denis.

French and foreigners alike began to discern developing national characteristics. The nation was 'sweet' France, already a land of culture and sophistication, of codes and rules, of valour and honour. The *Chanson de Roland*, composed sometime between 1100 and 1120, told the story of the loyal knight, abandoned by his sovereign, betrayed by villainy, dying in glory surrounded by swathes of the enemies he had struck down. In France, knighthood and martyrdom acquired a glamour that has subsequently been matched only by modern film stars and sports heroes. The ritual associated with the induction of a knight became ever more complicated, the vows of knighthood ever more awesome and demanding, the devotion of knights ever more absolute.

Both Louis VI and Louis VII attempted to check the power of the French barons. They established the Ile-de-France as the centre of their dynasty, a secure base from which they could play off one noble against another. In so doing, they made Paris the capital of France and the greatest city in the medieval world. Slowly but steadily the descendants of Hugues Capet, founder of the Capetian dynasty in 987, increased the extent of the lands under their direct control, though it was to be another two hundred years before this covered the majority of France.

For the peasantry, progress was measured in the number of children who survived, the number of mouths that could be fed, and, less satisfactorily, in the number of duties heaped upon them in feudal society. On top of the rent they paid in money or produce, they were expected to use the lord's oven, mill or wine press (for which they had to pay); to serve as soldiers; to construct fortifications – legal or otherwise; and to work directly on the lord's land. Life was not easy.

Louis VI (*above, left and bottom right*) was described by Abbé Suger as a 'famous youth...jolly, gracious, and benevolent, to such an extent that he was considered simple by some'. Louis' corpulence and gluttony earned him the nickname *le Gros* ('the Fat'), and from his mid-forties he was so large that he was unable to ride a horse. Much of his reign was spent trying to bring the turbulent nobility of the Ile-de-France to order, a feat he eventually accomplished, partly by increasing the power of the towns. (*Above, top right*) The Coronation of Louis VI. (*Opposite*) Louis grants the first royal charter to citizens of Paris.

NVS SVMES HOMES COM ILS SVNT
MEMBRES AVONS COM ILS ONT

Louis VII (*opposite*) was the second son of Louis le Gros. He was educated for the Church, but became heir to the throne of France on the death of his elder brother, Philippe. His marriage to Eleanor of Aquitaine (*right*) brought considerable territorial gains to France, but the pair became estranged, and Louis annulled the marriage in 1152. Eleanor then married the Comte d'Anjou, who became Henry II of England.

One of the most impressive Crusaders was Godefroy de Bouillon (*opposite and above, right*). He was a single-minded man who sank his heart and all his possessions in the cause of the First Crusade. After the capture of Jerusalem, Godefroy was elected 'Advocate' or Defender of the Holy Sepulchre. He rebuilt the city (*above, left*) and extended the territory held by the Christians. He died in 1100, at the age of forty.

The rebuilding of the church of Saint-Denis, Paris (*above, right*), from 1136 onwards, was largely the inspiration of Abbé Suger (*above, left*). It was one of the earliest, and finest, Gothic churches. Suger was a remarkable man. He believed that 'the English were destined by moral and natural law to be subject to the French'. He was a skilled politician and writer. And he was not a man to be denied what he wanted. He was told by the carpenters at Saint-Denis that it was impossible to find the vast oak trees whose timber he needed as the main supports for the nave. Suger refused to accept this, and set off one night to comb the huge forests round Paris.

After nine hours' search, he found what he wanted, deep in the forest of Yvelines – thirteen enormous trees which were duly marked and felled. Suger had ridden over 50 kilometres to find them. The church and the Chapel of the Virgin (*above*) were richly decorated inside, and coated with gold and jewels for its consecration in June 1144. It attracted criticism from Bernard of Clairvaux, abbot of the newly-established rival monastery at Clairvaux.

Saint-Bernard of Clairvaux (*above, right*) led a studious and ascetic life, and became known as the 'Mellifluous Doctor'. He was held in high regard by the poor and the powerful alike, not least by Pope Innocent II. In 1138 Bernard managed to achieve a reconciliation between Innocent II and the antipope Victor. (*Above, left*) The moment of reconciliation – Saint-Bernard stands before Innocent II, while Victor indicates that he has divested himself of papal regalia. Saint-Bernard was also largely responsible for France taking the lead in the Second Crusade, when Jerusalem was once more threatened. (*Opposite*) Bernard preaches the Crusade at Vézelay in 1146.

Saint-Bernard and other members of the Cistercian order gained in influence over the Crown throughout the reign of Louis VII. The austerity of the Cistercians was admired by many who condemned the display of the Benedictines. (*Above, left*) A member of the Cistercian order in contemplative mood. (*Above, right*) A lay brother of the Cistercians in working habit. The Cistercians were great horticulturists and pioneers of new farming methods. (*Opposite*) The church of Sainte-Radegonde at Talmont in the Charente-Maritime – an exquisite Romanesque building in a perfect setting. It was built in the first quarter of the 12th century.

Mont-Saint-Michel (*right*) was in many ways the finest example of a medieval stronghold in the whole of France. At high tide it was cut off from the mainland. In almost all circumstances it was impregnable. It was also a place of pilgrimage, and the sands surrounding the castle were the venue for tournaments and sports.

It was a time of prosperity for French builders and masons. Crusaders returning to France wished to build castles of their own as strong and impressive as those they had fought to capture in Asia Minor.

Rival patrons and monastic orders sought to raise churches, chapels and cathedrals to the glory of God. (*Opposite*) Building a church window in the 12th century, and (*above*) raising the tower of a castle. By this time, there were already clear divisions of labour among the workforce engaged in any major enterprise.

(*Left*) The keep and outer wall of the castle of Gisors in Eure, c.1170. Its octagonal construction was an advance in castle design, for it eliminated the blind spots near the corners of a rectangular tower.

In later times the Cathedral of Notre-Dame de Paris (*opposite*) came to symbolise the heart of medieval France. It dominated the Ile de la Cité, emphasising the power and prestige of the Church. From the top, gargoyles (*above, left*) looked down on the largest city in Europe. Hundreds of carvings (*below, left*) decorated the west front. And the cathedral's rich peal of bells (*below, right*) summoned the faithful and the fearful to mass, marked the passing hours, and tolled for the dead.

The epitome of chivalry in the 12th century was Roland, semi-legendary French knight of the 8th century and the hero of the 11th-century epic poem, *Chanson de Roland.* The story of how the brave Roland died at the pass of Roncesvalles, in the service of his uncle and emperor Charlemagne, was recited and repeated all over France. Roland was in command of the rearguard of Charlemagne's army, fighting the Basques – later described as 'the Saracens' — as they retreated over the Pyrénées from Spain (*above, right*).

Roland had been given a horn, which he was to sound if he needed help. Three times Roland refused to call for reinforcements. Eventually, he blew the horn (*opposite, left*). Three times he blew. Three times Charlemagne wished to turn back and help Roland. And three times the treacherous Ganelon told Charlemagne he was mistaken – the horn had not sounded. Roland and almost all his men were killed (*above, left*). Charlemagne turned back and discovered the body of his dead nephew (*above, right*). The faithful Roland had discharged his duties as a knight.

By the end of the 12th century the new Gothic style swept all before it. Even where sections of old buildings could be preserved, the preference was to remove all the old and create a totally new edifice. A fire destroyed much of Chartres Cathedral in 1194, and work began immediately on the vast new monument to the Virgin Mary (*opposite*). (*Above, right*) Stonemasons depicted in a window of Chartres Cathedral. (*Below, left and right*) Capitals in the north porch at Chartres.

Heloïse.

Peter Abélard (*opposite*) was one of the most brilliant scholars in all France. He was a lecturer in the schools of both Sainte-Geneviève and Notre-Dame in Paris, and the founder of rational theological inquiry. Among his pupils was Héloïse (*right*), a nun and the niece of Abélard's landlord, Fulbert. Abélard and Héloïse became lovers, which earned them swift retribution: indeed, Abélard was castrated. They were separated but maintained a passionate correspondence by letter. Abélard died in 1142, Héloïse in 1163. She was buried in the same tomb as her lover.

As life became more settled, roads became safer and trade opened up, the production of wine in France greatly increased. Most villages in the southern half of the country made their own wine, but already there were commercial vineyards in Gascony, the Médoc, Burgundy and elsewhere. (*Above*) A 12th-century painting of grapes being harvested from the vine.

(*Top*) An early depiction of the wine-making process – (right to left) the vine, harvesting the grape, treading the grape, and a barrel of wine. (*Above, left*) A more sophisticated way of extracting juice from grapes –– a 12th-century wine-press. (*Above, right*) Harvesting and treading grapes.

3
THE AGE OF CHIVALRY 1150–1200

(*Right*) The month of September – or the *cividade del fuiti* – as illustrated in the *Psautier de Sainte-Elisabeth*, a 13th-century French manuscript. The peasant is shown using a flail to separate the chaff from the wheat. The scales may well be a cynical and subtle gibe at the miller, to whom the peasant would take the wheat. Medieval millers were notorious for giving short measure to their customers. When the sun shone, these were good times for much of France. Agriculture was becoming a science and harvests had increased considerably in both quantity and quality.

Introduction

In 1186 Andreas Cappelanus published his *The Art of Love or How to Live Honourably.* In it he set down thirty-one rules that defined the age of chivalry. By modern standards, the rules are a strange mixture of the prim and the improper, the expected and the surprising, for they include:

> Marriage is no real excuse for not loving
> It is not proper to love any woman whom one should be ashamed to marry
> When made public, love rarely endures
> A man is always apprehensive,

and

> Nothing forbids one woman being loved by two men, or one man by two women.

In practice, the rules applied to a very limited section of society. A peasant woman who loved two men received short shrift in an age when marital justice was rough and ever ready. Members of the clergy were not supposed to love any woman at all. For the gentry, however, the problems of obeying or disobeying the code of Capellanus whiled away many an otherwise boring hour in between hunting expeditions and Crusades.

France was again the senior partner in the Third Crusade of 1189. In return for the extra taxes raised to finance the Crusade, Christendom received from Saladin the right of free access to Jerusalem. Few French people would have been in a position to take advantage of this concession, though its symbolic significance was important.

And there was more money around to pay the higher taxes. The science of agriculture made enormous progress. The advantages of practising a system of rotation of crops were recognised. Better methods of harnessing draught animals were devised. The landscape in Normandy and Picardy became dotted with windmills and watermills. Added to this, the late 12th century was a period of warmer and wetter weather throughout Europe, generally good for agriculture.

Economic expansion endowed much of France with an aura of prosperity. The glories of Gothic ecclesiastical architecture rose above the walls of wealthy cities, among them those at Châlons-sur-Marne, Amiens, Soissons and Bourges. The finest was Notre-Dame de Paris, the magnificent monument to its founder Philippe II. Castles and fortresses (Angers, Coucy-le-Château, Château-Gaillard) grew in grandeur as well as defensive strength. Town houses offered comfort, a vast improvement on what had previously been little more than a shelter for humans and animals.

Above all this fluttered the new fleur-de-lys, symbol of France for the next six hundred years.

Although the annulment of his marriage to Eleanor of Aquitaine placed Louis VII (*opposite*) in a position where he was surrounded by powerful enemies, his diplomatic and political skills enabled him to save and even strengthen the Capetian dynasty. He was one of the first French kings to use Paris as the base of his power, and also one of the first to become popular with the majority of his people. (*Above*) Louis kneels in prayer in a ward at the Hôtel-Dieu, Paris.

The marriage of the Capetian Philippe Auguste (*opposite*) to Isabelle of Hainaut (*right*) – last descendant of the Carolingian line – finally legitimised the Capetian succession. He was one of the leaders of the Third Crusade (*above*, shown landing in Palestine), though he had little affection for his fellow king and Crusader, Richard I of England. After the Crusade, Philippe made a bargain with Richard's brother John to divide and share Richard's French territories. Like his father, Louis VII, Philippe did much to strengthen France, adding Normandy, Maine, Anjou and Touraine to his kingdom, but his longest-lasting monument was the Cathedral of Notre-Dame in Paris.

The Third Crusade was largely a costly failure for all those who took part. Aspirations were high at the outset of the Crusade, and Europe experienced one of its rare moments of unity in 1190. (*Opposite, below*) The banners of the Pope, the Emperor Friedrich Barbarossa, France, England, Anjou and Sicily fly together as Crusaders leave for Asia Minor.

(*Right*) One of the few successes of the Third Crusade – a scene from the siege of Acre or Ptolemais. (*Opposite, above*) The city of Acre is surrendered to Philippe II and Richard I. The cost of the siege in lives and suffering had been appalling. (*Opposite, below*) A Saracen attack on a group of Crusaders, from the *Chroniques de Saint-Denis,* c.1200.

Sala al-Din al-Ayyubi (*left*) was known to the French Crusaders as Saladin. He was a doughty enemy – a man famed for his chivalry, piety, justice and greatness of soul. As well as being a skilled and brave warrior, he was an able administrator who supervised the building of castles, roads and canals. From his mid-thirties until his death in 1193 at the age of fifty-six, Saladin spent much of his time fighting the invading Crusaders.

(*Above, left*) An engraving by Doré of Saladin the warrior. (*Far right*) An earlier depiction of a clean-shaven Saladin, proclaiming to his army that he carried nothing with him into battle but his shirt. (*Above, right*) A page from the *Conquête de Jérusalem* showing Saladin's army besieging the Holy City, c.1190. (*Right*) A map of the Levant in the 12th century. At that time, Saladin ruled most of Syria and Egypt.

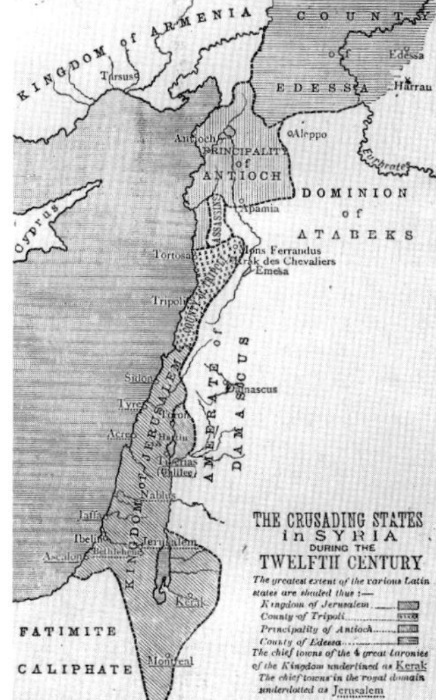

Much of the Crusaders' time was spent in attempting to capture the castles constructed by Turks and Seljuks in the Holy Land. These massive fortifications were larger than any in Europe and almost impregnable. Another great fortification was the Krak des Chevaliers (*right*), built by the Crusaders, and garrisoned by 2,000 men. It was situated some 750 metres above sea level, and incorporated all that the Crusaders had learnt from their struggles to capture Acre and Jerusalem. (*Opposite*) The effigy of a 12th-century Crusader in armour.

Richard the Lionheart became King of England, Duke of Normandy and Count of Anjou on 5 July 1189. He had already taken the Crusaders' vow, and in 1190 he and Philippe II set off together for the Holy Land. Richard enjoyed his wars, though he never reached – or even sighted – Jerusalem. For most of the period 1191 to 1194, he lived in tented splendour on campaign (*opposite, above*). After concluding a peace with Saladin, he returned to Europe.

The alliance between Richard and Philippe soon ended, and the two were at war. Richard was killed while besieging the castle of Châlus (*opposite*), and was buried at Fontevrault. Philippe continued the war, though he was now fighting the combined forces of England, Flanders and the Holy Roman Emperor. A major sea battle was fought off the English coast near Dover in 1217 (*below*). The French were defeated.

In the mid-12th century, the fleur-de-lys (the lily) (*right, above and below*) was adopted as the symbol of the French monarchy. The beauty and purity of the flower had been recognised by Christ himself, according to St Matthew's Gospel, chapter 6, verse 28, where the flower was favourably compared with 'Solomon in all his glory'. (*Opposite*) An early French depiction of King Solomon.

As in the case of so many medieval buildings, it was fire that gave the citizens of Amiens the chance to erect a completely new cathedral from 1220 onwards, under the supervision of Bishop Evrard de Fouilloy. The first architect was Robert de Luzarches, and he was succeeded by Thomas and Regnault de Cormont.

In many ways, the cathedral at Amiens was considered superior to those at Chartres and Rheims. By designing slender pillars, of the type used at Soissons, the architects and master-masons were able to add height but not cost to the building. (*Opposite*) A detail of the west front of Amiens Cathedral. (*Right*) The interior of the cathedral, looking east. Amiens was yet another outstanding example of the skill and imagination of French builders.

The importance of the French town of Conques-en-Rouergue in Aveyron (*left*) was that it lay on the pilgrim route from central Europe to the shrine at Santiago de Compostela in north-west Spain. Pilgrims stopped here for rest and refreshment, and to pray awhile in the church of Saint-Foy. Ahead lay another 600 or more kilometres, with the crossing of the western Pyrénées at Roncesvalles, and the long trek across northern Spain – then still a land of wolves, bears and brigands.

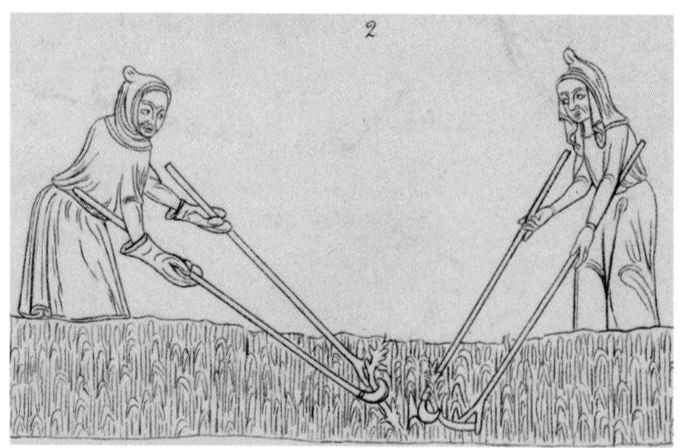
2

The seasons came and went and the farming year followed a familiar pattern. For those whose land gave forth good harvests, there was money to buy draught horses and new ploughs and harrows (*right*). For those a little less fortunate, there was money enough for oxen only (*opposite, above*). And for the very poor, all the hard work had to be done by human labour, whether it was harvesting (*opposite, below left*) or breaking up the ground (*opposite, below right*).

When it came, the medieval agricultural revolution centred on the use of machines – and in particular the mill. The most powerful was the windmill (*opposite, above*). The next was the watermill (*opposite, below left*). Handmills (*above and left*) relied on muscle power, but were a considerable improvement on older methods. And, when the corn was all safely gathered and separated from the chaff, it was loaded into bins (*opposite, below right*).

(*Left*) The Château-Gaillard, Eure. It was built by Richard I of England, to strengthen his hold on this part of France, but was captured by the armies of Philippe II in 1204 and subsequently dismantled. The weakness of its design was that it muddled practical use as a military stronghold, and propaganda use as a symbol of Richard's power. Its value today is as a picturesque ruin and a reminder of the struggle between England and France for supremacy in this part of Europe.

4
A PLAGUE OF TROUBADOURS 1200–1250

The first half of the 13th century witnessed an enormous leap forward in science and learning, comparable with that of the later Italian Renaissance. In France it was led by the great Villard, who came from the little village of Honnecourt, near Cambrai, in Picardy. His fame rests on the chance survival of his sketchbook, thirty-three parchment leaves now in the Bibliothèque Nationale in Paris. The book contains drawings of the wonders of the age – both practical and impractical – from flying buttresses to perpetual motion machines made of wood and quicksilver. (*Right*) A master in his study – medieval ideas are committed to parchment.

Introduction

Chivalrous behaviour found new missionaries in the troubadours of Languedoc and southern France – musicians and poets who spread the message of courtly love. Not all of them were wandering minstrels. They came from all classes and included women as well as men. Béatrice de Die was one of at least twenty well-known female troubadours in early 13th-century France, and some of the sensuality of the age is revealed in the passion with which she described the loss of her champion:

Naked-armed I held him tight
And pillowed on my breasts at night
I gave him joy with my caress.

Despite the problems of committing songs, thoughts, poems or chronicles to paper – in an age when everything had to be handwritten to a standard that all could read – France again produced a wealth of literature. Perhaps the

Louis VIII (*left*) was the son of Philippe II and the husband of Blanche of Castile (*opposite*). His short reign was largely taken up by wars. He fought the English, the heretics in the County of Toulouse, and the Albigensians, against whom he led the Crusade of 1226. After the death of Louis in 1226 (variously, if fancifully, attributed to poisoning, dysentery and even sexual starvation), Blanche ruled France as regent. Although scorned by powerful nobles, she proved herself a strong and capable ruler, putting down rebellion, leading the army into battle, and preparing her son to rule over one of the most illustrious periods in French history.

As castles grew in size and strength, the power of a local lord to challenge central government increased. New machines were needed to attack such strongholds of dissent (*above, left*). The science of siege warfare developed. The same catapults that were used to attack a castle could be used by the defenders (*below, left*). Both attackers and defenders used miners to undermine each other's fortifications. (*Opposite*) A range of catapults used to hurl rocks, stones and Greek fire into the camp of the opposition.

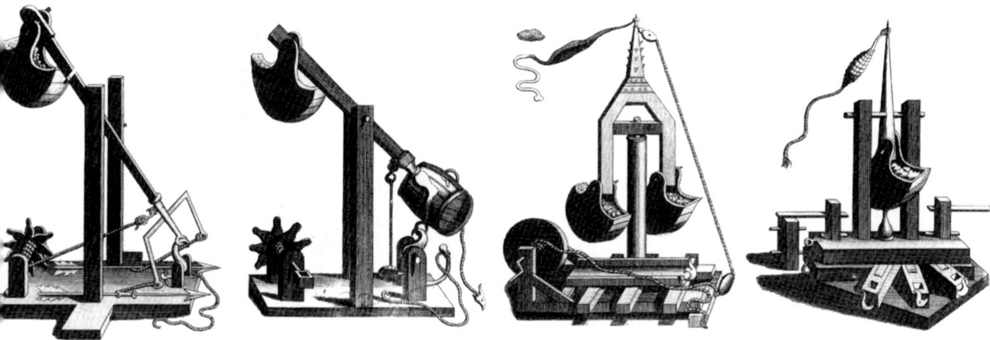

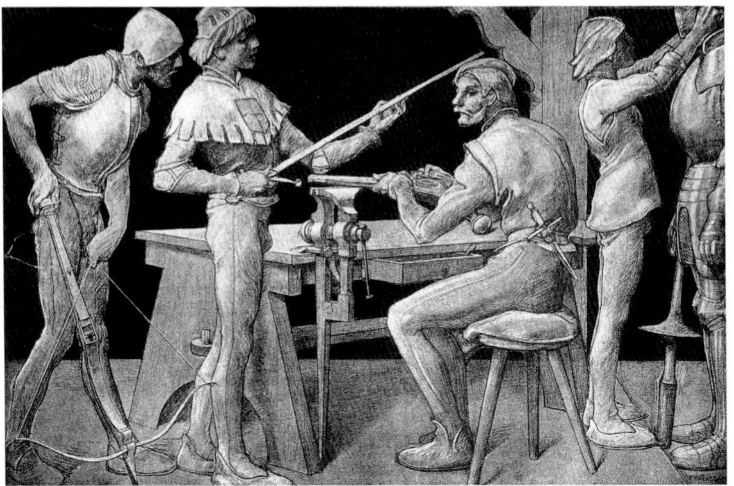

Individual soldiers also had new weapons in the 13th century (*above, left*). The crossbow was favoured by French archers; a fine sword by a fine gentleman – and the finest came from Spain. Any peasants recruited to fight would be armed with little more than a scythe or a billhook, though they might be lucky enough to pick up a pike fashioned at the village forge (*below, left*).

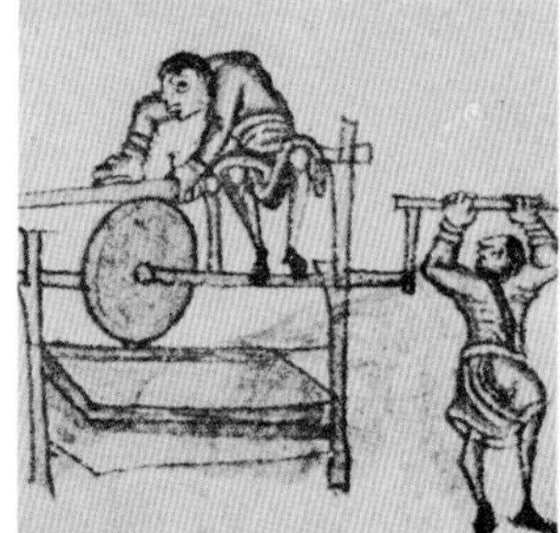

The manufacture of weapons was still very much a cottage industry (*above*). Swords were hammered by hand, and it required a keen eye to detect whether or not the edge of a blade was sufficiently sharp (*top, left*). A grinding wheel was used for this work (*top, centre*). In an unsettled age, most blacksmiths were overworked (*top, right*), for in addition to forging weapons and helmets, they were still required to attend to horses' hooves, farming machines and other tools.

The Crusade and expeditions against the Albigensians (formerly known as Cathars) were as much to do with economics as religion. What both popes and kings of France objected to was the refusal of the 'heretics' to pay tithes and recognise authority. One of the centres of rebellion was Carcassonne, in south-west France. In 1209 it was brutally occupied by the armies of Philippe II and heretics and believers alike were burnt to death in the cathedral itself. The castle was built as a future base and safeguard for royal authority (*above*).

Another centre of discontent was Toulouse; it was here that the beautiful church of Saint-Sernin had been built in the 11th century as a place of worship for pilgrims en route from central Europe and southern France to Santiago de Compostela.

The initiative for the Fourth Crusade of 1202 to 1204 came largely from Venice, whose rich trade in the Mediterranean was being challenged by Constantinople and the Turkish Empire. Though the vows made to God by the Crusaders spoke of their determination to restore the throne of Christ to the lands of the east, there was a strong economic motive behind the actions of many princes. Philippe II, a man of staunch faith, joined the Venetians and a joint French and Venetian army entered Constantinople on 12 April 1202 (*above, left*), to establish the Latin Empire.

(*Above*) Tintoretto's painting of the Battle of Zara, 1202. In the early 13th century, Zara was an important town on the trading route from Ankara to Persia through northern Turkey. The battle marked the high point of the Fourth Crusade as far as the French commitment was concerned. Philippe then had to turn his attention to his own kingdom, and to the trouble that was brewing in the south of France.

'This holy man loved God with all his heart,' wrote Louis IX's biographer, Jean de Joinville, 'and followed Him in all His acts...as God died for the love He bore His people, so did the king put his body in peril...' (*Above, left*) Louis IX receives the crown of thorns during the Seventh Crusade. (*Below, left*) The captive Louis is visited by his Saracen enemies and told that the promise made by the Sultan of Egypt will not be kept. The Sultan had promised to release Louis, but was later murdered. Behind Louis, to his right, is Jean de Joinville.

(*Right*) A better beginning to the Seventh Crusade. Louis IX wades ashore at Damietta at the head of his army. The French Crusaders captured the town, but were themselves later besieged and taken prisoner by the Saracens. Jean de Joinville spent six years in the company of Louis, both abroad and at home. He was impressed by the 'deeds and prowess' of Louis, but even more by the King's saintliness and good teaching.

By the middle of the 12th century in northern France it had become the practice to create effigies of the rich or powerful to lie over their tombs. These *gisants* were often richly carved and decorated. Many of the ruling Plantagenet line of England were buried in the abbey church at Fontevrault. The effigies placed over their tombs were in many ways the first attempts made at a true likeness of the people they commemorate.

The figures are carved to show how they appeared when ceremoniously laid out just after death, fully clothed in their robes, and at peace. One of the finest effigies is that of Richard I of England and his mother Eleanor of Aquitaine (*above*). It was executed some time early in the 13th century – Richard died in 1199 (at the age of forty-two) and his mother five years later (at the age of eighty-two).

(*Above*) The seal of the University of Paris in the 13th century. The rules of the University were strict. 'No one shall lecture in the University before he is twenty-one years of age...he shall not be stained by any infamy...he shall not lecture on the books of Aristotle on metaphysics and natural philosophy...'

Lectures were formal affairs and attendance at them was a required apprenticeship for students who aspired to become lecturers themselves. (*Above*) A lecture in progress at a medieval university. At the University of Paris the rules concerning the ages of the lecturers were also extended to the number of years of study that qualified them for the post.

Two mid-13th-century views of healing. (*Above*) Apothecaries at work making drugs from herbs. (*Opposite*) A medieval doctor in his laboratory. In cities, those who practised without permission from the 'masters of medicine' would be summoned to appear before a tribunal and their conduct would be scrupulously investigated. In country districts herbalists and quacks, apothecaries and 'old wives' ran no such risk. Old customs and new learning co-existed side by side, in reasonable peace and harmony.

(*Left*) A peasant at work, preparing the ground for a spring sowing – *Avril* from the *Psautier de Sainte-Elisabeth.* Spring was always a time of hope. The rigours of the winter were over, and one at least of the family had survived. With God's help and blessing, the ground would yield a good harvest, the animals would breed successfully, and Nature would provide. There would be honey from the bees, fruit and berries and nuts in the woods, fish in the streams and lakes, and the occasional hare or rabbit in the fields.

Three scenes from country life in medieval France. (*Above, left*) Oxen pull fine two-wheeled ploughs, from the Flemish *Trésors des Histoires*. (*Below, left*) Ploughing, sowing and pruning – activities which all took place in January and February. (*Opposite*) Ploughing and harvesting in September. The farm depicted here is a prosperous one. Horses are used instead of oxen. The farmhouse is substantial, with two storeys above the one in which the animals lived.

The economy of much of northern France depended on the woollen industry. Wool was produced in cottages and on farms – there were no factories as such. It was a man's job to shear sheep, but once the fleeces had been gathered in, women took over. (*Left*) A woman uses a distaff to produce a thread of wool. (*Above*) The more elaborate spinning wheel, quicker to use, but not so easy to take into the field and work with. On the right another woman is combing wool.

When the woollen cloth had been manufactured, it was often sheared again (*above, left*) to remove the wisps of wool and leave the cloth with a smoother, flatter finish. (*Above, right*) One of the final stages in the production of woollen cloth. A fuller rolls a bolt of cloth to cleanse and thicken it. The cloth has almost certainly already been dyed. The next step will be to make it into dress or jerkin, shawl or habit, hose or surcoat.

5
FIGHTING FOR POSSESSION 1250–1300

(*Right*) An illustration from a 15th-century French manuscript. King Meldiadus, brother of Tristan, is greeted by two knights – Esacabor and Arfasur – who pay homage to their king. The knight (or *chevalier*) was still an important figure in romance and real life in late 13th-century France, though he was later to outstay his welcome, and French armies who relied too heavily on the mounted warrior were to pay a heavy price. 'What is required of a good knight? That he should be noble. What means noble and nobility? That the heart should be governed by virtues. By what virtues...?' The four named by the author of this treatise on *The Chivalric Ideal* were strength, energy, boldness and fearlessness – the same qualities required of a horse.

ar-tus

Introduction

By the late 13th century reactionary influences were attempting to put a check on the French renaissance. In 1277 the Catholic Church published its *Execrable Errors*, condemning the teaching and the 'so-called' discoveries of the University of Paris. Ten years later, the Béziers monk named Matfre Ermengant wrote his *Breviari d'amor*, which sought to replace the eroticism of traditional courtly love with the more spiritual love preached by the Church. Practitioners of the old style were now told that chivalry was a ticket to Hell rather than Paradise.

In this age of greater piety, Louis IX, later to be venerated as Saint-Louis, set the tone, though the way was paved for him by his mother, Blanche de Castile. This remarkable woman – regent from 1226 to 1236 – resisted the challenge of rebellious nobles, led the French army and supervised her son's education.

The chivalric and spiritual ideals were combined in the character of Louis IX, king and saint (*above, right*). In his early life he was a man of action, courageous in battle, a great leader of men. In his later life he became more contemplative, forsaking glory and seeking to serve his people in a humble and modest manner. (*Above, left*) Saint-Louis serves a meal to the poor, from the *Petites heures d'Anne de Bretagne.*

(*Right*) Monseigneur Saint-Louis gives alms to beggars and helps attend the sick. (*Below, left*) Louis gives counsel and administers justice beneath the oak tree at Vincennes. It was said that all French people should have the right of access to the king. (*Below, right*) The death of Louis: '...the saintly king caused himself to be laid on a bed covered with ashes, and put his hands across his breast, and, looking towards heaven, rendered up his spirit to our Creator...' – Jean de Joinville.

Philippe III (*opposite, far left*), known as 'the Bold', was the son of Louis IX. Like many of his predecessors, Philippe worked hard to strengthen the power of central government, at the expense of what his adviser Pierre des Fontaines called 'poor and antiquated local customs'. However, Philippe the Bold was not an effective ruler. His son, Philippe IV (*opposite, right*), known as 'the Fair', was a much tougher character. His quarrel with Pope Boniface VIII eventually led to the establishment of the rival papacy at Avignon in 1305, when Philippe IV appointed Clement V as the first of the French popes. (*Right*) Isabella of Aragon, first wife of Philippe III, at the age of twenty-three in 1270.

Louis IX, Philippe III and Philippe IV all spent a considerable part of their reigns attempting to impose a stronger framework of government on France. The institutions of government were reformed, and placed on a firmer footing. (*Opposite, clockwise from top left*) An official dictates a report to a scribe; a session of the French parliament; promulgation of a 14th-century edict; and a French court of law in the Middle Ages. (*Above*) *The Judgement at Vendôme*, a miniature by Jean Fouquet. (*Above right, top and bottom*) Trial by combat, still a part of the French legal process in the 13th century.

The feudal system left few in doubt as to what was expected of them. It established a social and economic pyramid. At the top was the king, at the bottom were the serfs. From knights to peasants, each knew their rights, privileges and duties. Strict rules were laid down as to how many days work a serf owed his master, what dues he was to pay and what other services he was to supply. Women had to abide by what their husbands or fathers told them. (*Above, left*) The Lord of the Manor supervises the work of peasants on his land. (*Below, left*) A knight pays homage to his king.

(*Right*) Although the Lord of the Manor had many officers to carry out his orders, there were times when the serfs paraded before the lord himself to be told what they had to do. A similar system of social structuring was to be found in most towns, though it was perhaps less rigid and allowed a little more movement between the classes. (*Below, right*) The 13th-century seal of the Commune of Soissons, depicting the mayor (centre) and the sheriffs of the town.

Ce fu ou tans deste
Si ome ou moiſ de mai
ken maint lieu reſplendiſſent
Cler dou soleil li rai
Et q̃ arbre floriſſent
⁊ pre sont uert ⁊ gai
lorſ meſt priſ uolentes
q̃ tous iours maintenrai
De cele uolente ia ne me partirai

Throughout most of Europe the concept of knighthood was much the same. A knight was a man skilled in arms, valiant in danger, gentle yet resolute in manner towards the weak (especially women), and loyal at all times to his king. Promotion to the rank of knight could take place at a tournament, at Court, or (*below, right*) on the field of battle. (*Opposite*) A knight is invested with the trappings of his chivalric order. (*Right*) The accoutrements of knighthood – spurs and the sword.

In 1266 the French coinage was standardised by the introduction of the *livre tournois* throughout the country. It was an important step in the process of binding the disparate parts of the nation together. (*Left*) Two coining dies – the longer one has a spike with which it was fastened to a wooden bench. (*Far left*) A moneychanger at work. (*Below, left*) Two coiners hammer out the new currency.

One of the effects of the new coinage was to reduce the need to weigh individual coins to check that they contained the required amount of gold or silver (*above*). (*Right*) A later and more sophisticated machine for producing coins. The new coins served two purposes: to make payment of large amounts easier (for they were of high denomination) and to remind the rich of the power and sovereignty of the French king.

Much of the new French wealth was based on the wool and cloth industries. (*Opposite*) A bas-relief in the Cathedral of Chartres, in honour of the town's wool merchants. The wool trade brought prosperity to much of northern France, resulting in a general trade boom. (*Right*) A covered market in 13th-century France. (*Below, left*) A master-craftsman offers silver bowls and goblets for sale. (*Below, right*) Weighing goods in a market-place.

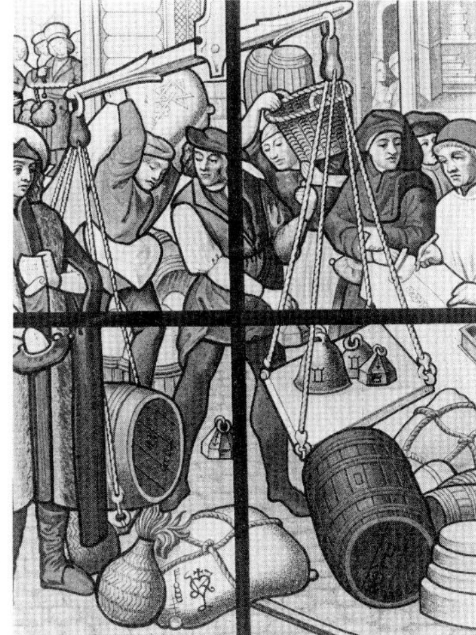

The first church of any stature in Rheims was built in the 9th century, and rebuilt some hundred and fifty years later. It was the church of Saint-Rémi, one of the finest examples of French Romanesque architecture (*above*). Later came the Gothic Cathedral of Notre-Dame (*opposite, left*), a bold attempt to rival and surpass the glories of Chartres, and rich in its decorative detail. (*Opposite, right*) The statue of an angel on the west front of Rheims Cathedral.

Throughout medieval times few generations of warriors, adventurers and freebooters were denied the chance of going on Crusade. It was the adventure of a lifetime – the chance to travel to a distant land, amass a fortune, large or small, and find death, glory or both on a battlefield. The Eighth Crusade of 1250 was no exception. Thousands of men-at-arms sailed from Western Europe to the Middle East, once more to drive the heathen from the Holy City. (*Above*) The French army embarks.

Many of the seeds of the Revolution of 1789 were sown in medieval times. The injustices of the feudal system itself lingered longer in France than in most other European countries, and a grievance peculiar to France was the regulation of supply and taxation of salt. Salt was essential as a food preservative. Without it many peasants were unable to ensure an adequate supply of food for their families throughout the winter. (*Opposite*) Weighing sacks of salt at a French harbour. (*Right*) Workers at a salt mine. The areas round La Rochelle and Aix-en-Provence were the main sources of salt.

In the 13th and 14th centuries, French scribes, monks and artists produced some of the most beautiful books of all time. The hours of patient work that went into them resulted in jewels of calligraphy and illustration. (*Left*) A page from *Les Merveilles du Monde*, showing Guillaume de Mandeville talking to the king. (*Opposite*) A page from the scriptures translated into French. Although a French version of the entire Bible was not published until the 14th century, extracts were produced earlier.

ICI FAIT HERODE OCIRRE LES INNOCENS

2

IST LI SIRE
AL ONEN SEIG
NVR SE DEVERS
LES OOEIES DESTRES
Desqucreopose
lestuens enemis:
escamel cleres piez·

4

'Woman should gather
roses ere
Time's ceaseless foot
o'ertaketh her,
For if too long she make
delay,
Her chance of love may
pass away...'

A sentiment and extract from *Le Roman de la Rose,* perhaps the greatest of French poems of the 13th century. (*Opposite*) *The Dance in the Garden of Pleasure,* an illustration from *Le Roman de la Rose.* (*Right*) A medieval illustration of the story of Lancelot and Guinevere.

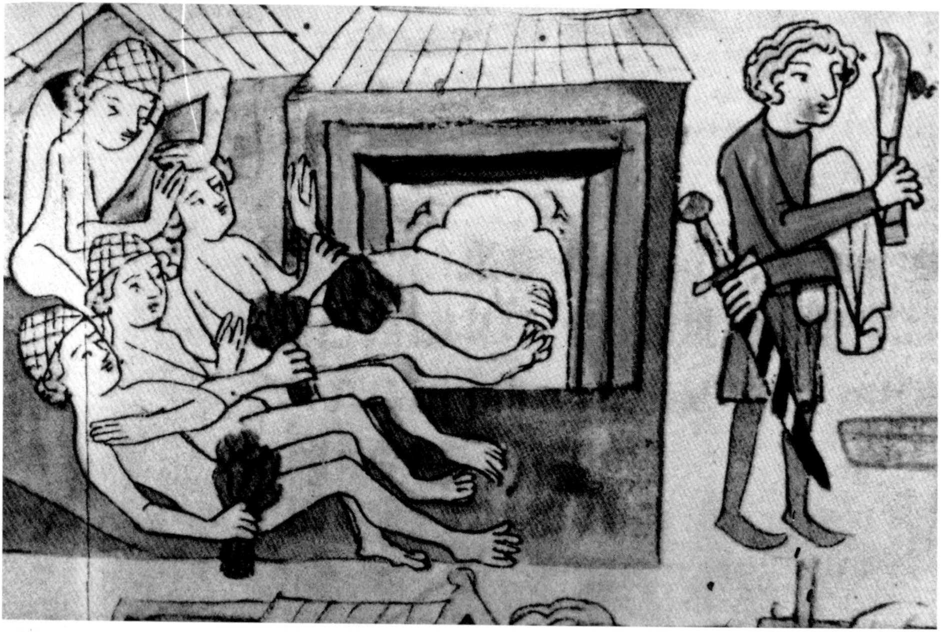

Many towns had public bath-houses. These were established as an aid to cleanliness and good health, and became meeting-places for gossips and friends. In many cases, however, the bath-houses deteriorated into dens of ill repute – the haunts of prostitutes and adulterers. (*Opposite, above left*) A man and woman take the plunge together. (*Opposite, above right*) A knight surprises a lady in her bath. He is wearing blinkers, but perhaps he should be wearing a blindfold. (*Opposite, below*) A medieval bath-house. (*Above*) Mixed bathing and merrymaking in a medieval bath-house. The presence of musicians is exceptional. It may well be that the scene represents a fête or public holiday.

The greatest sport of all was the combat of arms that took place at jousts and tournaments throughout France. More civilised than the old gladiatorial combats of Roman times, these were tests of strength and skill, a sharpening of the techniques that would be needed on the battlefield. (*Above, clockwise from top left*) A miniature of single combat from *Les Conquêtes de Charlemagne*; trial by ordeal – not a sport, but a contest to decide guilt or innocence; the Duc de Bretagne and the Duc de Bourbon in a contest of arms; and jousting in the lists at a tournament. (*Opposite*) The winning knight at a tournament is presented with his prize.

Second only to the thrill of the tournament – and more profitable to the stomach – was the hunt. (*Above*) A lady displays her skills in archery for the benefit of her attendants, and at the expense of a stag. (*Left*) The noble art of falconry – a duck has made the mistake of taking to the air. On water it would have been safe.

(*Right*) 'How to skin and cut up the stag' – from the miniature *Phebus, des deduiz de la chasse des bêtes sauvages* (Phoebus, hints on hunting wild animals). (*Below, right*) The day's kill having been cooked and eaten, the King of France distributes alms to the poor. The right to hunt was jealously guarded by the French nobility. Woe betide any peasant caught poaching on his lord's land – punishment was swift, merciless and extreme. Hunting was an aristocratic occupation and remained so until the Revolution of 1789.

6
WAR AND PLAGUE 1300–1350

On 26 August 1346, the French and English armies met at Crécy in Picardy, some 30 miles from the Channel coast. The French had pursued the English from Paris, though Philippe VI was 'mournful and anxious' at the thought of battle. The battle began late in the afternoon and continued until midnight, when Philippe, exhausted and wounded, was led from the field by the Count of Hainaut. 'Sire,' said the count, as he took the reins of the king's horse, 'lose not yourself wilfully.' The following year, the French Estates rubbed salt into the king's wound, reminding him that he had gone to Crécy 'in great company, at great cost', that he had been 'sent back scurvily and made to grant all manner of truces...' (*Right*) The Battle of Crécy.

S DENIS

Introduction

'In the year of Our Lord 1315,' wrote a contemporary French chronicler, 'famine arose in the land as if our God were displeased with our statutes. The corn would not ripen nor had bread the power to nourish. Therefore, as this hunger came to grip the whole land, mortality followed. Horseflesh was too pricey for some, who stole fat dogs to eat.' This was not the worst of it. Men and women ate their own (and other people's) children.

When they died, the poor could not afford timber coffins, for timber was in short supply and consequently expensive. All the poor could do was rent a coffin for the funeral service, and after the ceremony the undertaker tipped the body into the grave and rented the coffin to a new customer. It was a desperate and evil time.

In their misery, the people turned to their kings for help. They sought justice and a fairer share of the riches of life. The most important and immediate result of their supplications was an increase in the power of central government.

Power was exercised and justice dispensed in erratic ways. Jacques de Molay, master of the Order of Knights Templar, was tortured and publicly burnt in 1314. The financial skills of the Order, and the wealth and influence that this had gained for them, attracted the wrath of Philippe the Fair, King of France from 1285 to 1314. It made no difference that the Knights were a crusading order whose members took monastic vows, or that they spent much of their time defending the Holy Places and guarding the rights of pilgrims.

Life was cheap for women. A sliding scale of fines was imposed on anyone killing a woman. If the woman was past child-bearing age, the fine was 100 livres. If the woman was still of child-bearing age, the fine was 200 livres, and if the woman was pregnant, the fine was 700 livres.

Children, too, faced a harsh life from an early age. In his book *The Good Shepherd*, Jean de Brie listed a range of tasks for peasant children, graded according to age. The author of *The Knight of the Tour Laudry* recommended that parents of disobedient children 'take a smart rod and beat them'. The book was widely translated.

France now had its own Estates General, a centralised tax collecting system, the biggest city in Europe and a new university at Avignon. After the death of Pope Boniface VIII in 1303 (he had briefly been a prisoner of the French), it had its own pope, in the person of Clement V who voluntarily moved the papal residence from Rome to Avignon. It also had the world's first public clock, built in Paris in 1300 by Pierre Pipelart at a cost of 6 livres.

The Hundred Years' War raged to and fro across northern France. There were periods of peace and relative calm, but then a new English fleet appeared off the coast with a new invading army, and the fighting broke out once more. The principal sufferers were civilians – townsfolk and peasants in the country – whose lives and livelihoods were repeatedly at risk. (*Above, left*) The scaling of Pontandemer in the Hundred Years' War. (*Below, left*) Invading troops pillage a house in Paris.

The major battles – such as Crécy and Poitiers – tell only part of the story. There were frequent skirmishes for the capture of a village, a bridge, or even a farm. (*Below, right*) French and English soldiers battle for possession of a bridge: from a 14th-century French manuscript. (*Above, right*) Troops in full armour are more formally deployed on a battlefield, c.1350.

(*Right*) French troops under Philippe VI defeat a poorly equipped Flemish army at the Battle of Cassel, 23 August 1328. Despite their marked absence in the picture, victory owed much to the French crossbowmen. Crossbows were made of wood, steel and sinew. They were heavy to carry and cumbersome to use, but they had great penetrative power. A crossbowman usually carried some fifty bolts (arrows), though most of his equipment was transported to the battlefield in a waggon. The weapon was banned by the Church in 1139, but continued to be used for another three hundred years.

Following the English victory at Crécy, Edward III of England laid siege to Calais. The city was repeatedly attacked (*above*) by the English but held out gallantly for four months before surrendering on 4 August 1347. This was the high point for England in the entire war. Edward had assembled a group of extremely able soldiers, and most well-to-do homes in England were well stocked with booty from France. 'A woman who did not possess spoil from France,' wrote Thomas Walsingham, 'garments, furs, bed covers, silver vessels and cloth of linen, was of no account.'

A famous legend has grown up around the events that immediately followed the surrender of Calais. It is said that the burghers of Calais were paraded before Edward in chains, and that he announced his intention of having them executed. His wife and second cousin, Philippa of Hainaut, was in many ways a Francophile. The young Froissart was her secretary. She entered Edward's tent, fell on her knees before him, and interceded on behalf of the burghers (*above*). Edward spared their lives.

The rules governing a knight's behaviour were strictly regulated, though they allowed considerable latitude when it came to wooing a fair maiden. (*Opposite*) A knight sets out for war – 'he said goodbye to his good and beautiful wife with such tears and groans that she was ready to swoon...' (*Above, right*) The Count of Artois is received by the Countess of Boulogne and her daughter before a tournament, from the *Livre du très-chevalereux Comte d'Artois et de sa Femme*. (*Below, left*) 14th-century flower-power. (*Below, right*) A chivalrous author presents a poem to the object of his love.

On the morning of 26 August 1346, the English army took up a good defensive position above the village of Crécy. After a series of forced marches, the French troops were tired by the time they reached the battlefield (*above*). Nonetheless, with customary bravado the French knights charged the English lines. (*Left*) The Prince of Wales, known as the Black Prince because of his black armour, battles with King John the Blind of Bohemia.

(*Above*) Another view of the fight between the Prince of Wales and John of Bohemia. The standard bearing the words *Ich Dien* was that of Bohemia. It was captured by the Prince of Wales. The French knights launched attack after attack on the English lines, but were cut down by volleys of arrows from the English archers. Then the English knights advanced on foot, supported by pikemen and Welshmen with 'murderous knives'. The fighting was most ferocious at the foot of the hill (*right*), continuing through failing light and on into the darkness of night. When it ceased, 4,000 Frenchmen lay dead on the field.

In January 1348, the Black Death entered France via Marseilles. Within a year it overran the whole of France, from Provence to Normandy. Over eight hundred people a day died in Paris – 50,000 in all, and half the population of France. In Avignon bodies were thrown into the Rhône. In the Franciscan priory of Carcassonne every inmate died. In Amiens tannery workers believed the plague could be kept at bay by jollity.

(*Opposite, above and below*) Praying for relief from the plague. (*Right*) The plague hits the town of Tournai, 1349. (*Below*) Part of the aftermath of the plague – a group of travellers find many dying of famine in a French village. Contemporaries reported that oxen and asses, sheep and goats, pigs and even chickens also died of the plague.

It was an age of magic and superstition. The dancing lights of marsh gas or fireflies were seen as fairies, goblins, or even the souls of infants who had died unbaptised. Alchemy was the most popular science – the attempt to turn base metals into gold. Medicine was in its infancy, though knowledge of the human body and its many vicissitudes was increasing. (*Above*) Physicians bleed a patient, while others queue outside. (*Opposite, above left*) An apothecary grinds a powder with a pestle and mortar. (*Opposite, below left*) The laboratory of a successful – and possibly mad – alchemist. (*Opposite, right*) A page from a medieval manuscript on medicine.

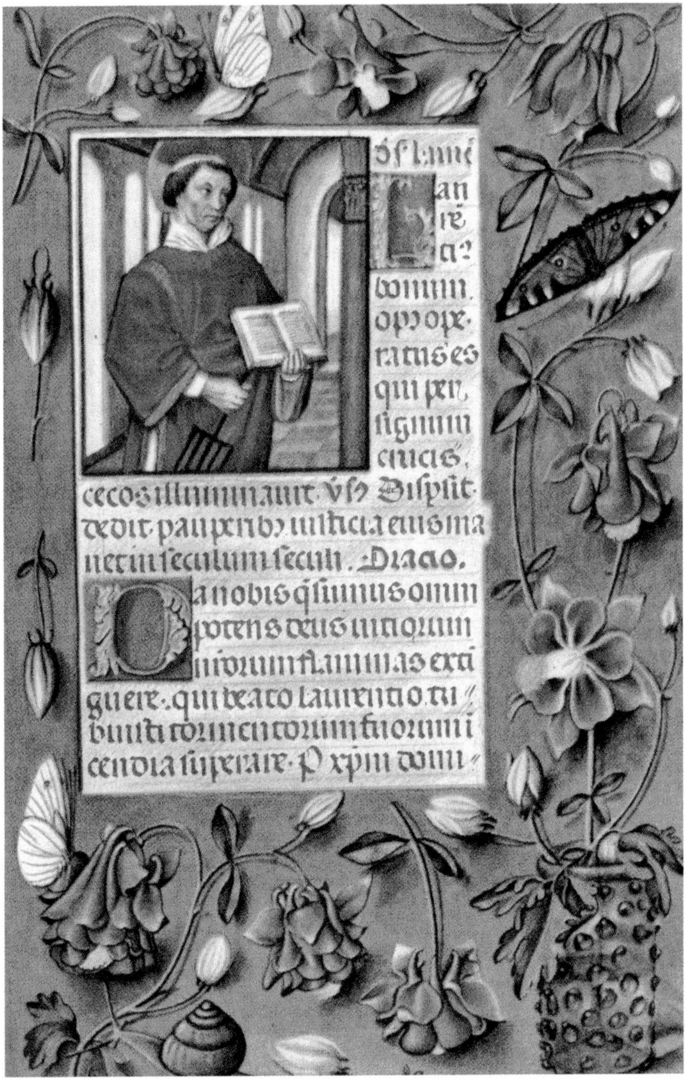

192
BONIFACIVS VIII Benedict. Caie-
tanus, Anagnin. creat. die 24. Decembr. an.
1294. Sedit an. 8. men. 9. dies 18. Obijt die 11
Octobr. an. 1303. Vac. Sed. dies 10.

Pope Boniface VIII (*opposite*) enjoyed poor relations with France. As papal legate he had raged against what he regarded as the presumptuous authority of the University of Paris: 'You Paris masters at your desks seem to think the world should be ruled by your reasonings. It is to us that the world is entrusted, not to you.' Philippe IV charged poor Boniface with heresy, blasphemy, murder, sodomy, simony and sorcery – and failure to fast on fast days. Later, Boniface was kidnapped by the French. This ultimately led to the papacy (Clement V) taking up residence at Avignon (*above*).

Philippe VI (*opposite*) was the first French king of the house of Valois. He succeeded to the French throne in 1328 on the death of Charles IV. His right to the throne was challenged by Edward III of England (*left*), who argued that by Salic Law succession was impossible through the female line. This clash between the two kings was the original cause of the Hundred Years' War, when Edward III claimed the French throne for himself in 1337.

The forests of Europe began to shrink rapidly in the 14th century. Timber was needed for houses, fuel, carts and wheels, fences, bridges, barrels and casks, looms and machines. As axes became stronger and sharper, the rate at which trees could be felled accelerated. (*Top, left and above, right*) Most trees were cut down simply as part of the process of clearing land to increase the area under cultivation.

A greedy consumer of timber was the shipbuilding industry (*opposite, below left and right, above and below*). It took a considerable number of trees to provide enough suitable timber for a single large ship (weighing up to 300 tons), and this was a time when nations sought to increase both merchant and military fleets. And yet it seemed that there would be enough timber to meet all possible human needs for ever...

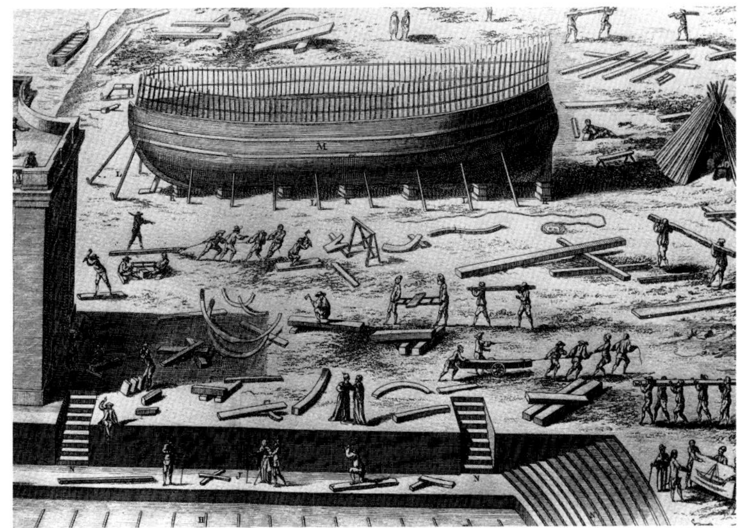

Spasmodic persecution of the Jews took place across Europe. In the period immediately following the Black Death, however, anti-Semitism became widespread. The first attacks occurred in Narbonne and Carcassonne. The Jews had few rights. The Church decreed that Jews should not be condemned without trial, and that they could not be robbed with impunity. On the other hand, Jews could not bring charges against Christians. They were held responsible for the Black Death, and accused of well-poisoning (an attempt to wipe out Christianity), and of drinking the blood of Christian children (*above*) or using it for their sinister magic rites (*opposite*).

As a succession of kings sought to strengthen their hold over France, the rich and powerful found themselves under attack. One of the richest orders in the country was that of the Knights Templar. The Templars were an order of monastic knights, formed during the Crusades as protectors of the Holy Land. Their original asceticism and poverty, however, were steadily replaced by arrogance and opulence. By the early 14th century they had 2,000 members in France, the largest treasury in northern Europe and a formidable fortress in the heart of Paris.

In 1307 Philippe IV had pounced. He had bullied Pope Clement V into authorising the trials of some two hundred Templars, who were hideously tortured and burnt alive. (*Right and opposite, below*) Jacques de Molay, Grand Master of the Order of the Temple. Broken by torture, he confessed to spitting on the Cross, 'and he would have confessed that he had slain God Himself if they had asked him that'. (*Opposite, above*) De Molay is led to the stake, 1314.

All branches of the Knights Templar in France, England, Scotland, Aragon, Castile, Portugal, Germany and Naples were subsequently abolished by the Council of Vienne in 1312. Their property was transferred to the Knights Hospitallers of St John, though Philippe IV managed to help himself to a generous portion. As de Molay died he cursed the pope and the king, saying they would die within a year. Clement V died a month later. Philippe lived only seven months more. (*Left and opposite*) Two members of the Templars. (*Above*) A meeting of the Order.

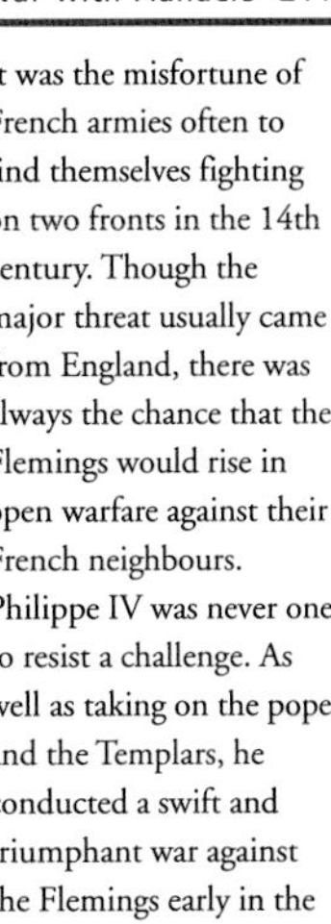

It was the misfortune of French armies often to find themselves fighting on two fronts in the 14th century. Though the major threat usually came from England, there was always the chance that the Flemings would rise in open warfare against their French neighbours. Philippe IV was never one to resist a challenge. As well as taking on the pope and the Templars, he conducted a swift and triumphant war against the Flemings early in the century. (*Left*) The French army defeats the Flemings at the Battle of Mons-en-Pévèle, 18 August 1304.

No city in the world could rival Paris in medieval times. It was perhaps the biggest in Europe, centred on the Ile de la Cité, on which stood the mighty Cathedral of Notre-Dame, the Hôtel-Dieu and the Palace of Saint-Louis. On the right bank of the Seine were the houses of industry and commerce, the markets and the wealthy residences. On the left bank was the University, the greatest seat of learning on the Continent. Some 150,000 people inhabited this crowded city. (*Opposite*) A map of Paris at the beginning of the 14th century. (*Above*) The Petit Pont de Paris.

7
STRUGGLING FOR NATIONHOOD 1350–1400

Both Charles V and Charles VI of France were lovers of music, and the late 14th century was a period of musical brilliance. This was the age of the Ars Nova, a freeing of style, the introduction of new rhythms, and more independently moving voice parts. Although many of these changes emanated from Florence, they were eagerly seized on by French composers and musicians, among them Philippe de Vitry, Guillaume de Machaut (the last of the French poets to compose his own music) and Johannes de Muris. (*Right*) French medieval stringed instruments – a lyre (left) and a lute – from an illustration dedicated to Louis de France, the Duc d'Orléans, c.1400.

Introduction

France produced the finest medieval cookbook, the *Viandier de Taillevent*, written by the chief cook to Charles V, in 1373. The elaborate recipes reflected the contemporary obsession with ceremony and presentation – stuffed pigs, stuffed heron, stuffed swans, peacocks roasted and then served with their feathers replaced, chicken glazed with honey.

A rich Parisian merchant entertained his guests with the following meal:

First course: meat in a cinnamon sauce, pasties of cod liver or beef marrow; eels in a spicy purée; loach in a cold green sage sauce; beef marrow fritters; joints of meat; saltwater fish; roast bream and darioles [small savoury side dishes]; sturgeon and jellies.

Second course: freshwater fish; broth with bacon; a meat tile – sautéed chicken and veal with a spiced sauce of powdered crayfish tails,

French fortunes reached a low ebb in the Hundred Years' War with the capture of Charles of Blois at the Battle of Roche Darien in 1347 (*opposite, above*). Then came a series of French successes until the English presence in northern France was limited to a few Channel ports (*above*). The war was renewed in 1385, with intermittent truces in 1389 and 1394. When Richard II of England married Isabella of France in 1396, the truce was extended to twenty-eight years, but broke out again in 1414, and the French were defeated (*opposite, below right*) and surrendered (*opposite, below left*) at the Battle of Agincourt in 1415.

For most French people, the Hundred Years' War was a bewildering succession of invasions and retreats. The country was in turmoil. In a single lifetime, a village could find itself now under the control of the English, now ruled directly by the King of France, now as a fief of the Duke of Burgundy. Towns closed their gates to invading armies, to sweat out a siege and await relief, which often never came. (*Top*) Heralds summon the citizens of Troyes to surrender: from the 14th-century manuscript *Les Chroniques d'Angleterre* by Jean Warrin. (*Above, left*) The King of France enters a fortified city during the Hundred Years' War. (*Above, right*) The citizens of Evreux ride out to meet their king.

The great chronicler of the exploits of this time was Jean Froissart, who gave up a career in the Church to write one of the most famous histories of war of all time. He began work on his *Chroniques* in the 1360s, but did not complete the work until thirty years later. The book covers the period 1326 to 1400, and includes descriptions of the affairs of England, Scotland, Flanders, Germany, Italy and Spain, as well as France. (*Above*) English troops use siege engines to capture a French town in the late 14th century – an illumination from Froissart's *Chroniques.*

On 19 September 1356, the French army under King Jean II and an Anglo-Gascon army under the Black Prince clashed near Poitiers. The result was another crushing defeat for the French. (*Right*) King Jean in action at the Battle of Poitiers, just before his capture. (*Opposite*) Three depictions of King Jean surrendering his sword to the Prince of Wales.

Ten years after the Black Death ravaged much of France, the revolt known as the Jacquerie broke out in the Beauvais area, north of Paris. It was not inspired by poverty, nor was it specifically directed against the king. Rather, it was a sudden eruption of resentment against the privations of war. Peasants rose against soldiers, attacking castles, killing their lords and masters, and raping the wives and daughters of the nobility. The rising was brutally crushed. (*Right*) The Comte de Foix defeats the rebels at the Battle of Meaux in 1358.

Despite war and plague, by the late 14th century food was in more plentiful supply. It was not uncommon for the better-off to serve dinners of six or more courses (*above and opposite, below*). 'First course: wine of Grenache and roasts, veal pasties, pimpernel pasties, black-puddings and sausages. Second course: hares in civet and cutlets, pea soup, salt meat, a soringue of eels and other fish. Third course: coneys, partridges, capons, luce, bar, carp and a quartered potage. Fourth course: river fish *à la dodine*, savoury rice, a bourrey with hot sauce and eels reversed. Fifth course: lark pasties, rissoles, larded milk, sugared flawns. Sixth course: pears and confits, medlars and peeled nuts, wafers...'

Hunting would have provided the hares, coneys (rabbits), partridges, and larks for such a meal. (*Above*) Huntsmen and dogs lead a group of ladies on a day's hunt. Bows and arrows were the most popular weapons, though spears were used to kill wild boar and deer.

The poor boiled their vegetables and occasional scraps of meat in pots over open fires, salted their home-slaughtered pork, and seldom had anything to pop into the local baker's oven. The well-to-do, however, were used to a variety of ways of preparing and cooking food – baking, roasting and spit-roasting, frying, steaming, coddling (poaching) and sautéing. (*Top*) Preparing and dressing meat in the 14th century. The two men on the right are taking the prepared dishes to the table. (*Above*) 'How a pig is caught with the help of dogs', from the 14th-century manuscript *Livre du Roy Modus*.

In the towns and cities, well-to-do families had their own cooks and kitchen attendants. In country districts, even the rich often relied on their serfs to prepare their food and cook for them. (*Above, clockwise from left*) Spit-roasting fowls and a suckling pig; using a giant pestle and mortar, possibly to grind salt; pounding the finished result to a fine paste, and boiling peas or legumes in large pots.

The relatively mild climate of medieval times permitted the cultivation of vines throughout almost the whole of France, though already the wine-making industry was concentrated around the areas of Bordeaux, Burgundy and the Loire. In the south almost every village produced its own wine, rough-and-ready stuff, and less alcoholic than modern wines. (*Above, left*) Tending a vineyard in medieval France. (*Above, right*) Tasting a cargo of wine – perhaps a little late in the day, since the wine is already in mid-shipment.

Four stages in the production of wine (*right, from top*): treading the grapes to extract the juice; drawing the young wine into casks; planting the young vines for next year's harvest; and picking the grapes. (*Above*) An illustration showing most of the stages in the production of wine at a 14th-century vineyard – including the all-important tasting.

Many of the weapons used in siege warfare (by both attackers and defenders of a town or castle) were little changed from those used in Roman times. What had changed was the strength of the fortified position. French military engineers had learnt a great deal from their expeditions as Crusaders to the Holy Land. They knew the advantages of circular towers over square ones, how to design a fortress that had the minimum of 'blind' or weak spots, where best to site a castle. (*Above*) Soldiers wearing chain mail load stones into a trebuchet – a powerful catapult, used in this case to hurl missiles from inside a castle.

(*Above*) An archer places his foot into the stirrup at the head of a crossbow, winding up the mechanism to prime the weapon. Crossbows were preferred by French archers to the English longbow. (*Right, above and below*) A wide variety of battering rams were used to break down the walls of a town or castle. In some cases these weapons were tipped with the replica of a ram's head, and were either driven against the wall by a file of men, or swung from a heavy wooden frame. In the top picture are two 'borers', vast drills used to grind their way through stone.

Despite innumerable setbacks over three hundred years, the French maintained their crusading zeal. (*Right*) A picture from the late 14th century of the departure of a joint Anglo-French expedition to the Holy Land.

For most Europeans, the Crusades were voyages of discovery. The Islamic civilisations of the Near East were far advanced in mathematics, science, astronomy and, surprisingly, cosmetics. Men dyed their hair black, using ingredients that ranged from the burnt claws of bears to cumin seeds. Women applied face make-up made from roots and leaves, or crushed insects, or even minced toads. To undo the damage caused to the skin by such primitive measures, there were remedial ointments made of 'asparagus roots, wild anise and milk of wild asses...aged in warm horse manure and filtered through felt'. (*Above*) An illuminated manuscript depicting a face specialist.

The great military hero of the late 14th century was Bertrand du Guesclin, Constable of France. Under his command, French troops defeated the English and recovered most of northern France. (*Opposite*) Du Guesclin accepts 100,000 livres from the papal legate, and agrees to by-pass the city of Avignon on his way to fight Pedro the Cruel of Castile, 1366. (*Left*) Charles VI and the Flemish nobles defeat the citizens of Ghent at the Battle of Roosebeke, 1382. The cloth merchants of Ghent allied themselves with the English for commercial reasons.

Charles V (*above*), known as 'the Wise', ruled France from 1364 to 1380, and had already acted as regent following the capture of his father, Jean II, by the English after the Battle of Poitiers in 1356. His wisdom lay in knowing when to leave matters of state alone and let others attend to problems. His own loves were beautiful manuscripts and his collection of treasures. None the less, by the end of his reign France was in a strong position. (*Above, right*) The signature of Charles V in a folio Bible.

(*Right*) The Coronation of Charles V, from an illustration in Froissart's *Chroniques*. Sixteen years later, on his deathbed and overcome with remorse at the amount of taxes he had wrung from the peasantry to pay for the wars of his reign, he abolished the hearth tax known as the *fouage*.

There was little that was wise about Charles V's successor, his son Charles VI. He was known as 'the Foolish', though 'unlucky' might be a fairer nickname. Beset by warring relatives, there was little Charles could do to prevent French fortunes plunging. (*Left*) Charles VI is accosted by a spectre in the Forest of Le Mans, 1392. The 1390s were a propitious time for spectres, and the madness of Charles made their appearance highly likely.

(Above) The anointing of Charles VI at his Coronation, 24 November 1380. (*Right*) Charles VI (left, with staff in hand) and his attendants, c.1400. (*Far right*) Isabella of Bavaria, wife of Charles VI and mother of the unhappy Charles VII. The people of France were kindly disposed towards poor Charles – aware of his madness and also aware of the pain that he suffered during his regular returns to sanity. The problem for the country, however, was that once again there was a division between the Crown and the exercise of political power. Berry, Anjou and Burgundy became satellite states, rather than integrated parts of the whole nation.

Jean Froissart travelled extensively. He visited England and Scotland as a young man, and toured Aquitaine and Italy – where he almost certainly met two great contemporary writers, Chaucer and Petrarch. As well as his famous *Chroniques*, he wrote a considerable quantity of poetry. (*Opposite*) Froissart presents a volume of his *Chroniques* to Queen Isabella. (*Right*) The Court of Charles V, from a miniature in Froissart's *Chroniques*.

One of the most beautiful books produced in Europe during the Middle Ages was the *Très Riches Heures du duc de Berry*. Sumptuously illustrated, it is far more an artistic treasure than a book. Two illustrations from the *Très Riches Heures*: (*opposite*) French peasants haymaking, with the Palais de Justice and the Sainte-Chapelle in the background; (*right*) the Duc de Berry's magnificent château at Saumur on the Loire.

8
THE MAID OF ORLEANS 1400–1515

Jeanne d'Arc was nine years old when the English overran the area around her home in Domrémy. Four years later she believed she heard the voices of St Michael, St Catherine and St Margaret telling her to free the Paris region from English control. The local commander, Robert de Baudricourt, conducted her safely through the English lines to Chinon, where she told her story to the Dauphin. Legend has it that the Dauphin was in disguise, and the unerring ease with which she identified him was taken as a sign of her extraordinary powers, and of the legitimacy of his claim to the throne. (*Left*) Jeanne d'Arc arrives at Chinon, 6 March 1429.

Introduction

The war dragged on. The plague returned with relentless regularity. In northern France the agony inflicted by both was at its worst. 'From Dieppe to Rouen,' wrote one Norman, 'there is not a recognisable track left; there are no farms, and, with the exception of a few bandits, no men.' As a united nation, France began to disintegrate. Burgundy entered into an alliance with England, and, after the defeat at Agincourt in 1415, poor Charles VI was persuaded (much against his will) to give his daughter's hand in marriage to the English king.

Three factors contributed to a swift change of fortune for France. The first was the influence of Jeanne d'Arc. Her claim that God had spoken to her, commanding her to drive the English from France, was readily accepted by many. The second factor was the astute diplomatic skill of Charles himself. He persuaded the Duke of Burgundy to change sides and the Duke of Brittany to join the French cause, all within the space of three years.

The third factor was the establishment by his successor Charles VII of a standing army of between 12,000 and 15,000 men from 1439 onwards, paid for by the *taille*.

The era of the knight in shining armour, bound to the code of chivalry, riding into battle on his faithful charger, was over. In 1449 the biggest artillery piece in the world was cast at a foundry in Mons. It was christened Mons Meg, and no knight, however heroic, could compete with such awesome, destructive power. Four years later, the French used more than three hundred cannon at the Battle of Castillon.

Between 1422 and 1483, Charles VII and Louis XI turned France into a fully centralised state. Mighty vassals ceased to be royal advisers and were replaced by lawyers, financiers and merchants. Separate departments were created to deal with money, justice and tax. By the Sanction of Bourges in 1438, the king obtained the right to influence appointments within the Church.

France breathed more easily. The fortress gave way to the château, with magnificent examples of the latter appearing at Amboise, Blois, Chambord and Chenonceaux. The first French printing press was established in Strasbourg in 1453, the second in Paris in 1470. The Gobelins, a family of dyers, founded their tapestry factory on the outskirts of the capital in the mid-15th century.

There was still time to eat. When Charles the Bold of Burgundy married Margaret of York (sister of Edward IV of England) in 1468, guests at the wedding feast consumed '200 fat oxen, 63 fat pigs, 500 kilos of lard, 2,500 calves, 2,500 sheep, 3,600 shoulders of mutton, 11,800 small chickens, 18,640 pigeons, 3,640 swans, 2,100 peacocks and 1,668 *crèmes*'.

As France's military fortunes declined in the early 15th century, so too did the power, prestige and authority of the French kings. Once again mighty vassals established rival courts – in Burgundy, Brittany and Provence. These rivals wore their own crowns of gold, openly flaunting their lack of respect for the monarchy. One of the most powerful of these rivals was René the Good, whose power base was the château in Tarascon (*above*), built to withstand the onslaught of any army. The greater the display of opulence, the greater the challenge to central authority.

René was Duke of Anjou, Count of Provence and Piedmont, and known as the 'Last of the Troubadours'. His court resided in Avignon, but his ambition roamed as far as Italy, where he had ambitions to become King of Naples. He became titular king in 1435 when he inherited Naples from his brother, Louis III. Later in life, when many of his political plans had come to little, he married his daughter to Henry VI of England and then settled in Aix-en-Provence, where he devoted most of his time to poetry and agriculture. (*Right*) The procession of René the Good to Aix, after a miniature in the *Bréveraire du roi René.*

Philippe the Good, Duc de Bourgogne (*above, left*), used the Hundred Years' War between the French and the English to his own advantage. At first he sided with the English, mainly to gain revenge for the murder of his father at the instigation of the Dauphin (later Charles VII). He claimed the crown of France and twice defeated Charles, then fell out with the English and made peace. He was lured back into alliance with England by the offer of money and the Champagne region. By 1430 he was one of the most powerful rulers in Europe. (*Above, right*) Isabella of Portugal, third wife of Philippe the Good.

In 1435 Philippe again broke the alliance with England and made peace with Charles. Together they drove the English out of northern and western France. For a while, Burgundy became the most prosperous and tranquil state in Europe. In 1454, however, the citizens of Ghent rebelled against the taxes imposed on them by Philippe. The Duke crushed the rebellion, killing 20,000 of the insurgents. (*Above, left*) Isabella of Portugal kneels before her husband, c.1450. (*Above, right*) Philippe the Good enters the city of Ghent after crushing the rebellion.

Charles the Bold (*above*) became Duke of Burgundy on the death of Philippe in 1467. Like him, Charles sought to make Burgundy a great kingdom, between France and the Holy Roman Empire, stretching from the Mediterranean to the North Sea. He was a patron of the arts and literature, and made sure that the Burgundian court was one of the most splendid in Europe. (*Left*) Charles appears before his council, to issue his ordinance regulating military levies, Trier, 1473.

(*Below*) The Burgundian parliament in the late 15th century. Charles' dreams of Burgundian glory came to an end in 1477, with his defeat by the French at the Battle of Nancy. The great state was dismantled, France taking the lion's share, but other princes gobbling up what bits they could. (*Right*) The tomb of Charles the Bold in Bruges Cathedral.

The story of Jeanne d'Arc is one of the most extraordinary in history, and one which can still arouse fierce debate. To her supporters, ancient or modern, Jeanne is a saint. To her detractors, she is either a fool or a witch, depending on their age. (*Above*) Jeanne's home at Domrémy. (*Far left*) Jeanne d'Arc's vision. (*Left*) Jeanne declares her mission to save France, while a sceptical clergy look on.

After her interrogation by ecclesiastics at Poitiers, Jeanne was allowed to join the French army at Blois. She had declared that her mission was initially to save Orléans, then under siege by the English. Clad in white armour and carrying her own standard – for someone had seen the propaganda value to France if she was successful – Jeanne entered Orléans on 29 April 1429 (*right*). Within ten days, the English had been routed.

Following Orléans, Jeanne and her army of 12,000 accompanied the Dauphin to Rheims, where he was crowned Charles VII. But he would go no further, and Jeanne set off without him to lift the siege of Paris and take on the Burgundians. She was captured at Compiègne, and sold to the English for 10,000 crowns. She was tried for heresy and sorcery by an ecclesiastical court of the Inquisition, presided over by Pierre Cauchon, Bishop of Beauvais.

Jeanne was found guilty, and taken out to be burnt in the courtyard of St Ouen. Here she broke down and recanted her error. She was returned to her prison. A few days later, she retracted her confession. On 30 May 1431, at the age of nineteen, she was burnt at the stake in the market-place of Rouen. Three images of Jeanne: (*opposite, above*) the sleeping warrior, watched over by angels; (*opposite, below*) the inspiring military commander; and (*right*) the young woman prepared for martyrdom.

Lucky the man or woman who was brought before a compassionate court or tribunal in the 15th century. The judicial process may have been swift, but it was certainly merciless – whether under the village tree (*opposite, above*) or within the dark confines of a city court (*above*). Most prosecutors believed that the quickest way to get at the truth was by using torture (*left*). The method was effective in extracting 'confessions': thousands of people confessed to crimes they had never committed to escape further torture. We hear the stories of those few brave souls who never broke; we do not hear the stories of the many who understandably did.

After confession came punishment – executed with little delay: it was not an age of appeal and retrial. Lucky the villain who was beheaded, for there were far worse fates. (*Far right*) Parading the head of a recently dispatched criminal. (*Right*) An accused is brought before a 15th-century court of law.

Despite wars and famines, rebellions and plagues, French architects and masons continued to erect masterpieces of Gothic architecture. One of the finest was the parish church of Saint-Etienne-du-Mont, Paris (*above, left*). Work began on the church at the end of the 15th century, but it took over one hundred and twenty-five years to complete. (*Below, left*) The pulpit at Saint-Etienne. (*Opposite*) The magnificent choir of the church, one of the glories of the French Renaissance period.

In the Middle Ages the city of Tours was known to its inhabitants as 'Martinopolis', for many were still proud of Saint-Martin, original patron saint of the Franks. It was a large and prosperous city, noted for its library, cathedral, university and fine houses (*above*). (*Left*) The courtyard of a grand house in the Rue des Trois Pucelles (Street of the Three Virgins).

(*Right*) The imposing west front of the Cathedral of Saint-Gatien in Tours, constructed between 1440 and 1537. The building was one of the earliest constructions of the period known as French Late Gothic. Although the doors and windows of the west front are of classic Gothic design, the tops of the twin towers have elements of the later Baroque style.

The most successful French king of the 15th century was Charles VII (*above, left*). When he came to the throne in 1422, France was in a desperate state. The whole of Aquitaine was under English control, and French armies had been forced south of the Loire by joint Anglo-Burgundian forces. Thirty years later, the English had been driven from northern France (with the exception of Calais), and the whole of the south was again under French control. The Hundred Years' War came to an end in 1453. (*Above, right*) Agnès Sorel, Charles VII's mistress from 1444, and a woman who exercised considerable influence over him.

(*Right*) A picture of Charles VII and his Court from the *Chroniques de Charles VII* by Jean Chartier. (*Far right*) The Court of Marie of Anjou, wife of Charles VII. Her chaplain, Robert Blondel, is presenting her with the book *Twelve Perils of Hell.* (*Below, right*) Another illustration from the *Chroniques de Charles VII*, showing the death of Charles in 1461.

Louis XI (*above, left*) made two unsuccessful attempts to depose his father, Charles VII, before succeeding to the throne on Charles' death in 1461. As Dauphin, Louis had married Margaret of Scotland (*above, right*), daughter of James I. A cunning and intelligent man, Louis managed to break the power of the 'mighty vassals' of France, prime among them Charles the Bold of Burgundy. By 1483, almost all France, with the exception of Brittany, was under the direct rule of the French king. Louis' last years were spent in terror and misery, for he had an excessive fear of death.

Louis XI was succeeded by his son Charles VIII, known as 'the Affable'. Charles died in 1498 and his cousin Louis XII (*above, left*) ascended the throne. Louis sought power through marriage. His first wife was the daughter of Louis XI. His second wife was Anne of Brittany, widow of Charles the Affable. His third was Mary Tudor, sister of Henry VIII of England. (*Above, right*) Louis XII rides out from Alexandria in a fruitless attempt to strengthen his hold on Genoa, one of several Italian possessions of the French crown at this time.

More than any other woman, Anne of Brittany (*above, right*) was a piece in the medieval game of international power-broking. Charles VIII (*above, left*) beat off a challenge for her hand in marriage from Maximilian of Austria in 1491. After Charles' death, Louis XII separated from his own wife to marry Anne and maintain the alliance between France and Brittany. Not until 1532 was Brittany finally incorporated into the French kingdom. The contemporary feminist, Christine de Pisan, was contemptuous of male views of women, and of the books that fashioned them: 'The books that so sayeth,' she wrote, 'women made them not.'

Although successful at first, the campaigns of Charles VIII to gain control over northern Italy ultimately failed. (*Above, right*) The entry of Charles into Naples, 22 February 1495. Five months later, he defeated the Italians under Gonzaga at the Battle of Fornovo (*below, left*). (*Below, right*) Charles receives a book from the French writer, Marc Picault, c.1495.

Fashion in the Middle Ages depended very much on the fortunes of war or the security of peace. During war (or plague) it was often impossible to obtain supplies of the more expensive and exotic materials – silks, taffetas, velvets and furs. Most clothes were made of wool, from cloth manufactured in Flanders or imported from England. For the well-to-do, they were lavishly cut, using plenty of material. Then, as now, the main aim of the wearer was to display wealth. (*Above, left*) Charles, Duc d'Orléans, in a thick fur-lined surcoat from the early 15th century. (*Above, right*) A woman of the Ursin family during the reign of Charles VI. She is wearing a rich brocade, fur-trimmed jacket over a woollen dress.

Typical costumes as worn at the French Court during the second half of the 15th century. (*Above, right*) The figures in the picture are (from left to right) a widow with her children, a marquis, a baron, a chevalier (knight) and a *cavalière* (trooper or cavalryman). (*Below, right*) Ladies of the Court.

(*Above*) The Three Virtues (Reason, Uprightness and Justice) urge Christine de Pisan to write a *Book of Ethics* for the instruction of women. She obliged. (*Left*) Christine de Pisan presents a copy of her poems to Isabel of Bavaria, Queen of France. The royal bedchamber is hung with tapestries embroidered with the fleur-de-lys of France and the Bavarian diamond.

(*Right*) Christine de Pisan at her writing-table. Her *City of Women*, which she wrote in 1404, was a devastating attack on male stupidity and insensitivity. The male attitude towards women played a large part in the fate of Jeanne d'Arc. Her English persecutors were as frightened of her habit of wearing male attire as of her alleged sorcery and witchcraft.

One of the longest lasting French institutions founded in the late 15th century was the Gobelins tapestry factory. The Gobelin family came from Rheims but established their business on the outskirts of Paris. (*Above*) Workmen at Gobelins softening the cloth on which the tapestries were embroidered. (*Left*) Producing a miniature embroidery at home. (*Opposite*) Bringing in the vintage – one of a series of tapestries depicting scenes from a noble life.

(*Opposite, above*) The château of Blois, built in the Italian style in the 15th century. (*Opposite, below left and right*) Two views of the interior of Blois. (*Above*) The château of Chenonceaux. (*Right*) One of the ornate statues at Blois. (*Far right*) The moathouse at Chenonceaux.

(*Left*) The fairy-tale château at Azay-le-Rideau. (*Opposite, above*) The château at Amboise, dominating the town below. Leonardo da Vinci died at Amboise in 1519. (*Opposite, below left*) The entrance to the chapel where Leonardo is buried. (*Opposite, below right*) A view of the courtyard at Amboise.

Introduction to Period 2 – 1515–1815

Old habits die hard. The mighty vassals returned to their former aggressive ways in the 16th century as France split in two over questions of religion, following the Reformation. The wars of religion in the second half of the century gave the bigots opportunities to assert their pugnacious devotion, the ambitious a chance to trade on others' misfortunes, and the truly devout the obligation to defend their faith – whatever that might be.

Frenchman fought Frenchman, sometimes solely in pairs, in duels between Catholic and Protestant; sometimes in gangs that roamed the streets of the cities, hunting whoever was in the religious minority; and, most evilly, in the macabre slaughter of the St Bartholomew's Eve massacre, when the cobbles of Paris ran with the blood of three thousand Huguenots.

The wars came to an end in 1598, when the Edict of Nantes promised the Huguenots toleration and the protection of their own garrison towns. But this promise was steadily whittled away. By 1622 only Montauban and La Rochelle were left to the Protestants. By 1685 Louis XIV had imposed the Catholic faith on all his subjects, and Abraham Mazel, a leader of the Protestant Camisard rebels, could write: 'I had several inspirations by which I was told to prepare and take up arms to fight with my brothers against our persecutors, that I would bring iron and fire against the priests of the Roman Church and that I would burn their altars... At dusk we set out for Saint-André-de-Lancize to carry out another order uttered by my mouth, which was to put to death the priest of the locality, to burn his house, to topple the altar and to set fire to the church...'

Mazel did exactly that, adding fresh horrors to a long history of violent sectarianism which continued well into the 18th century. In the Cévennes, fights between Catholics and Protestants amounted to open warfare, with bands of armed men roaming the Massif Central, hunting down their neighbours. Not until the Revolution of 1789 did these internecine attacks cease.

There was plenty of fighting to do elsewhere. The French fought the English in Canada, the Spanish and the Dutch in the Low Countries, and, across the Holy Roman Empire, the Austrians and the Prussians. They became masters of war, inventors of new siege tactics and experts in the use of artillery, though they were frequently defeated in the battles to raise taxes to pay for these military adventures. It took Napoléon Bonaparte to bring State and army together, to wage total war on an unprecedented scale.

Glorious though many of these escapades appeared at the time, France ultimately maintained a more lasting pride in feats less dashing and more intellectual. The roll of honour of French literary figures has never been equalled. From the bawdy novels of Rabelais in the 16th century, to the scientific theories and critiques on society of Ronsard, and on to the pre-revolutionary philosophical works of Rousseau and Voltaire in the 18th century, the list is staggering in its length and breadth. Descartes published his *Discourse on Method* in 1637, the first performance of Molière's *Tartuffe* took place in 1664, Jean Racine's *Les Frères ennemis* the same year. While the Sun King blazed in splendour at Versailles, State pensions were awarded to Corneille, La Rochefoucauld, La Bruyère and La Fontaine.

Writers met in salons, in houses, inns and coffee-shops, and at the home of Marie de Rabutin-Chantas, Marquise de Sévigné, herself a great letter-writer and a Court aristocrat, passionately interested in health and medicine. She had little time for the fashionable quacks of the age, men who believed that the best (or the only) treatment for any ailment was to bleed the patient copiously and regularly. Madame de Sévigné, who had very small veins and was not easy to bleed, rejected this rough-and-ready approach, as well as the 'powdered snake' and 'essence of human urine' offerings of contemporary apothecaries. She believed in the old remedies, in the new spa towns at Vichy and Alise Sainte-Reine, and in 'waters' generally – waters of emerald, of chicken, the Queen of Hungary's water, water of gunpowder. She lived to be seventy. Whether her unorthodox beliefs prolonged or shortened her life remains a mystery.

On, into the 18th century, words flowed from the pens of French writers. Denis Diderot published his *Encyclopédie* in 1751. Four years later came Rousseau's *Discourse on the Origins of Inequality*, eight years later Voltaire's *Candide*. The great minds now met at the dinner table, the card table, the billiard table – where Voltaire and

Diderot were joined by d'Alembert and the Marquis de Condorcet.

Eventually France picked up an empire in Canada, only to lose it on the Heights of Abraham in 1759; found another in Louisiana and sold it in 1802; won an empire in India and lost it at Plassey in 1757; fought for another in Europe, and lost it in the freezing wastes of Russia in 1812. World supremacy was more easily and comfortably achieved through the music of Couperin, Lully and Rameau, and the German-born Gluck; through the paintings of Poussin and Delacroix, Watteau and Jacques-Louis David; and, above all, in the wonders of Versailles.

Few have ever shared Saint-Simon's view of Versailles as 'the most wretched of places, without view, without woods, without water, without soil; for all there is shifting sands and marshes, consequently without air, which cannot be good here'. To Louis XIV, Versailles stood as the symbol of the glory of France – majestic, beautiful, meticulously arranged, wonderfully contrived and the envy of the entire world.

And so it remained for a hundred years, until the coming of the Revolution...

9
WARS OF RELIGION 1515–1598

Between 1562 and 1598, France was shaken by a series of eight internal wars. Collectively they were known as the Wars of Religion, though the prime cause of conflict was rivalry between two families to establish a new royal dynasty. On the Catholic side was the Guise family, on the Protestant, the Montmorency. The way for their feud was paved by the death of François II, the sickly heir of Henri II, who reigned for little more than a year. François was in turn succeeded by his two brothers – Charles IX and Henri III – but real power in France was exercised by their mother, Catherine de Médicis. Hatred between Guise and Montmorency burst into violence on the Eve of St Bartholomew, 1572, when over 3,000 Protestants were slaughtered on the streets of Paris. (*Right*) Grieving Huguenots seek to comfort the bereaved, while others gaze in terror at the carnage below.

Introduction

In 1519 Leonardo da Vinci died at Amboise, a little market town some 15 miles east of Tours on the River Loire. He was one of many Italians who had been persuaded to visit France by the young king François I, who loved all things Italian. In 1534, Jacques Cartier stood on the banks of the St Lawrence River in Canada, with 3,000 miles of forest and plain, mountain and lake stretching westward before him.

Where did the future of France lie? Which way to go? Like a modern tourist, uncertain where to invest his or her limited time and money, the leaders of France hesitated, and then decided Canada could wait. There were greater riches to be found in Europe. Here was where France would assert itself, once it had put its own house in order.

The first step was to establish the French language. By the Edict of Villers-Cotterets in

1539, French became the language of diplomacy, of legal and official documents. Ten years later, the poet Joachim du Bellay published his *Defence and Illustration of the French Language*, recognising the preferability (if not superiority) of French over Latin for all communications. The translation of the Bible into French, and its ready availability thanks to the printing press, dealt a crippling blow to Latin, and to other vernacular languages such as Occitanian and Picard.

But the publication of a French Bible also served to fuel the religious controversy that had raced westwards from the little town of Wittenberg in Germany. This was accompanied by a succession of weak French kings and a lessening of control by central government. Aristocrats recovered much of their influence in provincial France, and the scene was set for the Wars of Religion that tore France apart between 1562 and 1598.

It was a tragedy of catastrophic proportions. In the early 16th century France had much to commend it as the most civilised country in Europe. There was wealth in plenty for those with luck and ability, and even the poorest families could look to their local town government to find help and support in their weeks and months of need. In the 1520s programmes of poor relief were established throughout France, providing alms, work, or, in the case of the 'undeserving', punishment.

It was a livelier, happier time, reflected in the boisterous writings of François Rabelais, whose *Great and Inestimable Chronicles of the Grand and Enormous Giant Gargantua* first appeared at the fair at Lyons in 1532.

But there were dark days and terrifying nights ahead as Catholic and Huguenots (as the Protestants were known) took up arms.

In an age of splendour and opulence, the meeting between François I and Henry VIII of England at the Field of the Cloth of Gold (*left*) was outstandingly ostentatious. Temporarily at least, the two countries were at peace, and François needed an English alliance against the Emperor Charles V. French military ambitions were turned to Italy, prized and coveted by François as the home of the Renaissance, a rich land, ripe for plunder.

François himself (*right*) was a man of large, if not always healthy appetite. He was a strong ruler and a doughty warrior, though Mars frequently made way for Venus. (*Opposite, bottom row, left to right*) Three mistresses of François I: Anne de Pisseleu, created Duchesse d'Etampes, a woman who completely dominated François from 1526 to his death in 1547; La Belle Ferronière, an earlier mistress; and Diane de Poitiers, Duchesse du Valentinois, who was also the mistress of Henri II.

The wealthy families of France maintained their position in society and their power over the local peasantry. At times when the Crown was weak, their estates became petty kingdoms over which they exercised absolute control. The French Parliament (the Estates General) had almost ceased to exist, and the *seigneurs* were judges, juries, landlords, tax collectors and military leaders in their own domains. As they grew richer, and as their stranglehold over the provinces tightened, they built new homes – grand houses that replaced the old castles, more comfortable, more graceful and far more lavishly equipped and furnished.

One of the finest was the château of Chambord (*above and opposite*), built – like so many – on the banks of the Loire. A Renaissance masterpiece, although its architect is uncertain both concept and design have been attributed to Leonardo de Vinci, who had been installed by François I at Clos Luce, near Amboise, in 1516.

Warfare in the early 16th century finally proved that the knight on horseback was no longer a military force of any consequence. This was the age of the arquebus and the musket, the cannon and the siege mortar. Horses were still vitally important to get guns and warriors to the battlefield, to carry scouts and messengers, but pikemen and musketeers were rapidly replacing archers and cavalry. With a collection of Swiss and German mercenaries, as well as their own French troops, first François I (*above*) and then Charles IX invaded Italy.

At first all went well. Big siege trains battered down the walls of many a north Italian city (*above*) and the French captured these jewels of the Renaissance. In 1525, however, François was defeated and captured at the Battle of Pavia (*opposite, below*) and subsequently forced to accept the humiliating terms of the Treaty of Madrid. He responded by making new alliances with German Protestant states and with the Ottoman Turks.

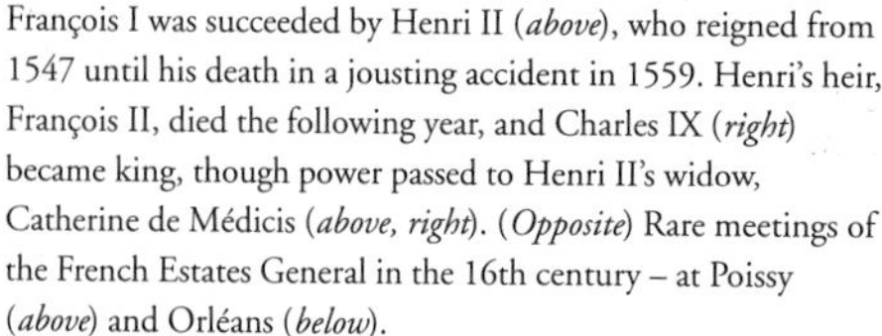

François I was succeeded by Henri II (*above*), who reigned from 1547 until his death in a jousting accident in 1559. Henri's heir, François II, died the following year, and Charles IX (*right*) became king, though power passed to Henri II's widow, Catherine de Médicis (*above, right*). (*Opposite*) Rare meetings of the French Estates General in the 16th century – at Poissy (*above*) and Orléans (*below*).

Charles IX was succeeded by Henri III, third son of Henri II and Catherine de Médicis. As Duc d'Anjou (*above, right*) he had defeated the Huguenots at the battles of Jarnac and Moncontour in 1569. At his mother's insistence, Henri accepted the Polish throne in 1573, but had to hurry back to France following the death of his elder brother Charles in 1574. (*Above, left*) Henri III's younger brother François, Duc d'Alençon, who died in 1584.

There were over twenty known assassination plots against Henri III during his reign. Some were hatched by those seeking to usurp his authority and gain the throne for themselves. The more dangerous were those initiated by religious fanatics. (*Above*) The death of Henri III in 1589. He was murdered by a Catholic bigot and friar named Jacques Clément, who was incensed at Henri's opposition to the militant Catholic League. Clément was in turn killed by the (ineffective) royal guards.

The later 16th century witnessed ferocious persecution of Catholic by Protestant and vice versa. (*Above, left*) A Catholic view – Catholics are chained together in pairs and starved into madness and death; a Catholic is dragged along a taut rope until cut in two. (*Below, left*) A Protestant view – a Huguenot bookseller from Avignon is burnt at the stake for selling translations of the Bible.

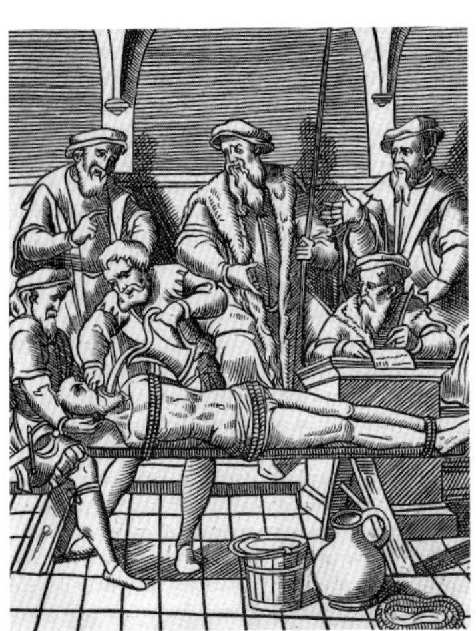

(*Left*) A group of Huguenot worshippers is attacked by Catholics. Those who attempt to escape by climbing on to the roof of their meeting-house are shot. (*Far left*) Water torture is used to extract a confession. (*Below*) Jean Calas, a Huguenot, is broken on the wheel. In 1551 Protestantism was made a capital crime throughout France.

The preferred Protestant religion in France was Calvinist rather than Lutheran. Jean Calvin (*opposite, left and right*) was born in Noyon, near Compiègne. He studied in Paris, but decided the rigidity of Catholic views there was ill-suited to his own religious principles. He settled in Geneva in 1541, the year in which his *Institutions* was published in French. He was present at the Council of Geneva in 1549 (*above*), through which he became the ruler of the city.

Calvin's simple faith gained a large following in France, especially in the south and south-west, Poitou, Normandy, Alsace and Lorraine. Calvinism was more popular among the middle classes than the peasantry, and in towns rather than in the country. The exception to this was the Cévennes region, which became staunchly Calvinist, despite the efforts of lord and bishop to stamp out this 'heresy'. Despite fines, imprisonment, torture and execution, the people of the Cévennes remained true to their new faith.

History regards Catherine de Médicis and Charles IX as equally responsible for the massacre of the Huguenots on St Bartholomew's Eve, 24 August 1572. At first Charles was reluctant to issue the order for the slaughter, but few can resist the wishes of a mother, and he finally consented (*left*). Among those killed was Admiral Gaspard de Coligny, a prominent member of the Montmorency family, then visiting Paris for the wedding of Charles' sister Marguerite to Henri de Navarre.

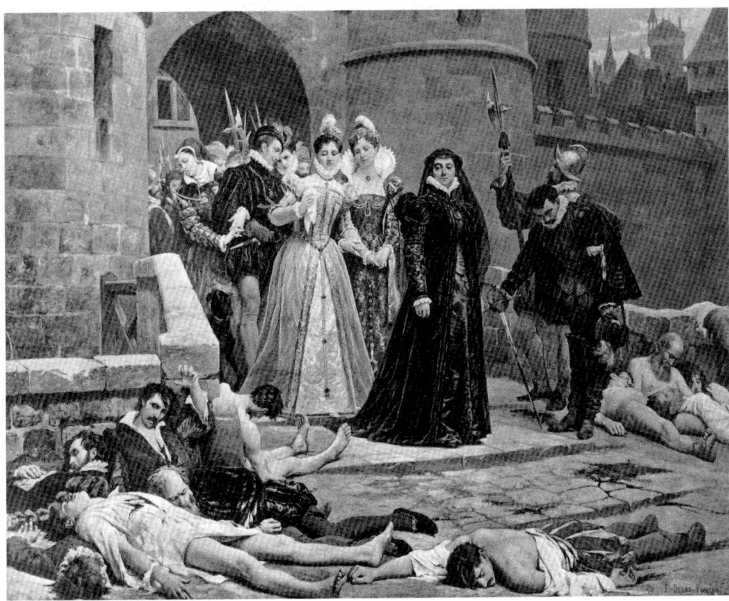

Three views of the massacre. (*Above, left*) The murder of Coligny in his hotel room. (*Above, right*) The slaughter in the streets. (*Left*) Catherine de Médicis surveys the carnage on the morning after the killing.

The main Huguenot strongholds during the religious wars were along the lower reaches of the Loire, in Gascony and the Midi, and in some of the areas around Paris – though these last were the first to suffer Catholic attack. The strongest bastions of all were La Rochelle and the Ile de Ré, on the west coast. Here the Huguenots looked for help from England, by then a Protestant nation. (*Opposite*) Part of the Hôtel de Ville in La Rochelle. (*Right*) The Phare des Baleines on the far west tip of the Ile de Ré.

To a casual observer it might seem that there was a curse on the Guise family, for violence seemed to stalk them. The dynasty was founded by Claude of Lorraine, created first Duc de Guise in 1527 for his part in suppressing a peasant revolt in Lorraine. His son François (*above, left*) succeeded to the title in 1550 and spent much of his life fighting the Huguenots. He was shot by a Huguenot at the siege of Orléans in 1563 (*above, right*).

François de Guise and his brother, Cardinal Charles de Guise (*opposite, below left*), virtually ruled France during the reign of François II. In 1563 the title passed to Henri, the third Duc de Guise (*opposite, below right*). Henri was known as Le Balafré ('the Scarred'). He spent much of his life fighting for the Catholic cause and was one of the instigators of the St Bartholomew's Eve massacre. Though close to Henri III, he was not trusted by the king. (*Above, right*) Henri, Duc de Guise, greets Henri III on the way to Mass, 22 December 1588. The duke was unaware that the king was plotting his assassination. (*Below, right*) The death of the duke the following day.

Henri de Navarre (*above, left*) was the leader of the French Huguenots for much of the 1560s and 1570s. On the death of Henri III in 1589, he marched on Paris, then in the hands of the Catholic League. 'Paris,' declared Henri, 'is worth a Mass,' so he changed his faith and secured his succession to the throne of France. (*Below, left and right*) Marguerite de Valois, first wife of Henri de Navarre, and Marie de Médicis, his second wife and mother of Louis XIII. (*Above, right*) The interrogation of Jean Chatel, who had attempted to assassinate Henri in 1594. The method of torture used here is *le brodequin*. A physician stands by to make sure that the accused does not die.

(*Right*) Henri de Navarre, now Henri IV of France, defeats the Catholic League at the Battle of Ivry, 14 March 1590. (*Below*) Spanish soldiers and their followers leave Paris through St David's Gate after Henri IV declares war on Spain in January 1595.

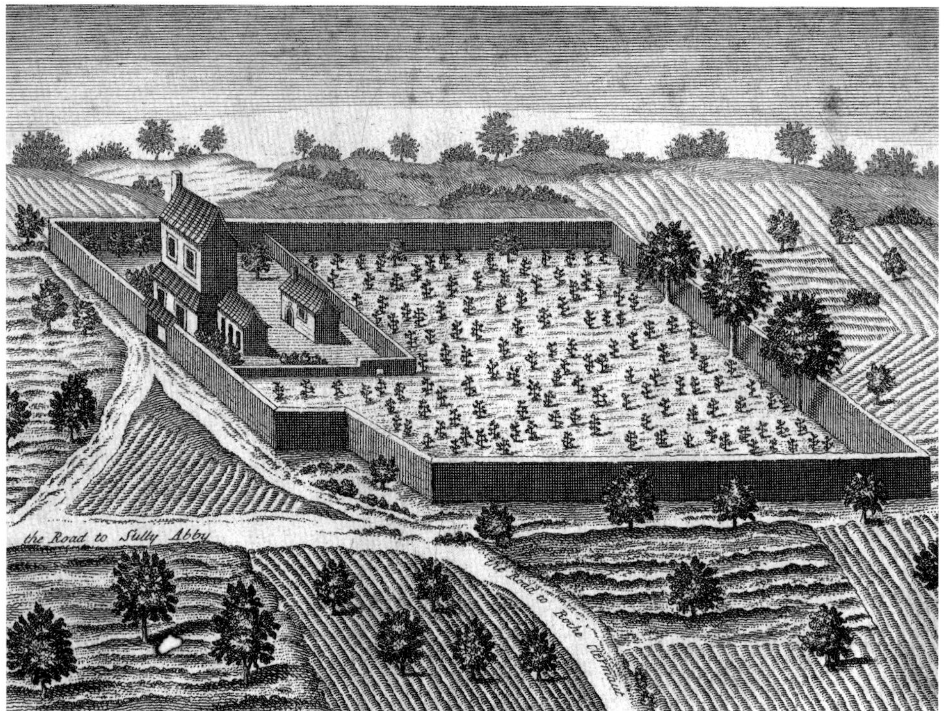

François Rabelais (*opposite, above right*) was born at his father's farmhouse near Chinon (*above*) around the year 1494. He trained as a novice of the Franciscan order, but came to loathe Franciscan life. With the pope's permission, he transferred to the Benedictine order. Rabelais began writing in the 1530s, his first works being *Pantagruel* and a successor to the *Grand Gargantua* of 1532 – Rabelais almost certainly did not write the original. He followed these books with a series of almanacs called the *Pantagrueline Prognostications*, a mixture of serious ideas and nonsense.

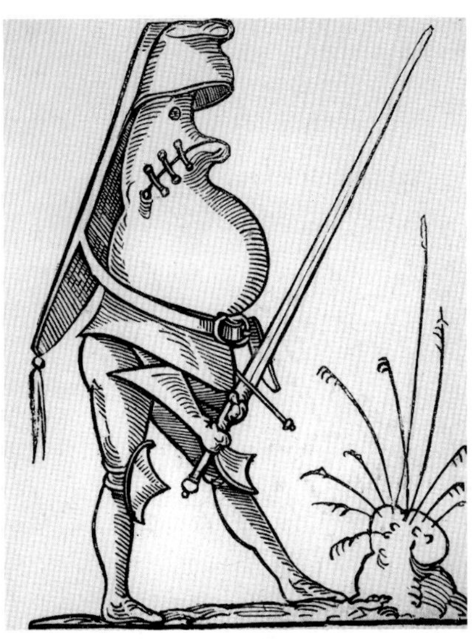

All his works have a riotous energy, a monstrous wit that bubbles to the surface, and – often – a licentious tone. As a writer he has seldom been out of fashion. (*Left*) A publisher's blurb for a 19th-century edition of Rabelais. (*Above, left*) A caricature by Rabelais of Charles de Bourbon, Governor of Milan, c.1520. Apart from his books, Rabelais was responsible for bringing the melon, the artichoke and the carnation to France.

Many of the best images of late 16th- and early 17th-century France are from the etchings and engravings of Jacques Callot (*left, above and below*). Callot was born in Nancy but joined a band of gypsies at the age of twelve and travelled to Florence. He was sent home, but returned to Italy to train as an artist.

On his return to Nancy he found patrons first in the Duc de Lorraine and then in Louis XIII, who commissioned him to provide pictures of the siege of La Rochelle and other aspects of war which Callot published under the title *Miseries of War.* (*Above*) A view of Paris along the Seine, one of the many engravings of France produced by Callot early in his career.

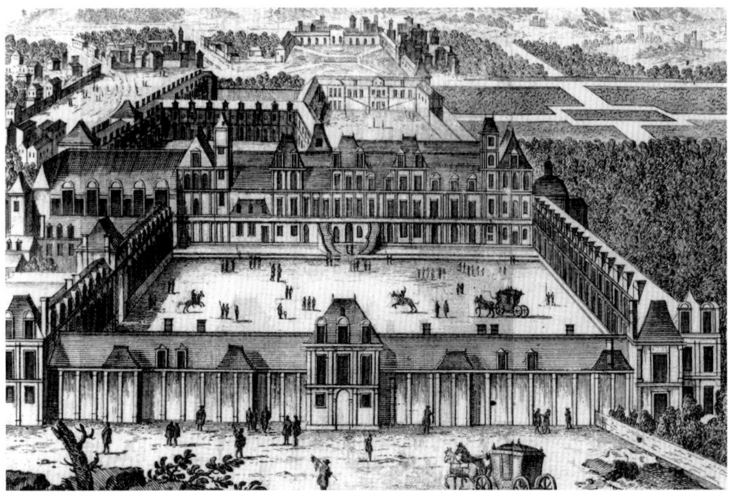

The great joy of the palace of Fontainebleau (*above, left*), to many of its royal occupants, was its distance from unruly Paris. Here, in the tree-lined walks (*opposite, above*) or in the Fountain Court near the Galleria d'Ulisse (*below, left*), François I and his successors strolled and picnicked, safe from the Paris mob. (*Opposite, below*) The lavishly decorated Gallery of Henri II, Fontainebleau.

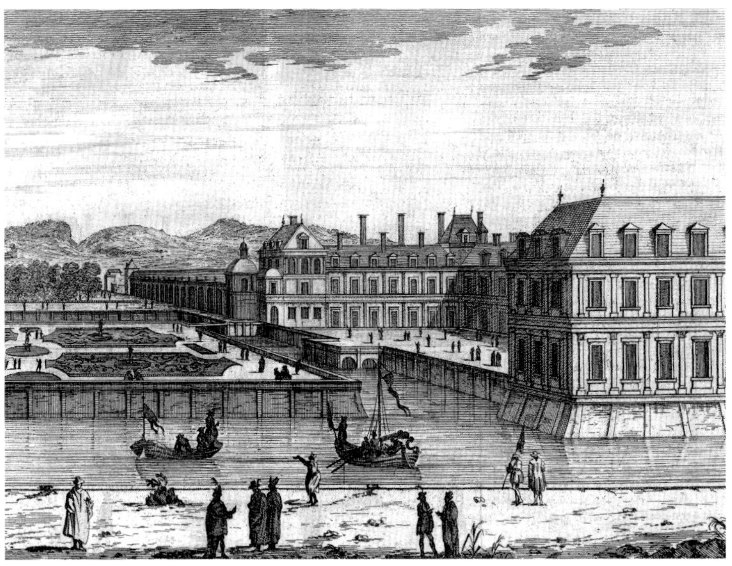

Michel de Notredame (*left and opposite*) was a French physician and astrologer who became better known as the prophet Nostradamus. He was born at Saint-Rémy, Provence, in 1503, and trained as a doctor of medicine. Not until 1547 did he set himself up as a prophet, and his *Centuries of Prediction* have made him famous throughout the world. It has been said that he foretold the Revolution of 1789, the sinking of the *Titanic*, the First World War and the rise of Hitler. Most of his predictions, however, are very vaguely phrased. Charles IX had no doubt as to the wisdom of Nostradamus, and appointed him royal physician-in-ordinary in 1550.

10
EMINENCE GRISE
1598–1648

(*Right*) A triple portrait by the artist Philippe de Champaigne of the French statesman and ecclesiastic, Cardinal Armand Jean du Plessis, Duc de Richelieu. Richelieu originally trained as a soldier, but there were richer pickings to be had in the Church for a smart and ambitious young man. At the age of twenty-nine he became adviser to Marie de Médicis and regent for her son Louis XIII. He was a cardinal in his mid-thirties and minister of state to Louis before he was forty. For the next eighteen years he had more power than any man in France, and he used his power ruthlessly to achieve what he wanted.

Introduction

As the dust settled on the first round of the Wars of Religion, the kings of France set about reclaiming some of the power and authority they had lost. Significantly, they used cardinals of the Catholic Church to help them – first Armand Jean du Plessis, the great Richelieu, and then Jules Mazarin. For almost forty years between them, they dominated the King's Council, lending their sometimes sound, always strong advice to the newly-established Bourbon dynasty.

The two cardinals also played a leading part in the French counter-reformation, a reassertion of the old faith in a leaner, keener mode. The new Church emphasised the importance of good works, and the devout leapt to centre stage. In 1608 Saint-François de Sales and Sainte-Jeanne de Chantal founded the Order of the Vistardines and published the *Introduction à la vie dévote*. At much the same time, Saint-Vincent de Paul established the Lazarist missionary order and the nursing order of the Daughters of Charity. The pious Sainte-Louise de Marillac worked with Vincent de Paul, but not all loyal Catholics had quite such holy aims. The Company of the Holy Sacrament, founded by the Duc de Ventadour in the late 1620s, was a secret society of lawyers, clerics and nobles who combined a programme of good work in hospitals, in schools for the poor, and among prostitutes, with plots and plans to reduce the rights of Protestants.

Comparative peace at home gave France the chance to rebuild and expand towns and cities, which it did with aplomb. New splendours arose in Paris: the Place Royale, the *Académie française*, the Hôtel Lambert, and the Pont-Neuf, the first bridge to span the Seine. France's first national newspaper, *La Gazette*, appeared in 1631.

In the countryside, life was less peaceful. The struggle against hunger and famine continued. Massive tax increases were imposed to pay for the lengthy war against Spain in the first half of the 17th century. Individual acts of violence (rick-burning, the maiming of animals, attacks against the agents of landowners) were common. Widespread revolt flared with dangerous regularity – in the south-west in 1624 and 1636, in the Loire valley in 1636, and in the Normandy rising of the *Va-nu-pieds* ('bare feet') in 1639.

Central government was under pressure to learn how to cope with direct action. Force required money. Money came from taxes. Taxes led to direct action. It was a cycle that the *Ancien Régime* never managed to break.

The marriage between Louis XIII (*above, left*) and Anne of Austria (*above, right*) was arranged by Louis' mother, Marie de Médicis, when he was only fourteen years old. Two years later, Louis banished his mother to the provinces. On Louis' death, Anne herself became regent of France. (*Left*) Anne's advisory council – on the extreme right is Saint-Vincent de Paul.

(*Above, left*) Henri Coiffier-Ruzé d'Effiat, Marquis de Cinq-Mars – friend and favourite of Louis XIII. (*Above, right*) Louise Motier de Lafayette, a former nun who became mistress of Louis XIII. (*Right*) Louis receives lessons in horsemanship from his instructor, the Marquis de Pluvinel.

(*Above, right*) Champaigne's portrait of Richelieu at the height of the cardinal's power. (*Above, left*) The tomb of Richelieu in the Chapelle de la Sorbonne, Paris. Early in his career, Richelieu made it his business to destroy the Huguenots. He laid siege to their stronghold, La Rochelle (*left*), and starved the garrison into submission.

Richelieu's talent was manipulating people and running the affairs of France, but he had misplaced ambitions as a writer. His plays have sunk into merciful oblivion, but his other works (*above*) are still occasionally read. (*Right*) Richelieu and Father Joseph – a menacing portrait of the *éminence grise* who ruled France from 1624 to 1642.

Shortly before his death, Richelieu recommended to the king that Cardinal Jules Mazarin (*opposite*) should succeed him as principal adviser to the Crown. When Louis died a year later, Mazarin used his influence over the king's widow, Anne of Austria, to maintain power. Anne and Mazarin (*left*) were close confidantes. There is no proof that they were secretly married, but Anne certainly loved her stiff-necked, authoritarian and largely unpopular chief minister. Regarded as a foreigner by Parisians (he was born in Italy), and hated in the provinces, Mazarin thought it wise to move the French Court to Saint-Germain, but soon faced civil insurrection.

Samuel Champlain (*left*) was the French founder of Canada. He crossed the Atlantic to the New World three times between the years 1603 and 1608, exploring the coast and the interior and establishing the city of Quebec. He was also the first Frenchman to forge treaties with the Hurons, the native North Americans who dominated the north-east of the continent – a powerful alliance which controlled eastern Canada for one hundred and fifty years.

The main enemies of the Hurons were the Iroquois Five Nations (*below, right*). On 29 July 1609, Champlain and the Hurons attacked and overran Iroquois camps near the St Lawrence (*right*). Although Champlain set up forts and trading stations for the rich fur trade, his main aim (like that of so many other explorers) had been to find a north-west passage to the Orient. In 1629 he published his *Les Voyages de la Nouvelle France* (*below, left*), an account of his wanderings and discoveries over the past twenty-five years. He died in 1635.

LES
VOYAGES
DE LA
NOVVELLE FRANCE
OCCIDENTALE, DICTE
CANADA,
FAITS PAR LE S^r DE CHAMPLAIN
Xainctongeois, Capitaine pour le Roy en la Marine du Ponant, & toutes les Descouuertes qu'il a faites en ce païs depuis l'an 1603. iusques en l'an 1629.

Où se voit comme ce pays a esté premierement descouuert par les François, sous l'authorité de nos Roys tres-Chrestiens, iusques au regne de sa Majesté à present regnante LOVIS XIII. Roy de France & de Nauarre.

Auec vn traitté des qualitez & conditions requises à vn bon & parfaict Nauigateur pour cognoistre la diuersité des Estimes qui se font en la Nauigation. Les Marques & enseignements que la prouidence de Dieu à mises dans les Mers pour redresser les Mariniers en leur routte, sans lesquelles ils tomberoient en ce grands dangers, Et la maniere de bien dresser Cartes marines auec leurs Ports, Rades, Isles, Sondes, & autre chose necessaire à la Nauigation.

Ensemble vne Carte generalle de la description dudit pays faicte en son Meridien selon la declinaison de la guide Aymant, & vn Catechisme ou Instruction traduicte du François au langage des peuples Sauuages de quelque contrée, auec ce qui s'est passé en ladite Nouuelle France en l'année 1631.

A MONSEIGNEVR LE CARDINAL DVC DE RICHELIEV.

A PARIS.
Chez PIERRE LE-MVR, dans la grand' Salle du Palais.

M. DC. XXXII.
Auec Priuilege du Roy.

While Richelieu and Mazarin sought to strengthen the Catholic hold on France by persecuting the Huguenots, other Catholics did what they could to reform and purify the Catholic Church itself. Foremost among these new saints was Vincent de Paul (*above, right*), founder of the Lazarist missionary order and co-founder with Sainte-Louise de Marillac (*opposite, left*) of the nursing community known as the Daughters of Charity. As a young man, Vincent had been captured by corsairs in the Mediterranean and sold into slavery in Tunis. Later he did what he could to rescue those who had been sentenced to work as galley slaves (*above, left*).

Sainte-Jeanne de Chantal (*above, right*) was the co-founder with Saint-François de Sales of the Order of Visitation. Such foundations offered women the otherwise rare chance to work independently of husband or father. They also did much to raise the standards of hygiene, care and medical practice in 17th-century hospitals throughout France. Their work was widely publicised by word of mouth. Their sombre costumes were recognised all over the country. Within a short time, they attracted the attention of many wealthy supporters.

Blaise Pascal (*opposite and right*) was an outstanding mathematician of prodigious natural talent. He was born in Clermont-Ferrand in 1623 and educated by his father, though Blaise discovered as much on his own as his father taught him. He was also a philosopher, physicist and inventor. He made the first mechanical adding machine and established the mathematical laws of probability. His greatest invention, however, was the barometer. He climbed to the top of the Puy de Dôme with two glass tubes of mercury inverted in a bath of the same substance. As he climbed, he noted the fall of the mercury columns with increased altitude.

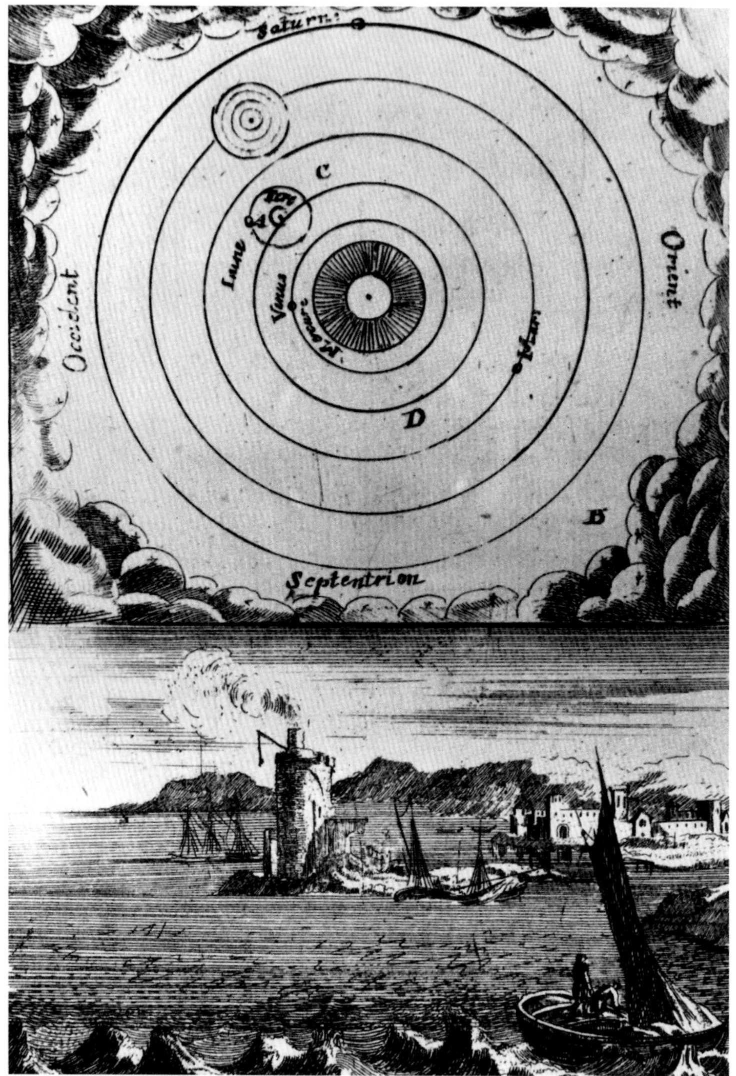

Many great French minds were at work in the 17th century. Out of the chaos of the struggle between Catholic and Protestant, and the ferment of ideas sparked by the Renaissance, came a new fascination with learning and experiment. René Descartes (*opposite*) was one of the greatest philosophers and mathematicians of all time, though even he suppressed some of his thoughts and findings for fear of provoking the wrath of the Catholic Church. (*Left*) Descartes' diagrammatic representation of the movement of the planets around the sun, from a book published in 1685.

Although Savinien Cyrano de Bergerac (*opposite*) was famous in his lifetime as a writer and dramatist, he was best known for fighting over a thousand duels – mostly with those who dared insult his fine (long) nose. His work is full of comic invention and flights of fancy. (*Left*) Cyrano heads for the moon, powered by the magic phials fastened to his waist – an illustration from his *Histoire comique des états de la lune et du soleil*. Much of Bergerac's work was unpublished during his lifetime, for Richelieu and Mazarin imposed regimes of heavy censorship on French writers, scientists and free-thinkers.

From the middle of the 17th century to her death in 1696, Marie de Rabutin-Chantal, Marquise de Sévigné (*left*), ran a one-woman crusade to improve the medical care of the French. Like the playwright Molière and many of her contemporaries, she had little respect for doctors, but she showered them with advice on how to treat and avoid a thousand and one diseases and ailments.

Part of Madame de Sévigné's dislike of the medical profession stemmed from the fact that she had small and well-hidden veins, so that it was difficult for doctors to bleed her – bleeding being the preferred treatment for most conditions. She was as prepared to take advice as to give it, collecting her wisdom from quacks, irregular practitioners, 'old wives' and folklore. The earnestness with which she passed on such information caused many to regard her as a sage. (*Right*) The house of Madame de Sévigné. She died of smallpox, after nursing her beloved daughter through a long illness.

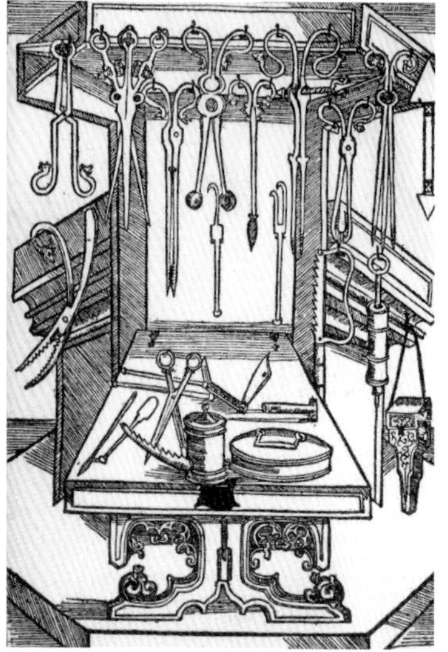

Slowly, and often unsteadily, superstition and quackery gave way to more scientifically based medical practice. The tool-kit of the surgeon (*above, left*), though grotesquely crude by modern standards, became larger and better equipped to deal with delicate work. (*Above, right*) An illustration from a treatise of 1597 on 'rhinoplasty'. (*Below, left*) Cauterising a leg wound. (*Below, right*) First aid on the field of battle – a wound to the chest is cauterised. Many patients died of the shock of such treatment.

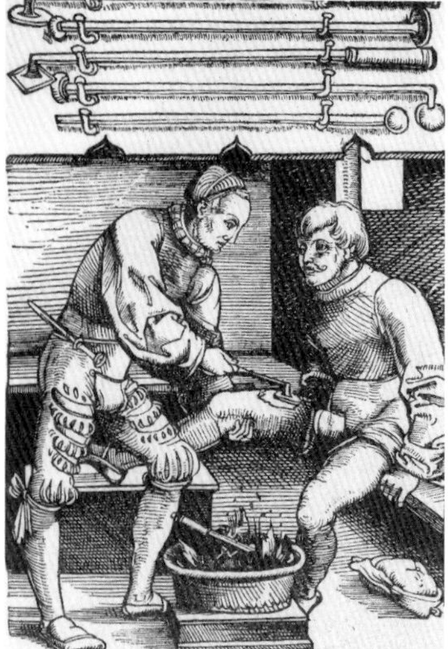

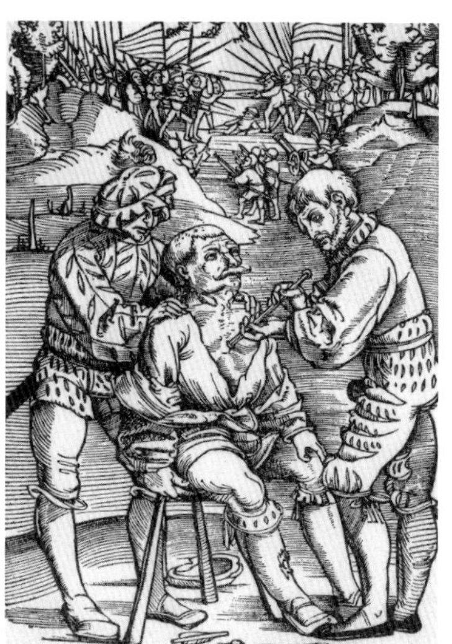

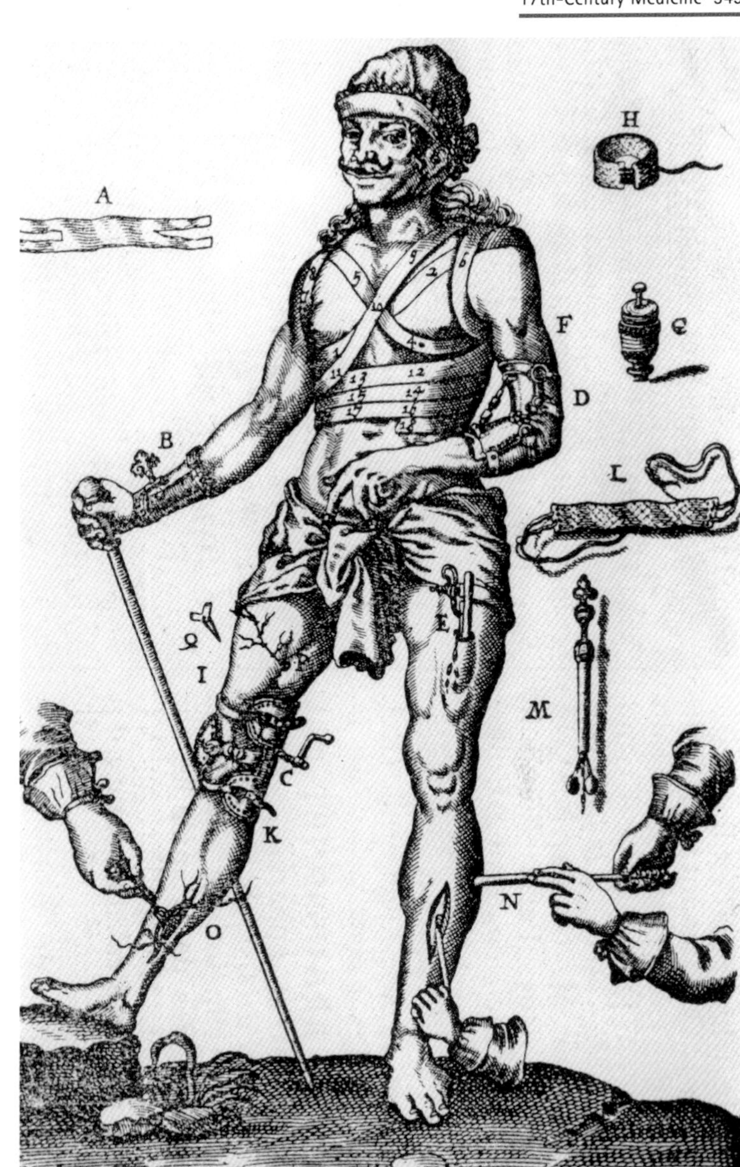

An illustration, probably used as the frontispiece to a treatise on surgery, dating from 1656. The lettered instruments – which look more fitted to torture than treatment – suggest that ingenious minds were working to establish improved ways of helping the body's recovery from a large variety of wounds or accidents. Though crude in many ways, they were probably a vast improvement on older methods, where amputation, cauterisation or death (or any combination of the three) were more likely outcomes.

Paris was the 17th-century wonder of the world – the most elegant city in Europe, bejewelled with Gothic glories, decorated with statues of the nation's heroes, a centre of learning and art, the capital of the most powerful country. Among the city's new wonders was the Pont-Neuf (*left*), the first bridge to span the entire width of the River Seine. The grand building standing on wooden piles is the Hôpital de la Samaritaine.

11
THE SUN KING
1648–1715

Louis XIV believed that a great king deserved a great setting, and he therefore commissioned the building of the Palais de Versailles. He left the members of his academy of fine arts in no doubt as to the importance of the task ahead of them. 'I entrust to you,' he said, 'the most precious thing in my world, my renown.' In an age of absolute rule, it was a daunting responsibility, but the men who designed, furnished and decorated this temple to *le Roi-Soleil* (the Sun King) rose to the occasion. (*Right*) Visitors to the new Palais de Versailles throng the great courtyard, c. 1680.

Introduction

There was one more cloud to be dispersed. In 1648 the civil war known as *La Fronde* broke out. It was named after a children's catapult and was confined mainly to the regions around Paris and Bordeaux. Nevertheless, it was a serious challenge to the absolutism that Richelieu and Mazarin had worked so hard to impose on the country. Mazarin himself was exiled (three times in four years) and the young Louis XIV was virtually a prisoner of the Paris mob. The worst of the rising was over by 1652, though it smouldered on until 1661, when Louis' minority came to an end and he took control of France.

And then the Sun blazed in all its magnificence. Le Nôtre, Le Brun, Le Vau, Hardouin-Mansart and the Francine brothers merged their considerable talents to create the Palace of Versailles – a mixture of self-glorifying monument to *le Roi-Soleil*, and pleasure-dome for Louis the man. It took twenty-one years to build, and during that time consumed 5 per cent of the entire State income.

To be fair to Louis, it was not just his own importance that he wished to recognise. In 1661 the Academy of Dance was set up, followed by the Academy of Inscription (1662), the Academy of Science (1666), the Academy of Architecture (1671), of Music (1672), and the *Comédie-française* in 1680. The French East Indies Company was founded in 1664, Canada became a province of France, and a thriving colony was established in Louisiana. Long before other European nations realised the commercial possibilities of inland waterways, the Canal du Midi was completed in 1681, linking the Mediterranean with the Atlantic.

Had Louis been less profligate in his spending, and less eager to go to war on the slightest pretext, the French economy would have been healthy enough in the late 17th and early 18th centuries. But the French navy increased in size from eighteen ships to two hundred and seventy-six in the first part of his reign, and by the end of it France had to support a standing army of 400,000 men. As the public debt soared, new and unpopular taxes were introduced, and offices were sold across the board in a frenzied attempt to avoid financial disaster.

As Louis lay dying in 1715, François de Salignac de la Mothe Fénelon pithily described the state of a nation worn out by war and internal strife: 'All France is just one great desolate hospital lacking provisions.'

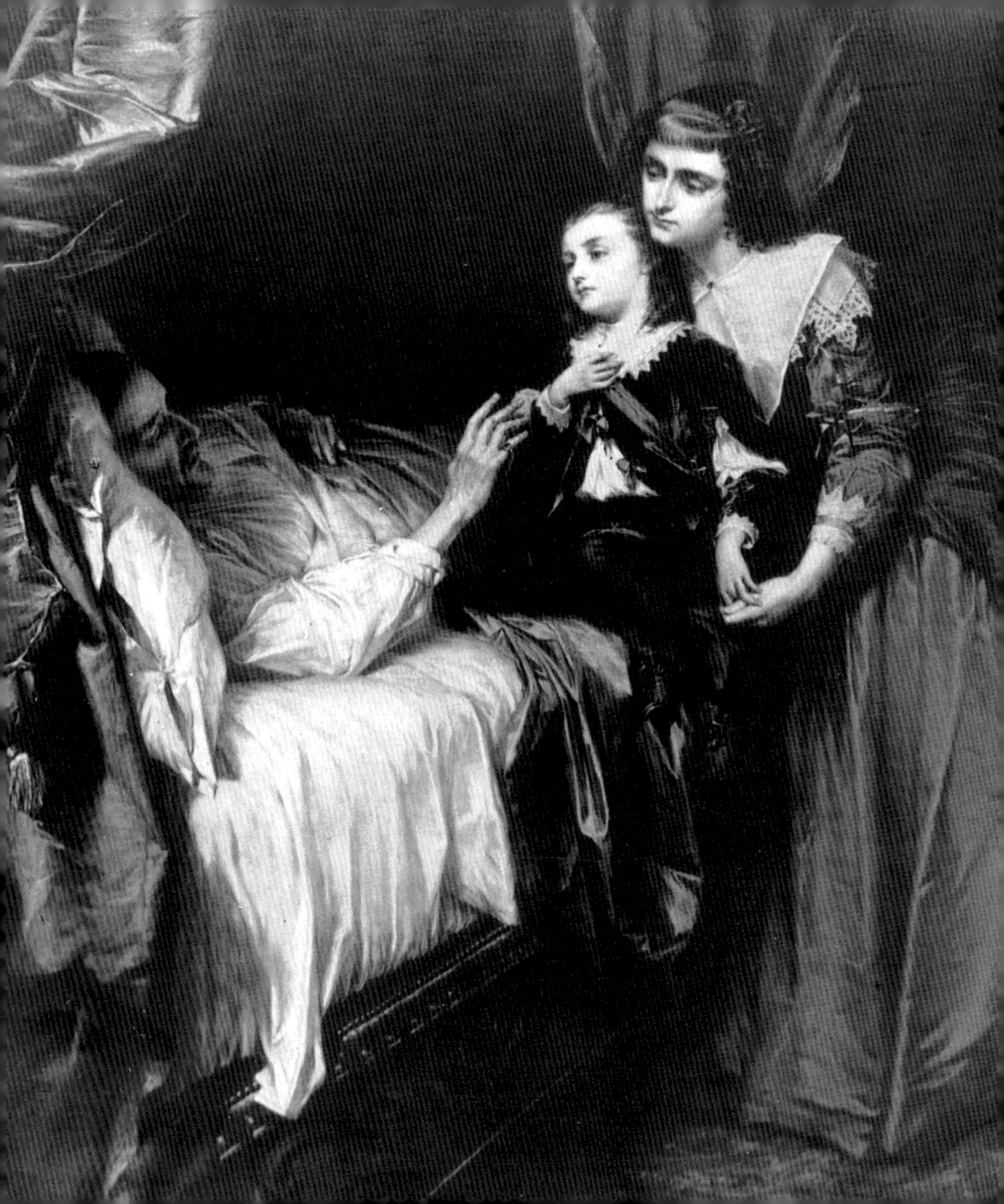

Louis XIV was the son of Louis XIII and Anne of Austria. He succeeded to the throne at the age of five in 1643. The little boy was brought to his dying father after his own christening (*opposite*). 'What is your name?' asked the king. 'Louis Quatorze,' replied his son. 'Not yet, my boy,' said Louis XIII, though the time was fast approaching. (*Right*) Fifteen-year-old Louis XIV in costume as the Sun King, a rare drawing of 1653.

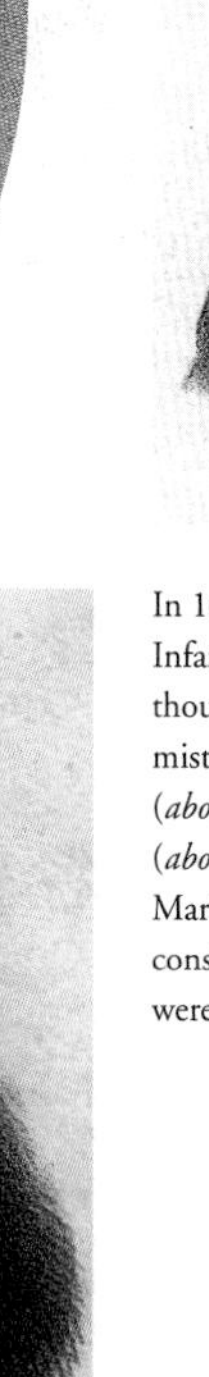

In 1660 Louis XIV married Marie-Thérèse of Austria, the Infanta of Spain (*left*). Their marriage lasted twenty-three years, though Louis was by no means true to his wife. Among his many mistresses were Françoise Athenaïs, Marquise de Montespan (*above, left*), and Françoise d'Aubigné, Marquise de Maintenon (*above, right*), whom Louis married after the death of Marie-Thérèse in 1680. The Marquise de Maintenon had considerable influence over Louis, both before and after they were married.

Louis recruited his mistresses from a wide variety of sources – from his Court, from the houses of his friends, and from the most fashionable of nunneries. (*Above, right*) Louis entreats the Duchesse de La Vallière to leave her Carmelite retreat in Paris. He had more worldly gifts to offer her. (*Below, right*) The meeting between Louis and his future father-in-law, Philip IV of Spain, to decide the fate of Marie-Thérèse – a Gobelins tapestry from the painting by Charles Le Brun at Versailles.

Louis was utterly convincing in his role as absolute ruler of France. His Court was sumptuous, his entertainment lavish, and his will unyielding. (*Above*) Louis grants an audience in his bedchamber at Versailles to the pope's nephew, summoned to apologise for a slight to the French ambassador in Rome. (*Left*) The meeting between Louis XIV and James II of Britain at the Court of Saint-Germain, shortly after James's flight from London.

(*Above*) A moment of relaxation from the affairs of state – Louis enjoys a game of billiards at Versailles, c.1694. The game was already well over one hundred years old when this picture was painted by Trouvain. (*Right*) Louis XIV and members of his close personal staff in walking-out costume. Few of those around Louis were allowed any power or influence. Within a year of the death of Mazarin in 1661, Louis ordered the arrest of his chief minister, Nicolas Fouquet.

The reign of Louis XIV (*left*) was the longest of any monarch in European history. During the seventy-two years he was King of France he had two main ambitions: to unite his country and to crush his enemies abroad. Never again, as far as he was concerned, would Protestant factions threaten the stability of life at home, and never again would foreign armies dare to cross the French frontiers.

(*Above*) A painting by Nicolas de Largillière of Louis XIV and his family, all of whom predeceased him. From left to right: the Duchesse de Ventadour (governess to the royal children), the Duc de Bretagne (1707–12, great-grandson of the king), Louis, le Grand Dauphin (1661–1711, the king's son), Louis XIV, Louis, Duc de Bourgogne (1682–1712). When Louis XIV died in 1715, he was succeeded by another great-grandson, the Duc d'Anjou, who became Louis XV.

(*Above*) The heart of Paris in 1650, from Boisseau's painting of the Palais de Justice on the Ile de la Cité. Despite the removal of the Court to Versailles, Paris continued to be the heart of France. The city had had its periods of decline and moments of setback: half the population died during the Black Death in the mid-14th century.

By 1550, however, the population had once again reached well over a quarter of a million and the city was indisputably the greatest in Europe. Long before the Revolution of 1789, kings and ministers feared the Paris mob, that seemingly uncontrollable mass of people who were prepared to challenge authority in the most outrageous manner.

Today the Tuileries also lends its name to a Métro station, but three hundred years ago it was an immense royal palace in the heart of Paris (*left*). The gardens surrounding the Tuileries (which still survive) were laid out by André Le Nôtre in the mid-17th century. Le Nôtre also designed the tree-lined avenue, extending the royal view from the palace, which came to be known as the Champs-Elysées, perhaps the most famous street in the world. The Palais des Tuileries was destroyed during the Communard uprising in 1871.

The Vieux Louvre (*above, left*) was a medieval fortress built more to protect the kings of France than as a symbol of their wealth and power. Over the centuries it was rebuilt and enlarged, but the greatest changes to the palace were those of the 17th century, supervised by Louis' chief minister, Jean-Baptiste Colbert. (*Below, left*) Building the new Louvre. (*Opposite, above*) The Louvre as it was towards the end of the 17th century. (*Opposite, below*) View of the Louvre and the Grande Galérie as it neared completion. Many architects worked on the project, notably Antoine Houdin, Charles Perrault and the Italian architect Lorenzo Bernini.

ARMIDE
Dessiné par M. Johannot
Gravé par Geille

Jean-Baptiste Lully (*opposite*) was born in Florence in 1632. The Chevalier de Guise recognised the talent of the young musician and took him to Paris, where Lully soon became Louis XIV's composer of music for the dance. Lully became famous for his operas, among them *Atys* (*right*). He also became extremely rich. The Court of France was a hotbed of vice, and Lully happily succumbed. It is said that only his genius saved him from serious punishment. He died from an abscess induced by striking his foot with his own long baton while conducting a performance of the *Te Deum.*

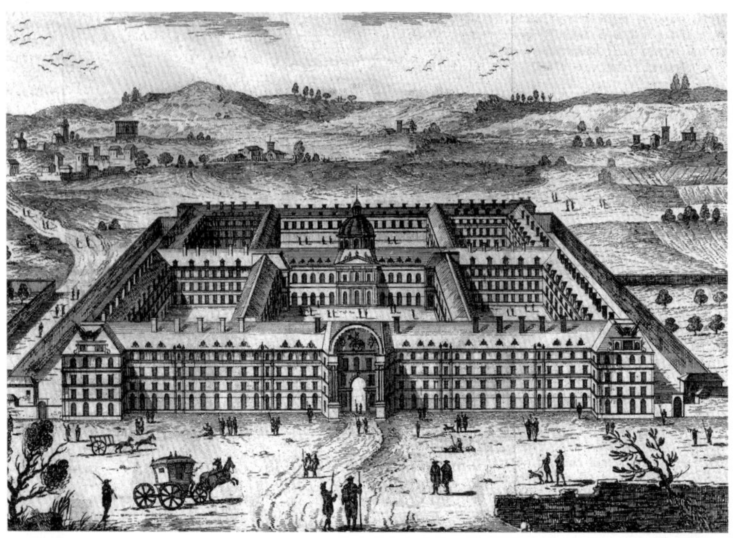

The Hôtel des Invalides (*opposite and above, left*) was built by Louis XIV to house veterans of his armies who had been wounded in the many wars of his reign. It was founded in 1670. Although often cited as evidence of the charitable side of Louis' nature, its main purpose was to prevent ex-soldiers begging, stealing, filling the streets and generally causing havoc. (*Below, left*) Nuns cleaning and tending patients in a contemporary convent hospital in France.

Louis founded the French academy of architecture in 1671. Its role was to train young architects, by which means it established State control of any major new buildings. Among the buildings for which members of the academy were responsible were the Sorbonne (*above*) and the Collège des Quatre-Nations (*opposite*). The Collège was designed by Louis Le Vau and François d'Orblay, and was built between 1662 and 1672.

In the late 17th century, the Palace of Versailles (*above*) was the marvel of the age. There was nothing anywhere to compare with it. It cost a fortune to build and almost crippled the French exchequer, for Louis spared no expense in its construction. It was the product of the combined genius of France's finest architects and designers – chief among them Louis Le Vau, André Le Nôtre, Jules Hardouin-Mansart (who built the Grand Trianon), Philibert Le Roy (the Marble Court) and Charles Le Brun (the Salon de la Guerre and the Galérie des Glaces). The Sun had never shone so brilliantly.

From conception to completion the Palace took almost fifty years to build. The Palace Chapel (*opposite*), designed by Hardouin-Mansart and Robert de Cotte, alone took twenty-one years to build and was not completed until 1710. The Fountain of Latone (*above*) was the work of Le Nôtre and Hardouin-Mansart. With the Grand Canal, it too took over twenty years to build. At one time more than 30,000 workers were employed on the construction of the Palace and its surrounding gardens. It was the Sun King's crippling legacy to his successors, a *tour de force* that played its own part in bringing down the French monarchy.

(*Left*) Joseph Vernet's study of ships of the French navy. On the left is a battleship flying the flag of France, in the middle a galley flying a red flag. The vessel on the right is a merchant ship, which flies a blue flag with a white cross. (*Opposite, above*) Disaster – the French fleet is destroyed by the English at La Hague, 22 May 1694. (*Opposite, below*) Triumph – French corsairs under Jean Bart defeat the Dutch fleet at the Battle of Texel, 1694.

Robert Cavelier, Sieur de La Salle (*above, left*), was a man of 'inexhaustible pride', 'inflexible purpose' and 'insatiable intellect'. He was also overbearing, courageous and brilliant. He learnt a dozen Native American dialects, covered 1,000 miles in a canoe in sixty-five days, and blazed a trail through North America from Michigan to the Gulf of Mexico. In his wake came Jean-Baptiste Lemoine de Bienville (*above, right*), an early governor of the enormous tract of land named Louisiana after the greatest of all kings of France.

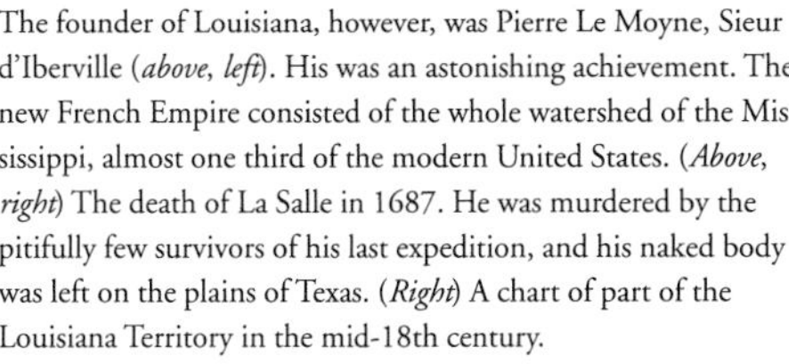

The founder of Louisiana, however, was Pierre Le Moyne, Sieur d'Iberville (*above, left*). His was an astonishing achievement. The new French Empire consisted of the whole watershed of the Mississippi, almost one third of the modern United States. (*Above, right*) The death of La Salle in 1687. He was murdered by the pitifully few survivors of his last expedition, and his naked body was left on the plains of Texas. (*Right*) A chart of part of the Louisiana Territory in the mid-18th century.

It was not easy to find enough volunteers to sail the Atlantic and help to build this vast new French Empire in the Americas. Where persuasion or bribery failed, force was used. There was a particular shortage of women in the Louisiana Territory. One way to solve this problem, and to sweep a little dust under the carpet, was to transport prostitutes to the colonies.

(*Opposite, above and below*) Young paramours, debauched old rogues and wealthy clients bid farewell to their harlots. There were many protestations of heartbreak, but consolation was doubtless close at hand – for all parties. (*Right*) Gendarmes raid a brothel and drag the occupants off to the harbour. (*Below*) A round-up of prostitutes for service overseas.

Jean-Baptiste Colbert (*opposite*) was an administrator of the highest ability. Almost single-handedly he revolutionised the economy of France, doubling the revenues and saving the country from bankruptcy and chaos. His aim was to establish France as the greatest country in the world in every sphere of achievement – commerce, art, science and literature. Had he found a way of curbing Louis XIV's military ambition, he would certainly have succeeded. (*Above*) The Gobelins tapestry celebrating the life and work of Colbert.

Part of the aim in establishing the Academy of Science in 1666 was, in modern parlance, to raise the profile of science. It worked. Young, brilliant, enquiring minds went to work in workshop and laboratory, shaping and reshaping the world around them. Among them was the French physicist Denis Papin (*left*). Papin was born in Blois in 1647. In his early career he helped Christiaan Huygens and Robert Boyle in their experiments.

Papin's own inventions included the steam digester of 1679 (*below, right*). It was a forerunner of the modern domestic pressure-cooker. Of greater promise were Papin's designs for an atmospheric condensing steam engine. Unlike his English contemporary Thomas Newcomen, however, he never actually built one. (*Above, right*) The power unit of a steamship, designed by Papin in about 1690.

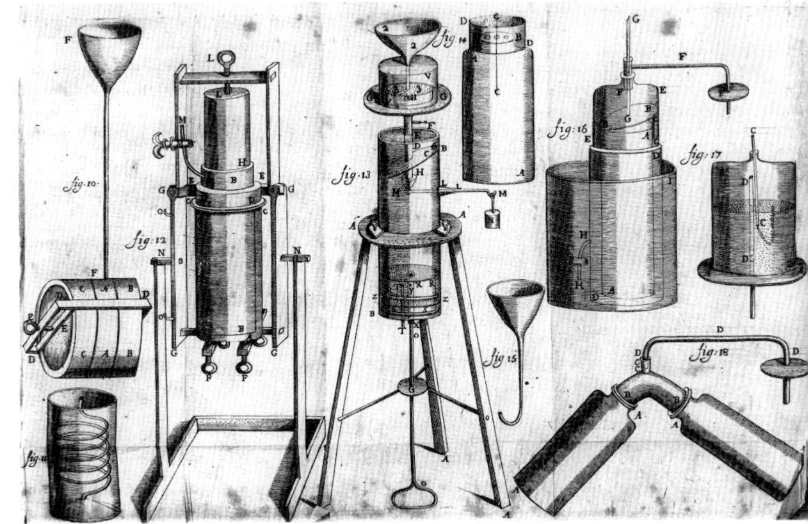

(*Above, left*) The painter Louis Boullongne works on a portrait of the composer André Campra and his librettist, Danchet. Campra composed many opera-ballets, among the most popular being *L'Europe galante* and *Fêtes venitiennes*. (*Below, left*) The painters Pierre Mignard and Charles Le Brun. Le Brun was a co-founder of the Academy of Painting and Sculpture in 1648, and also the first director of the Gobelins tapestry works.

A quartet of famous painters. (*Clockwise from top left*) Claude Gellée, otherwise known as Le Lorrain, a major influence on landscape painting for the next two hundred years; Nicolas Poussin, considered by many the finest French painter of the 17th century; Antoine Watteau, whose sketches and paintings catalogued the fashions of the *Ancien Régime*; and Jean Jouvenet.

Individually they were brilliant, together they offered the most comprehensive and magnificent works of literature in the world. (*Opposite, left*) Jean de La Bruyère; (*opposite, above right*) Charles Perrault, creator of Little Red Riding Hood and Sleeping Beauty; (*opposite, below right*) Jean-Baptiste Poquelin, better known as Molière. (*Right, clockwise from top left*) The playwright Pierre Corneille; the dramatist and poet Jean Racine; Jean de La Fontaine, poet and wit; and Charles Marguetel de Saint-Denis, Seigneur de Saint-Evremond, wit and satirist.

For the well-to-do, life was increasingly comfortable. Houses were cleaner, brighter, airier. Food was more plentiful and better prepared. Clothes, even boots and shoes (*opposite, below*), were more comfortable. A day's pheasant shooting (*left*) could be followed by a pleasant evening of wining and dining (*above*).

And there were diversions to charm the eye and please the intellect. (*Above, left*) Fireworks explode from the frame of a swimming lion. (*Above, right*) An aristocrat sings to his own accompaniment on the lute. In the summer, there was dancing on the village green (*centre, right*) to the music of the local band. Not all classes could join in, though they were allowed the pleasure of watching.

Philippe, Duc d'Orléans (*above*), was the grandson of Louis XIII. He was born in 1674, and spent his early adult life as a soldier, commanding with success in Italy and Spain. He preferred life at home to life at court, where he dabbled in chemistry and the fine arts, and lived with his wife, the daughter of Louis XIV and Madame de Montespan. His testing time came in 1715, when Louis XIV, on his death-bed, appointed him the duke regent of France during the minority of Louis XV.

Though he was credited with the founding of France's first National Bank, his initial popularity was undermined by the part he played in promoting John Law's Mississippi Scheme. He made alliances with England and Holland, expelled James Stewart, the Pretender to the British throne, from France, and debarred the *parlement* of Paris from engaging in politics. (*Above*) The Palace of the Duc d'Orléans at Villers-Cotterets.

12
THE OLD REGIME 1715–1789

The Revolution of 1789 was not a chance or sudden happening. The sun was setting even before the death of Louis XIV, and the *Ancien Régime* drifted aimlessly and ignobly into its twilight years. For many of the rich, fashion and style were everything. What matter if the country was bankrupt or losing international prestige? There were still balls to attend, theatres to visit, songs to applaud, and beautiful clothes to wear. All that was effete and ridiculous reached its most bizarre in the piled and powdered hairstyles of the ladies. (*Left*) 'One must learn to suffer for one's beauty' ('*Faut apprendre à souffrir pour être belle*') – a contemporary cartoon from the *Ancien Régime.*

Like his great-grandfather, Louis XV (*left*) was a womaniser, with a prodigious sexual appetite. Though enjoying hundreds of casual affairs, Louis was comparatively constant to at least two of his mistresses – Jeanne Antoinette Poisson, Marquise de Pompadour (*opposite, above left*), and Marie Jeanne Gomard de Vaubernier, Comtesse du Barry (*opposite, above right*). Of the two, Mme de Pompadour had the greater influence over Louis, appointing her own favourites to control public affairs for some twenty years. (*Opposite, below*) Officers of state at the Coronation of Louis XV, 25 October 1722.

Josèphe Jeanne Marie Antoinette (*above*) was the fourth daughter of the Empress Maria Theresa and the Emperor Francis I. She was married to the Dauphin (afterwards Louis XVI) in 1770 at the age of fifteen. Sadly, she was a spendthrift and a meddler, someone whose personal extravagance and interference in affairs of state cost France dear. She was reactionary in her tastes and views, and her influence over her husband proved fatal to both.

Louis XVI (*right*) enjoyed a brief period of popularity at the beginning of his reign. He had inherited a debt of 4,000 million livres, but this had been substantially reduced by his ministers, Maurepas, Malesherbes and Turgot. Further reforms were rejected by Court, aristocracy and Church, and by his wife Marie Antoinette. The last fifteen years of his reign saw a series of botched attempts to repair the damage done to France by privilege and autocracy.

One of the most extraordinary characters at Louis XVI's court was the Chevalier d'Eon (*left and opposite*). In 1762 he was sent to work at the French Embassy in London, but was recalled in 1774 under suspicion that he might betray secrets to the British government. His sentence was that he should henceforth wear female attire (he had often disguised himself as a woman in his government work). He returned to London in 1785 and lived there until his death in 1810 at the age of seventy-two. His post-mortem was a lively event.

The early writings of Denis Diderot (*opposite*) brought him little success. His *Pensées philosophiques* was publicly burnt by order of the Paris *parlement* in 1746, and three years later he was imprisoned for *Lettre sur les aveugles* (Letters on the Blind). His great work was the *Encyclopédie, ou Dictionnaire Raisonne des Sciences, des Arts et des Métiers*, which first appeared in 1751. To produce it, Diderot hired the best writers of the age as contributors, and the work took twenty-five years to complete. (*Above and below right*) Two illustrations from the *Encyclopédie* – an 18th-century laboratory, and a rolling mill for the production of wrought iron.

Jean-Jacques Rousseau (*opposite*) led a wandering life before finally settling in France in the mid-18th century. He was one of the contributors to Diderot's *Encyclopédie*, but is best known for his *Discours sur les sciences et les arts*, *Le Contrat social* and *Emile, ou l'éducation*. He was a profound thinker, a founder of the Romantic school and one of the philosophical forerunners of the Revolution. (*Above*) Rousseau's home at Montmorency.

François Marie Arouet de Voltaire (*opposite, above right*) lived from 1694 to 1778, although he had not been expected to survive infancy. Indeed, he might have lived longer, but the 'royal' welcome he received on his last visit to Paris (*right*), including the reception at the theatre for his last tragedy, *Irène* (*opposite, below*), brought on a fatal illness. (*Opposite, above left*) Voltaire's house at Ferney, on the Swiss border, near Geneva.

Charles de Secondat, Baron de la Brède et de Montesquieu (*left*), was a French philosopher and jurist, critical of the institutions and laws of his country. When he published his *De l'esprit des lois* anonymously in 1748 it was immediately placed on the Catholic Index of banned books, but passed through twenty-two editions in less than two years. Despite his criticisms, Montesquieu was a member of the French Academy from 1728 until his death in 1755.

Honoré Gabriel Riqueti, Comte de Mirabeau (*below, right*), was a politician and an orator, as well as a writer, and was imprisoned for his forthright views. His most audacious work was the *Essai sur le despotisme*, published in the 1770s. (*Below, left*) Marie Antoinette seems understandably hesitant at meeting Mirabeau. (*Right*) Mirabeau addresses a court of law.

One of the finest writers of the late 18th century was Anne Louise Germaine Necker, Madame de Staël (*opposite*), only child of the French minister and financier Jacques Necker, the man who propped up the *Ancien Régime* in its last few years. Seldom has any country produced so many great writers as France at this time. (*Right, clockwise from top left*) Claude Adrien Helvétius, philosopher and publisher, contributor to the *Encyclopédie* and author of *De l'esprit*; the Abbé Antoine François Prévost d'Exiles, soldier and novelist; Pierre Carlet de Chamblain de Marivaux, playwright and novelist; and the playwright Pierre Augustin Caron de Beaumarchais.

The French wool industry had long been centred in north and north-east France. Production of the raw material in the 18th century had changed little since medieval times. Fleeces were hand-combed (*opposite, above*) and woollen thread was still made on hand-turned spinning wheels or hand-frames (*above, left*).

The finest woollen creations came from the Gobelins factory on the outskirts of Paris. Here were designed and manufactured the superb tapestries that graced Versailles, the Tuileries and the palaces of those rich enough to afford them. (*Below*) A new Gobelins tapestry is revealed to its purchaser. (*Opposite, below and above, right*) Two illustrations from Diderot's *Encyclopédie* showing stages in the Gobelins process of manufacture.

Joseph Michel de Montgolfier (*opposite, below left*) and his brother Jacques Etienne were paper manufacturers and inventors of the hot air balloon, called the Montgolfière. (*Below, right*) Pilatre de Rozier and the Marquis d'Arlandes take off on the first manned flight by balloon, November 1783. (*Opposite, above right*) Jacques Charles and Nicolas Robert land after a flight of twenty-seven miles. (*Opposite, below right*) The first passengers – a cockerel, a duck and a sheep – plunge to earth, September 1783. (*Above, right, and opposite, above left*) Two views of the first crossing of the Channel by Jean Pierre Blanchard, 7 January 1785.

One of the few military successes of the 18th century was the French alliance with the colonists in the American revolutionary war. The decision to support the Americans was taken by the Comte de Vergennes (*opposite, above right*). Both the Comte de Rochambeau (*opposite, left*) and the Marquis de La Fayette (*opposite, below right*) fought in America. (*Right*) The first meeting between La Fayette and George Washington. (*Below*) The British surrender at Yorktown to American and French forces.

In the early 18th century, civic pride prompted many provincial cities of France to commission large-scale developments. The new wealth that had poured into Bordeaux, Lyons, Nantes, and Toulouse was spent in building new squares, government offices, opera-houses and theatres. The city of Nancy at this time was the seat of Stanislas Leszczynski, son-in-law of Louis XIV. He became the patron of the architect Emmanuel Heré de Corny, who designed the Palais du Gouvernement in 1715. One of de Corny's finest works was the fountain and elaborate railings (*right*) that became the centrepiece of the Place Royale (now the Place Stanislas).

The Paris *Opéra* (*above*) was the home of high culture, of theatre and music, of Gluck's magnificent *Iphigénie en Aulide* – though not of Mozart's frivolous *The Marriage of Figaro*, which was staged at the *Comédie-française*. By the late 18th century, however, there were signs that 'money', as well as class, was gaining an *entrée* into the auditorium.

François Couperin (*right*) was the son of the organist and composer Charles Couperin. Like his father, François was for many years organist at the church of St Gervais in Paris (*above*), designed by Salomon de Brosse. In 1717 Couperin became composer-in-ordinary of chamber music to Louis XV, and, as a composer, he had a profound influence on J.S. Bach.

Radically rebuilt and redeveloped in the 18th century, Bordeaux emerged as one of the most elegant cities in France. At the heart of the old town was the Porte de Caillou (*above, right*), but it was the new buildings that brought grandeur to the city. (*Above, left*) The staircase of the Grand Théâtre, designed by Victor Louis and built between 1777 and 1780. (*Opposite, above*) The river front of Bordeaux, on the west bank of the Garonne. (*Opposite, below*) The centre of Bordeaux towards the end of the 18th century.

The island of Corsica was under Genoese rule during much of the 18th century. It had its own king – Theodore Antony I (*left*) – but was in a constant state of turmoil, neither independent nor happily bound to Genoa. In 1768, the Genoans more or less gave the island to France. They were almost certainly glad to be rid of their troublesome appendage, but in so doing they unwittingly shaped the history of the whole of Europe.

For Ajaccio, Corsica's capital, was the birthplace of the second son of Charles Bonaparte, named Napoléon. He was born in 1769, just one year after the island became part of France, as a result of which he received his free education in France and was allowed to join the French army. (*Right*) French troops on Corsica. The fate of France had been decided by events on the island of Corsica, some twenty years before the Revolution.

Early in the 18th century, French agriculture appeared to be in a healthy and thriving condition. New crops such as buckwheat and maize, which had been introduced from the New World a hundred years earlier, had greatly increased the amount of food available for humans and animals. New methods of farming had led to richer soil and better harvests. (*Above*) The harvest is gathered in: an illustration from *Le Nouveau Théâtre d'Agriculture et Ménage des Champs*, published by Le Sieur Liger in 1723.

(*Above, left and right*) Two illustrations from *La Nouvelle Rustique*, published in 1755 – ploughing and breaking up the soil (left), and hay-making (right). The promise of better times ahead was not fulfilled. In the 1780s France experienced a succession of poor harvests, leading to famine in many areas. Landowners resorted to lowering wages, increasing rents and enclosing land to maintain their profits. The brunt of the recession fell on the peasants.

While the peasants starved, the nobles played – the statement may not be entirely true, but that is how it seemed to the 'have-nots' of the time. (*Above*) A fancy-dress masquerade of the mid-18th century. The ballroom is brilliantly lit by chandeliers, the costumes are of the finest materials, the setting is magnificent. The days and nights of such diversion were numbered.

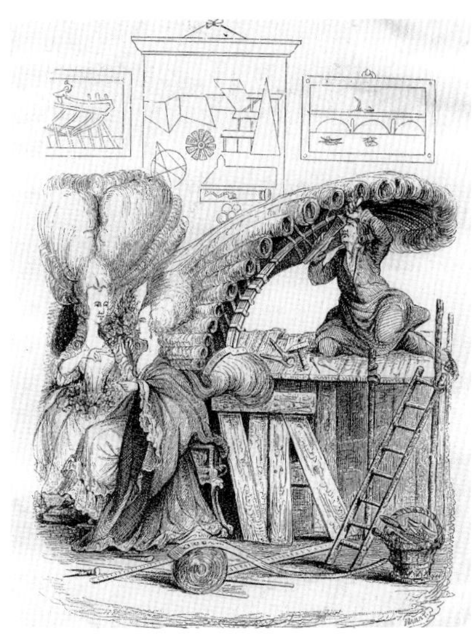

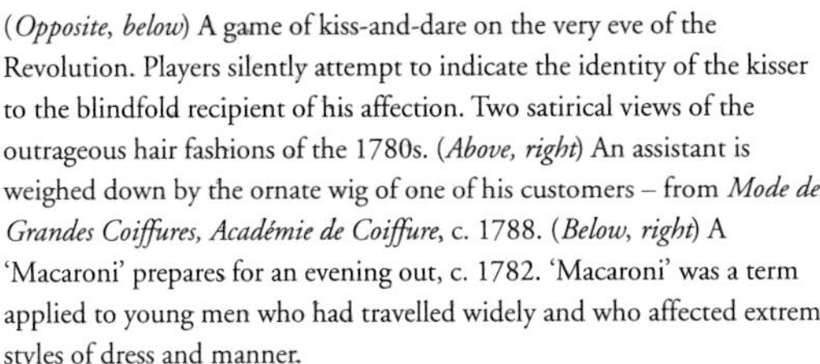

(*Opposite, below*) A game of kiss-and-dare on the very eve of the Revolution. Players silently attempt to indicate the identity of the kisser to the blindfold recipient of his affection. Two satirical views of the outrageous hair fashions of the 1780s. (*Above, right*) An assistant is weighed down by the ornate wig of one of his customers – from *Mode des Grandes Coiffures, Académie de Coiffure*, c. 1788. (*Below, right*) A 'Macaroni' prepares for an evening out, c. 1782. 'Macaroni' was a term applied to young men who had travelled widely and who affected extreme styles of dress and manner.

Love of money may not be the root of all evil (*pace* the Bible); lack of it often is. Louis XVI turned with growing desperation to a succession of advisers and ministers as the French financial crisis worsened during the 1780s. Foremost among them was Jacques Necker, satirically portrayed as the financial saviour of France (*left*). Necker was in and out of favour during the years leading up to the Revolution. His plans to reform taxes and recall the Estates General were haughtily opposed by Marie Antoinette, and he was banished from Paris.

Necker was also criticised by Charles de Calonne (*below, left*), who replaced Necker as controller-general of finances until he, too, was banished in 1786. (*Below, right*) An earlier dabbler in economic matters – John Law of Scotland. Law ran a bank in France early in the 18th century, but his promotion of a Mississippi joint-stock company led to enormous losses by speculators, and to riots on the streets (*above, right*).

The end of the *Ancien Régime* came suddenly. On 20 June 1789 deputies of the Third Estate, fearing an attack by the king, the nobles and the clergy, met informally on a tennis court at Versailles (*left*). Together they swore that they would not disband until the basis of a new constitution had been established. At first Louis XVI appeared to succumb, promising that the Third Estate would be the main component of a National Assembly. The king was, however, preparing a *coup d'état*. When news of this reached Paris, the city erupted. It was the beginning of the end.

13
REVOLUTION AND EMPIRE 1789–1815

The chaos and political spite that had brought death to many and anarchy to the streets of Paris was ended in 1795 by the celebrated 'whiff of grapeshot' (*left*). The young artillery officer from Corsica, Napoléon Bonaparte, saved France from the mayhem of the counter-revolution with a single volley of cannon. The rows and wrangles, *coups* and counter-*coups* were no more. 'The Revolution is completed,' Napoléon declared. In its place he established a military-technocratic state of such power that all who opposed it, at home or abroad, were swept aside…until the saviour of the Revolution made the fatal mistake of taking on the might of the Russian winter.

Introduction

It was a time of fury. Crowds, mobs, gangs and armies thronged the streets of Paris and roamed the French countryside. Revolutionary fashions changed too rapidly for many to keep safely abreast of which faction was in power and which in disgrace. Nobles fled, families were divided. Châteaux were looted, churches burned. The country spun out of control, yielding now to one wing of the revolutionary chamber, now to another.

A young Corsican artillery officer cleared the streets of Paris with a whiff of grapeshot, and rose rapidly to command all the armies of France. Prussia, Russia and Austria declared war on France and ordered that not a hair of King Louis XVI's head was to be harmed. The head may not have been otherwise harmed, but it was severed from his body by the newly-established Madame la Guillotine on 21 January 1793.

France had a new anthem in the *Marseillaise*, a new flag in the tricolour, a new currency, a new code of law, a new calendar, new *départements* and new conquests. Napoléon Bonaparte occupied Europe from the Atlantic Ocean to the marshes of Poland, from the North Sea to the deserts of Egypt. But a chill wind blew from the east, freezing the *Grande Armée* and driving its few survivors back to France. The Emperor abdicated and went sullenly to the isle of Elba in enforced exile. He escaped, and for a hundred days led the rest of Europe a dizzy dance until his reputation as a military genius was shattered at Waterloo.

Much of what he had accomplished remained. Paris now had an Arc de Triomphe worthy of ancient Rome to celebrate Bonaparte's victories, and a Champs-Elysées that became renowned as one of the grandest avenues in the world. The metric system – modern, efficient and comprehensible – swept aside old units of measurement.

The *émigrés* who trickled back never recovered their composure or their standing. For women, the Revolution and its bustling aftermath offered a new place in society which many were quick to occupy. Angélique Brulon helped to defend Corsica in seven campaigns between 1792 and 1799, first disguised as a man, then openly as a woman. She was awarded the *Légion d'Honneur*. An estimated 8,000 or more women fought as front-line troops for the Revolution. Olympe de Gouges proved too revolutionary even for the Revolution and was executed in 1793 after issuing her *Declaration of the Rights of Women*.

The Revolution of 1789 was the first in a series of four revolutions within ten years – the others taking place in 1792, 1794 and 1799. It was the most shattering in that it threw the entire social and political structure of France into the melting-pot. From it emerged a new vocabulary, with words such as 'citizen', 'equality', 'fraternity', 'left wing' and 'right wing' thrusting aside the old concepts of privilege and feudalism.

There were also new symbols, of which perhaps the longest-lasting was that of Liberty herself (*opposite*), the figure of a young woman in a simple (and often revealing) white dress, with a tricolour sash and the cap of liberty, carrying a sword and radiating purity. Other revolutionary characters were depicted just as heroically, but less attractively. (*Above, from left to right*) A member of the Commune of 1793, a gaoler from the Tower of the Temple, one of the strong-arm men who carried out the dictates of the many revolutionary committees, and the all-important drummer boy, who helped beat up a crowd wherever one was needed.

On 14 July 1789, the citizens of Paris stormed, captured and destroyed the Bastille (*above, right*), symbol of the old France. 'Is it a revolt, then?' asked Louis XVI, from the temporary safety of Versailles. 'No, sire,' came the answer. 'It is a revolution.' The event has traditionally been seen as the starting point of the Revolution, to be celebrated each year on the same day. (*Below, right*) A bonfire celebrating the fall of the Bastille, 14 July 1792. (*Opposite*) Though long seen as the symbol of royal despotism and injustice, the Bastille held few prisoners when it was captured.

The first stage of the Revolution lasted from 1789 to 1791. It was a period of great political change, of the swift move from absolutism to a constitutional monarchy, of hope and ideals. The National Assembly (*above, left*) removed feudal restrictions, granted religious toleration to all (including the Jews), and reduced state control of trade and industry. Events placed the new Utopia under an unbearable strain. In June 1791, the royal family attempted to escape from France. The shock that this provoked among Parisians and the relief felt on hearing that Louis had been recaptured (*opposite, above and below, left*) were caricatured by the British cartoonist James Gillray. A new constitution was drafted in September 1791 (*opposite, below right*) which Louis was compelled to sign – his signature is on the left of the document. The Revolution entered a new phase, in which terror was to replace idealism (*below, left*).

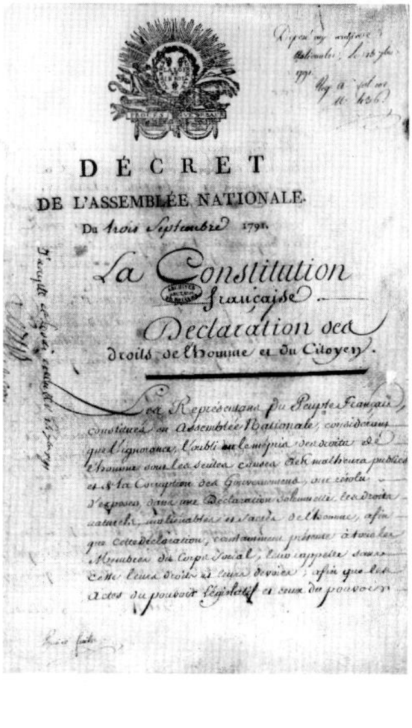

DÉCRET

DE L'ASSEMBLÉE NATIONALE.

Du trois Septembre 1791.

La Constitution françaiſe.

Déclaration des droits de l'homme et du Citoyen.

Les Représentans du Peuple Français, constitués en Assemblée Nationale, considérant que l'ignorance, l'oubli ou le mépris des droits de l'homme sont les seules causes des malheurs publics et de la Corruption des Gouvernemens, ont résolu d'exposer, dans une Déclaration solennelle, les droits naturels, inaliénables et sacrés de l'homme, afin que cette déclaration, constamment présente à tous les Membres du Corps social, leur rappelle sans cesse leurs droits et leurs devoirs; afin que les actes du pouvoir législatif et ceux du pouvoir

The importance of keeping a close watch on Louis XVI and the rest of the royal family had been noted early in the Revolution. Louis was a weak man, but not without a certain cunning – there was no knowing what plots he might hatch from the relative safety of Versailles. On 5 October 1789, a large crowd of soldiers, accompanied by women from the markets of Les Halles, marched to Versailles to bring the 'baker' and the 'baker's wife' to Paris (*right*). Since Marie-Antoinette had commented, on hearing that the people of Paris had no bread to eat, 'Let them eat cake', the royal family had been dubbed 'bakers'.

Swift, efficient and thereby merciful was how Joseph Ignace Guillotin (*left*) viewed the instrument of execution that he had perfected in the early days of the Revolution. Guillotin was a physician and deputy to the Estates General of 1789. Similar machines had been used in Scotland, Germany and Italy, but from 1791 onwards, the guillotine (*above*) despatched moderates, royalists, extremists, traitors, aristocrats and criminals with breathtaking ease. (*Opposite*) A revolutionary executioner.

pardonnés moi mon cher papa d'avoir disposé de mon existence
sans votre permission, jai vengé bien d'innocentes victimes, jai
prevenu bien d'autres desastres, le peuple un jour desabusé, se
rejouira d'être delivré d'un tyran, si jai cherché a vous persuadé
que je passais en angleterre cesque jesperais garder lincognito mais
jen ai reconnu limpossibilité, jespere que vous ne serés point tourmenté
en tous cas je crois que vous auriés des defenseurs a Caen, jai pris
pour défenseur gustave Doulcet, un tel attentat ne permet nulle
defense cest pour la forme, adieu mon cher papa je vous
prie de moublier ou plutot de vous rejouir de mon sort la
Cause en est belle, jembrasse ma soeur que jaime de tout
mon Coeur ainsi que tous mes parens, noubliés pas ce vers de
Corneille

le Crime fait la honte et non pas lechafaud

Cest demain a huit heures que lon me juge, ce 16 juillet

Corday

Jean-Paul Marat (*above, right*) was editor of the radical *Ami du peuple* ('Friend of the people'), a newspaper that preached extremist policies and called for the death of priests, aristocrats and royalists. Charlotte Corday d'Armont (*above, left*) was a moderate revolutionary, appalled at the slaughter of the Girondins. In July 1794 she gained admittance to Marat's house and murdered him in his bath (*opposite*). Corday was arrested, tried and executed. (*Left*) A facsimile of a letter from Charlotte to her father, written in prison the day before her trial, 16 July 1794.

Marie anne Charlotte
Corday au citoyen
Marat.
À MARAT,
DAVID

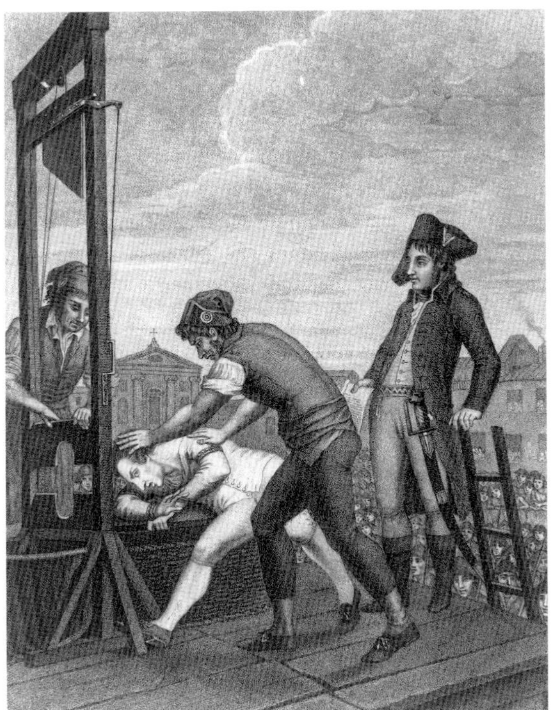

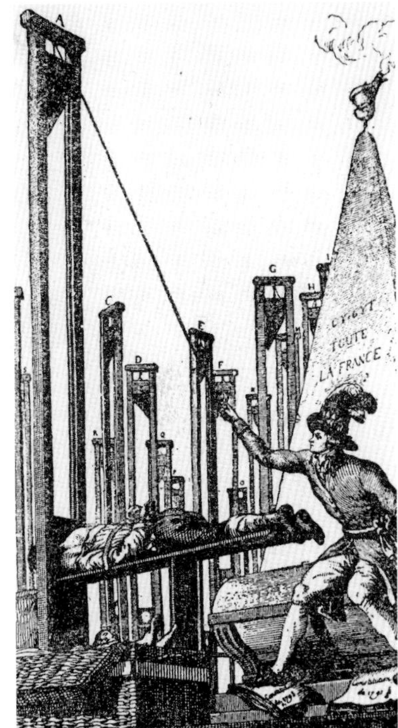

The Reign of Terror, as the period of mass executions and murders came to be known, lasted for much of 1793 and 1794. Thousands of people died; some 150,000 emigrated. Those who called for clemency were swept aside. Old comrades were betrayed and executed. Maximilien Robespierre (*opposite, below left*) denounced his fellow Jacobin, Georges Jacques Danton (*opposite, below right*), and the latter was executed with Camille Desmoulins (*opposite, above*). A cartoon suggested that the violence would end only when Robespierre executed the executioner (*above, right*) and there was no one else left in France, but Robespierre himself went to the guillotine on 28 July 1794 (*above, left*).

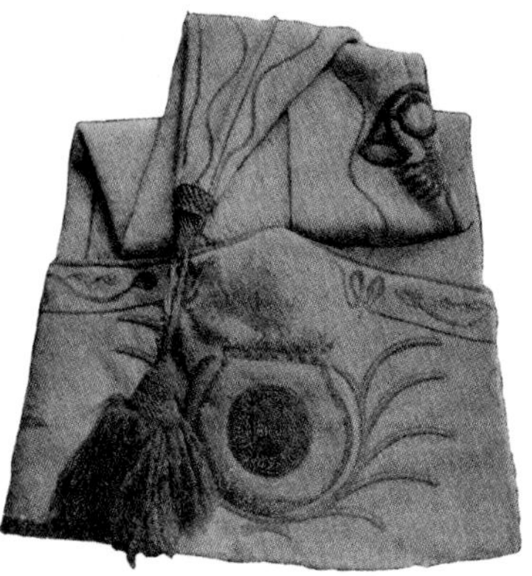

(*Above*) The Jacobin Club, or the *Société des Amis de la Constitution.* The Jacobins took their name from the convent in which they established their headquarters (*opposite*). (*Left*) The emblem of the Jacobins, and (*far left*) a Jacobin bonnet.

On the day the Republic was ratified, new words were added to the slogan 'Liberty, Fraternity, Equality' – 'Unity and Indivisibility...or Death'. Few responded to the call of these words more readily than the Jacobins, who in many ways saved the Revolution, though history has since condemned them for the blood they shed in so doing. The end came for the Jacobins in the summer of 1794. On 27 July, Robespierre (having been elected first deputy for Paris in the National Convention) was vehemently attacked in the Convention. A deputy proposed his arrest. Robespierre fled to the Common Hall. That night he was arrested. The following day he was executed.

To the sentimental, the deaths that shocked most during the Revolution were those of the aristocrats. Many nobles emigrated, fleeing to England or the Holy Roman Empire. Those that stayed, or were caught, were given short shrift. The blood-letting began in earnest in September 1792. Aristocrats in the Prison des Carmes were slaughtered by the mob (*left and opposite, below*).

(*Opposite, above*) The massacre at the Abbaye Prison, September 1792. (*Above*) *The Last Roll Call of the Condemned*, by Charles Louis Muller. An officer of the Revolutionary tribunal reads a list of those about to be executed. Kneeling beside him is Madame Leroy, an actress from the *Comédie-française*. Seated in the centre is the French poet André de Chénier, whose pamphlets had offended Robespierre. The cleric seated on the right is Saint-Simon, Bishop of Agde.

Claude Joseph Rouget de Lisle (*left*) composed the *Marseillaise* in 1792 when stationed at Strasbourg as a captain of engineers. The original title of the march was *Chant de guerre pour l'armée du Rhin.* It became the battle hymn of the Revolution, sung to inspire and encourage whenever France was in danger, whenever doubt and hesitancy threatened. (*Opposite*) The opening bars of the *Marseillaise* and a picture of the attack on the Tuileries, during which it was sung. (*Above*) Rouget de Lisle sings his anthem for the first time.

THE CELEBRATED MARSEILLAISE HYMN.

No. 186.

At the Tuileries there was no resistance. The Troops of the Line withdrew, the people entered and went over the whole of the Palace dancing and singing but pillaging nothing except the Throne which they promenaded afterwards along the Boulevards. Most of the populace sung the MARSEILLAISE HYMN and shouted "VIVE LA RÉPUBLIQUE." *Galignani's Messenger.*

In June 1791, the French royal family, disguised as servants, slipped out of Paris by coach (*above*) and headed east. Their hope was that they would reach the protection of the Emperor Leopold II, a fellow despot and an opponent of all that the Revolution stood for. They were recognised, captured at Varennes and brought back to Paris by a triumphant mob (*left*).

From that moment, there was little hope that the royal family and the institution of monarchy could survive in the new France. Louis XVI, Marie-Antoinette and their children were imprisoned in the Temple. The disastrous war with Austria and the advance of the Prussian army to Louis' rescue led to the proclamation of the French Republic. Louis was accused of treason, condemned to death on 20 January 1793, and executed the following day (*above, right*). Marie-Antoinette spent the next eight months in the common prison known as the Conciergerie, before she too was sentenced to death and followed Louis to the guillotine (*above, left*).

The *sans-culottes* comprised the citizen armies of revolutionary France. They were militia men and women, who made up for their lack of military training with the zeal and loyalty with which they fought. Royalists and reactionaries mocked their efforts. (*Left*) The *sans-culottes* are blinded by the royal sun after erecting a statue to La Nation.

(*Above, left*) A satirical print of a noble *sans-culottes.* (*Above, right*) An openly sympathetic portrait of male and female *sans-culottes.* The first tests of *sans-culottes* valour took place during the wars of 1793. France faced a formidable coalition of enemies – Austria, Prussia, Britain, Holland, Spain, Sardinia, Tuscany and Naples. (*Opposite, below*) A defeat for the *sans-culottes* and the death of General Dampierre, 3 May 1793.

One of the most successful of the *émigré* nobles was the writer and politician François René, Vicomte de Chateaubriand (*left*). He was born in Saint-Malo in 1768, joined the army and then sailed to America, where he spent eight months gathering material for his *Voyage en Amérique*. He returned to France briefly, but then fled to London where he stayed until the turmoil and violence came to an end.

For a while Chateaubriand held office under Napoléon, but his Catholic beliefs were incompatible with prevailing French politics. He was, however, a great survivor, travelling extensively during the Empire, returning to support the restored monarchy in 1816, becoming a Liberal in the 1820s, and reverting to royalist during the reign of Louis-Philippe. (*Right*) An illustration from the memoirs of Chateaubriand, published posthumously.

One area of France that remained loyal to Louis XVI was La Vendée, in the west. This was a deeply Catholic area, hostile to any lessening of the Church's wealth or power. The introduction of conscription in 1793 provoked open rebellion. (*Opposite, above*) The Vendéans march on the city of Nantes, 29 June 1793. (*Opposite, below*) A peasant is taken from his home and family and forced to join the army. (*Above*) The pacification of the Vendée. It came at a price. Between 150,000 and 200,000 Vendéans and Chouans were executed, and another 300,000 killed in the civil war.

The Revolution was not all death and terror. As in all liberation movements, sacrifice and hard work were punctuated with fêtes and national holidays. Bastille Day was early adopted as a time for celebration, and from time to time mass rallies were organised to celebrate the new spirit of the country. On such occasions the new flag of France – the tricolour – was prominently on display (*left*).

One of the biggest celebrations was that held on the Champ-de-Mars on 14 July 1790, the first anniversary of the fall of the Bastille and the start of the Revolution. The festival centred around a mammoth parade of the military might and splendour of the new nation, prompting an emotional response from the crowds that had gathered to watch. 'Bliss was it in that dawn to be alive...' – but few of those present could guess at the terror that was to come.

The revolutionary ideas and ideals quickly spread across the world. In Haiti they were eagerly endorsed by François Dominique Toussaint Louverture (*left*), whose last name derives from his skill in creating a breach in the enemy's ranks. Toussaint was born in 1746, the child of African slaves. In 1777 he was freed, and fourteen years later joined the black insurgents against French rule in Haiti.

The French forces on the island were still loyal to Louis XVI at that time, and the fight for freedom was fierce and long (*above*). In 1797 Toussaint was made commander-in-chief on the island by the revolutionary French government. He defeated invasions by the British and the Spanish, and fought on to establish Haitian independence. Napoléon opposed such a radical idea, and Toussaint was arrested and taken to France, where he died in prison in 1803.

In the chaos and confusion that raged in Paris during the early wars against Britain, Austria and Prussia, the Revolution seemed in constant danger of collapse. In 1795, counter-revolutionaries were crushed by a young brigadier named Napoléon Bonaparte (*left*), who cleared the streets with 'a whiff of grapeshot'. He was promoted and appointed commander of the army of Italy the following year.

His early career had not been without its moments of danger. He was temporarily removed from the army list in 1792 for concerning himself more with the revolution on Corsica than with the demands of his regiment. In 1794 he was arrested and charged with conspiring with the Jacobins, for he had been a friend of Robespierre. The charges against him were not proven and Napoléon was released. On the eve of leaving for the Italian campaign, he married Joséphine, widow of the General Vicomte de Beauharnais, a man who had been executed during the Reign of Terror. (*Above*) Napoléon and Joséphine in their garden.

Bonaparte's campaign in Italy was a series of brilliant victories. By 1804 he had secured the safety of France, and had overthrown the old revolutionary constitution. On 18 May he crowned himself emperor (*above, left*). After a brief truce, France was again at war. Bonaparte gathered a large army at Boulogne (*left*) for the proposed invasion of England.

Wars cost money, however, and Bonaparte was forced to sell Louisiana to the United States for $2 million. (*Right*) US President Thomas Jefferson coughs up the money for the Louisiana Purchase. Bonaparte marched against the Russians and defeated them at the Battle of Friedland, 14 July 1807 (*opposite, above right*). (*Above, left and right*) The new Empress and Emperor of France.

The Arc de Triomphe (*right*) was built to celebrate Bonaparte's victory over the Austrians at Austerlitz on 2 December 1805. Work began in 1806 on Chalgrin's design, but the arch was not completed until 1836. In all, it cost 10.4 million francs. It is a huge construction, 50 metres in height and 45 metres wide. The vast central arch is itself 30 metres high. The Arc is decorated with lions' heads, masks, swords, the names of warriors and lists of French military victories. The whole is topped by a frieze depicting *The Departure of Volunteers* in 1792.

Bonaparte's downfall was precipitated by his disastrous invasion of Russia in 1812. The *Grande Armée* of 600,000 men marched to Moscow, but was forced to retreat through the snows and gales of a viciously cold winter (*above*). The end came rapidly. Bonaparte was defeated at Leipzig by a coalition of British, Prussian and Austrian armies ('The Battle of the Nations'), and was forced to abdicate.

His new home was the tiny island of Elba. It was not big enough to contain him. On 26 February 1815, Bonaparte escaped (*above*) and sailed to the south of France. Here he was greeted with wild enthusiasm by the army sent to arrest him (*right*). And so began the Hundred Days leading up to the Battle of Waterloo. Louis XVIII was forced to flee, the allied armies hastily reconvened, and France welcomed back her 'Little Corporal'. (*Opposite, below*) Bonaparte's last home on the island of Saint Helena.

The end came with ignominy. At Waterloo in modern-day Belgium, Bonaparte saw his Imperial Guard heroically attempting to stem the British and Prussian advance, and then hurried from the battlefield (*left*). It was left to the Comte de Cambronne to surrender to the allies. Sober accounts of the moment report that the Comte said 'The Guard dies but never surrenders'. Those present heard him say '*Merde!*' Both remarks seem fitting. (*Above*) Bonaparte, in full uniform, stands on the cliffs of Saint Helena reflecting on the glories and horrors of his past.

Introduction to Period 3 – 1815–2000

The new spirit set in motion by the Revolution of 1789 allowed France little time to draw breath during the 19th century. The archaic magnificence of the Coronation of Charles X at Rheims in 1825 was followed by a succession of ill-conceived moves, the most bizarre of which was the restoration of the death penalty for blasphemy. It could not last. After *Les Trois Glorieuses*, three days of insurrection from 27 to 29 July 1830, Charles was forced to abdicate.

Louis-Philippe, the unassuming 'citizen king', forsook the notion of Divine Right, carried an umbrella when he walked through the streets, reduced censorship, and wooed the bourgeoisie. His government, however, did little for the urban or rural poor. 'Whatever the lot of the workers,' declared one of Louis-Philippe's ministers, 'it is not the manufacturer's responsibility to improve it.'

That Louis-Philippe survived so long may be attributed to the fact that France still had a predominantly rural population. By 1830 there were more town-dwellers than country folk in Britain. By 1870 the same was true of Italy, by 1900 of Germany. Not until the 1930s did the urban population of France exceed the rural. Nevertheless, where protest raised its head, it was slapped down. Whatever flags were waved on the barricades (the tricolour of the Orléanists, the black flag of the anarchists, or the red flag of the workers), the powerful combination of the Church, the right and the bourgeoisie made sure it did not fly for long.

Then came a series of bad harvests, and yet another French government was doomed. Louis-Philippe obligingly packed his bags and departed by steam-packet for England and obscurity. Republicanism returned to Paris, and then to the rest of France. Elections were held against a background of fighting in the streets. Louis-Napoléon, nephew of the great Bonaparte, was elected president for four years. Within three years he had manipulated the system sufficiently to have himself elected president for life. A year later he assumed the title Napoléon III and became emperor. Martial law was declared in thirty-one *départements* and 10,000 discontented peasants were deported.

Now began a hurly-burly in which the Church strengthened its grip on education, later enacting a Syllabus of Errors that attacked freedom of speech, religious tolerance, socialism and what it sneeringly referred to as the 'cult of science'. Teachers were forbidden to wear beards (the badge of anarchy).

Paris was rebuilt by Baron Haussmann. French literature was graced by the talents of Hugo, Flaubert and Baudelaire (hot on the heels of Stendhal and Balzac). Liberty suffered, banks prospered. There was a massive railway boom. Wine-growers made fortunes; even the peasantry bought pianos. Paris gained a new opera-house (a bomb had been thrown at the emperor in the old one) and the Bibliothèque Nationale. France gained a new empire in West Africa, Indo-China and the Pacific. France also secured Nice, in return for backing the unification of Italy. Then came the ignominy of Sedan and the emperor's temporary imprisonment in Germany following the Franco-Prussian War. He never returned to France.

The crazy progress continued. The Commune and its suppression brought death to tens of thousands on the streets of Paris. The Palais des Tuileries and the Hôtel de Ville were razed to the ground. Columns and statues commemorating the glories of the past were toppled and shattered. A hundred years were to pass before Paris was once again permitted to have its own mayor.

Out of the rubble rose a new Paris and a new France, with a roll of honour that no nation could match. This was and still is the France the whole world knows: of the Impressionist painters – Renoir, Degas, Monet, Cézanne, Sisley, Pissarro and a dozen others; of Rodin, Zola, Proust, Maupassant, Verlaine, Rimbaud, Mallarmé, Debussy, Saint-Saëns, Fauré, Ravel, Pasteur, the Curies, Poincaré, Bergson, Charcot, Durkheim, Panhard, Michelin, Blériot, Bernhardt, Méliès, the Lumière brothers, Pathé. It was the land of *haute cuisine*, perfume, *haute couture*, elegant carriages, the can-can, champagne, *opéra bouffe*, grand hotels, the Métro, *La Vie Parisienne*, Château-Lafite and Château d'Yquem, and all the best that life had to offer. How much of this contributed to the survival of the Republic is incalculable.

La Belle Epoque came to a bloody end with the slaughter of the First World War. Every city, every town, every village in France has its poignant war memorial listing all the names of the million and a half men who died, though there are no monuments to the three million who were disabled. It took the French economy twenty-five years to recover, and by then it was time for the Second World War. There was no Miracle of the Marne in 1940 to match that of 1914, and the Third Republic came to an end with the arrival of the German army and the division of France into the Vichy and Occupied Zones.

As always, there was much activity on the French artistic front in the years between the wars. France produced and nourished the leaders of the Surrealist movement (Breton, Desnos, Eluard, Perot, Dali, Magritte, and André Masson). Leading French writers included Sartre, Barbusse, Victor Margueritte and a gaggle of right-wing authors under the patronage of Charles Maurras's *Action Française* clique. The great fashion houses (Chanel, Balenciaga, Dior) dressed the rich in sumptuous elegance, wherever they came from. Life at all levels was brilliantly chronicled by the photographer Henri Cartier-Bresson.

The spirit of joy and renewal that marked the Liberation of France in 1944 and 1945 did not last long. The economy prospered, but France suffered military defeat in Indo-China, came close to civil war when President de Gaulle executed a volte-face over the matter of *Algérie française*, and flirted with revolution in the excitement of May 1968.

Then came the end of de Gaulle, but not the end of Gaullism, another staggering economic recovery, the fruits of the European Community, the threat of socialism under François Mitterrand (it never amounted to the real thing), and a resurgence of national pride in the triumphs of French sport and technology in the final decade of the millennium. The century had been one of immense suffering, but it all came right in the end.

14
SEEKING SOLUTIONS 1815–1848

The painting by Eugène Delacroix of *Liberty Leading the People*, 1830, captures the spirit of the revolution that drove out Charles X. Romanticism was now embraced by the left, and the picture was exhibited in the 1831 Salon. The event itself centred on *Les Trois Glorieuses*, the three days from 27 to 29 July when radicals and progressives won the battle for possession of the streets of Paris. Once again revolution had come to France, and once again the background had been poor harvests and high prices. Throughout Europe conservative governments wondered if the dark days of the 1790s would return.

Introduction

With the help of the Church and the restored nobility, Louis XVIII and Charles X did what they could to drive France back into the years of the *Ancien Régime*. The tricolour was outlawed and the white flag of the Bourbons restored. The *Marseillaise* was banned. The storming of the Bastille was no longer celebrated as a national holiday on 14 July each year.

There were some things, however, that could not be changed back to their pre-revolutionary state. Despite protests and much indignation, the Church failed to regain the land that had been taken from it in the years between 1789 and 1815. Nor did the returning *émigrés* recover their old estates, most of which had been divided and subdivided several times since their flight during the reign of terror.

Even the most reactionary of regimes cannot stand in the way of all progress, all change. The first French railway was opened in the 1830s. The new mode of travel was to play a leading role in the break-up of the old rural society which had survived all that the Revolution had hurled at it.

A new age of French literature produced *Le Dernier Chouan*, the first novel of Honoré de Balzac, in 1829. Victor Hugo's *Odes et poésies diverses* was published in 1822, and he was even granted a pension by Louis XVIII. Marie-Henri Beyle, better known as Stendhal, served in Napoléon's army for twelve years before entering the civil service and becoming the French consul in Trieste. His three great romantic novels – *Armance, Le Rouge et le Noir* and *La Chartreuse de Parme* – were published in 1827, 1830 and 1839 respectively. Armandine Lucile Aurore Dupin, Baronne Dudevant, adopted the pen name George Sand, male attire and a bohemian lifestyle while writing *Rose et Blanche*, *Indiana*, *Valentine* and a host of other novels.

Brave women continued to struggle for their rights. 'The most oppressed man can oppress one being, his wife,' wrote Flora Tristan, a Utopian socialist who was the illegitimate child of a Peruvian *seigneur* and a French migrant to Spain. Tristan returned to France in 1816, the year in which the liberal divorce laws of the Revolution were repealed by Louis' Restoration government. She managed to shake herself free from her deranged husband after he attempted to shoot her in the street, and travelled to Britain, where she wrote *Promenades in London*, an account of working-class depression worthy of comparison with the work of Engels later in the 19th century. Like her contemporary George Sand, Flora Tristan shocked and distressed the male-dominated society in which she lived.

There are those who believe that it is still too early to assess the effects of the Revolution of 1789. Certainly the restoration of Louis XVIII (*above, left*) in 1814 was an unexpected effect, and not one likely to last. Louis returned 'in the baggage train of the allies'. He brought with him no queen, for his wife, the Comtesse Marie de Provence (*above, right*), had died in 1810. (*Left*) Louis lands at Calais, 24 April 1814.

There were those who greeted Louis XVIII with fulsome respect and self-interested joy (*above, right*). The 'White Terror' which then spread through France killed hundreds of revolutionaries and Protestants. Others, however, were more critical. As early as 1815 there were satirical cartoons depicting the returning king as a fool riding an ass (*below, right*). Perhaps it was as well for Louis that he died in 1824, before anti-royalist feeling reasserted itself.

Both Louis XVIII and his brother Charles X (*left and opposite, left*), who succeeded him in 1824, made the mistake of seeking to re-establish the absolutism of the *Ancien Régime.* Blind to the changes that had taken place in France, they obstinately set out to return to the old days of press censorship, despotic rule and religious intolerance. Charles' Coronation set the tone for his reign – a pageant that recreated the spirit of the 1500s and was indeed a conscious attempt to put the clock back.

The people barely tolerated Charles as their king for six years, before the events of *Les Trois Glorieuses* toppled him from the throne and forced him to abdicate. Charles and his family fled to England, then Scotland, and finally moved to Prague. He died in Gorz of cholera in 1836. (*Above, right*) A contemporary cartoon of Charles X embarking for England with his private belongings but without any '*bon voyage*' wishes from his people.

When Charles ascended the throne in 1824, he was supported by a right-wing ministry and a Chamber of Deputies, two-thirds of whom were nobles. In the country there was official encouragement for schemes that demanded a collective penance for the 'sins' of the Revolution of 1789. The register of electors was manipulated to reduce the number of those entitled to vote. Two successive elections in 1830, however, returned majorities hostile to Charles' government. Charles responded by invoking emergency powers. The battle lines were drawn. Violence broke out in late July. Gendarmes seized the printing presses (*above, right*) in an attempt to limit freedom of expression. On 28 July three columns of the army were ordered to attack the Hôtel de Ville (*above, left*).

Wherever the army advanced, street barricades were constructed behind them. It was impossible to crush the revolution. Rebels captured royalist cannon in the Rue Saint-Honoré (*right*) and elsewhere. The tricolour was once more carried through the streets (*above*). By 29 July, the struggle for power was virtually over, and the royalist cause lay in ruins.

When Charles abdicated, the crown was offered by the Marquis de La Fayette, the old campaigner of the American War of Independence, to Louis-Philippe, Duc d'Orléans (*above, left*) (whose father had renounced his title during the Revolution to become Philippe-Egalité – but was guillotined nonetheless). Louis-Philippe ruled as a 'citizen king', and adopted a humble manner. However, he was as ineffective as he was modest, and opposition from republicans, socialists and nascent communists grew throughout his reign.

J'abdique cette Couronne
que la voix nationale m'avait
appellée à porter, en faveur
de mon petit fils le Comte de
Paris. Puisse-t-il réussir
dans la grande tâche qui lui
échoit aujourd'hui.
24 Fev.r 1848 — Louis Philippe

In February 1848 Paris rose against him. Louis-Philippe dismissed Guizot, his chief minister, and promised reforms, but the offer came too late to save him. On 24 February 1848, he signed a deed of abdication (*above*). On the same day he left Paris (*top, left*) and travelled to England. He took up residence at Claremont, a few miles from London, where he lived simply as 'Mr Smith'. (*Above, right*) Louis-Philippe and his wife, Marie-Améli, daughter of Ferdinand I of the Two Sicilies, at Claremont, c. 1849.

Though the events of 1848 were less violent and less traumatic than earlier revolutions, blood was shed. (*Opposite, above*) The burning of royal carriages at the Château d'Eu, 24 February 1848, and (*opposite, below right*) the burning of the electoral lists at the Porte Saint-Denis. This was the first revolution to be photographed. (*Below, left*) A photogravure of the remains of barricades in the Rue de Rivoli. (*Opposite, below left*) A young revolutionary of 1848. (*Above, left*) Possibly the first ever news photograph – a daguerreotype of an arrest in France, 1847.

(*Right*) A seating plan of the French Chamber of Deputies for the session of 1832. The left and right wings of the Chamber are clearly shown (*Côté Gauche* and *Côté Droit*), and each seat is marked with a number and the name of the deputy who sat there. Seat No. 14 belonged to François Guizot, later to replace Louis Adolphe Thiers as the king's chief adviser. Thiers, then Minister of the Interior, and later the suppressor of the Commune of 1871, sat in seat No. 13. At the very back of the Chamber were seats allotted to journalists, evidence of progress towards a more enlightened democracy.

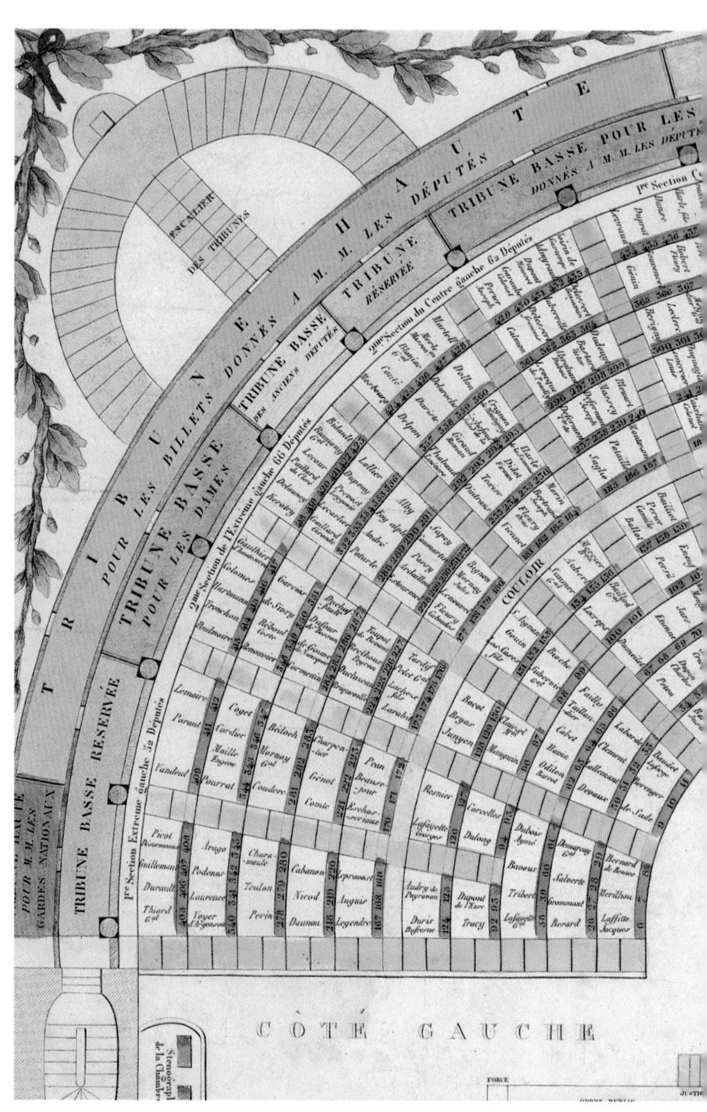

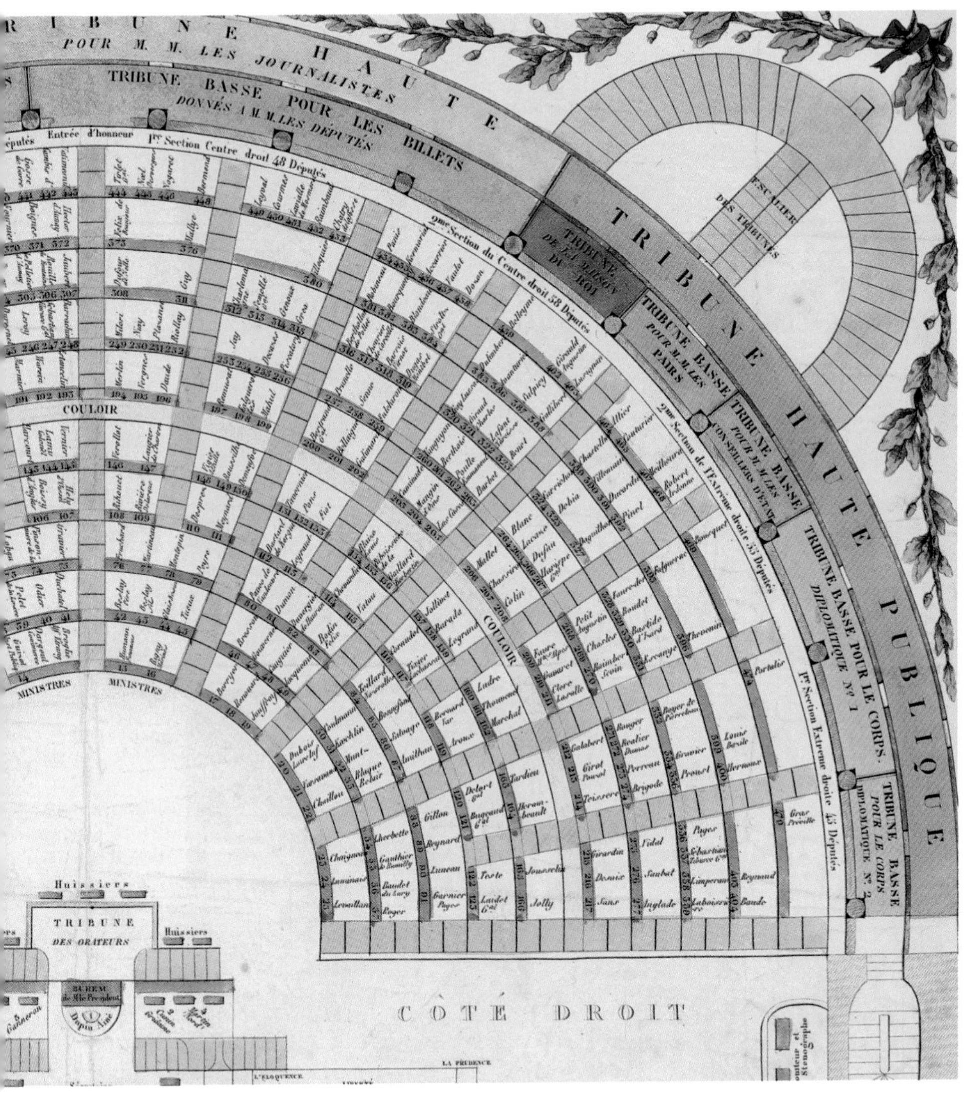
TRIBUNE HAUTE POUR M. M. LES JOURNALISTES
TRIBUNE BASSE POUR LES BILLETS DONNÉS A M. M. LES DÉPUTÉS
Entrée d'honneur
1re Section Centre droit 48 Députés
2me Section du Centre droit 58 Députés
2me Section de l'Extrême droite 53 Députés
1re Section Extrême droite 45 Députés
TRIBUNE DE LA MAISON DU ROI
TRIBUNE BASSE POUR M. M. LES PAIRS
TRIBUNE BASSE POUR M. M. LES CONSEILLERS D'ÉTAT
TRIBUNE BASSE POUR LE CORPS DIPLOMATIQUE No 1
TRIBUNE BASSE POUR LE CORPS DIPLOMATIQUE No 2
TRIBUNE HAUTE PUBLIQUE
ESCALIER DES TRIBUNES
COULOIR
COULOIR
MINISTRES
MINISTRES
Huissiers
TRIBUNE DES ORATEURS
Huissiers
BUREAU de Mr le Président
CÔTÉ DROIT
LA PRUDENCE
L'ÉLOQUENCE

Charles Louis Napoléon Bonaparte (*opposite, above left and below right*) was the third son of Napoléon's brother, Louis Bonaparte. He made two abortive attempts to seize power in France, in 1836 and 1840. He was first elected President in 1848, and was re-elected (for ten years) in 1851. (*Left*) The result of the 1851 election – over 7.5 million votes cast for Napoléon, just over 1 million against.

A year later, after another plebiscite, Napoléon assumed the title of Emperor Napoléon III (thus maintaining the fiction that Napoléon I's son had been the rightful Napoléon II) and made a triumphal entry into Paris (*opposite, above*). His rise to absolute power had been astonishingly rapid. The Constitution had been overthrown, and France had moved from republic to empire within three years. Napoléon's supporters wasted no time in establishing the cult of empire. (*Above, right*) The bust of Napoléon III is enclosed in a laurel wreath and surmounts a menacing imperial eagle. The names inscribed on the wreath are those of Napoléon's later victories.

Pierre Joseph Proudhon (*right*) and Louis Blanc (*opposite*) were too young to appear in the seating plan of the 1832 Chamber of Deputies. Blanc was born in 1811 and first made his name as a historian. He was a member of the provisional government after 1848, but was accused of violence and fled to London. Not until the fall of Napoléon III was he elected to the National Assembly. Proudhon was a journalist, the author of the famous socialist slogan 'Property is theft'. He attempted to establish a bank offering interest-free credit, preached revolution and was imprisoned for three years. In many ways he was a forerunner of Marx.

Louis-Philippe, like so many rulers before and after him, attempted to bolster his sagging popularity at home by embarking on a series of military adventures. After the loss of so many colonies following the defeat of Napoléon in 1815, there were many in France who were prepared to support expeditions to gain territories abroad.

The designated target was North Africa, and French troops were landed in Morocco (*above*) in the early 1840s. French fleets bombarded Tangiers (*opposite, above*), where the war came to an end with the signing of a treaty in September 1844. Seven years later French troops were again in action, bombarding the port of Salee (*opposite, below*). By gaining new colonies, the way was prepared for future anguish and bloodshed.

Marie-Henri Beyle (*left*) was born in Grenoble in 1783. As a young man he was offered a post in Bonaparte's Ministry of War, and he followed the military campaigns in Italy, Germany and Russia. He is more famous, however, as Stendhal, the brilliant novelist and author of *Le Rouge et le Noir* and *La Chartreuse de Parme.* (*Opposite, left*) The title page of Stendhal's *Vie de Rossini.* (*Opposite, above right*) A sketch by Stendhal for a proposed novel. (*Opposite, below right*) Stendhal dancing in an inn at Pont-Saint-Esprit.

Vie de Rossini,

PAR

M. De Stendhal;

Ornée des Portraits de Rossini et de Mozart.

Laissez aller votre pensée comme cet insecte
qu'on lâche en l'air avec un fil a la patte.
Socrate. *Nuées d'Aristophane.*

PREMIÈRE PARTIE.

Paris,

CHEZ AUGUSTE BOULLAND ET CIE, LIBRAIRE

RUE DU BATTOIR, N° 12.

1824.

Aurore Dupin, Baronne Dudevant (*above, left and right*) was the illegitimate daughter of the Maréchal de Saxe. She left her husband and children to enter bohemian society in Paris and to write under the name George Sand. Her lovers included politicians and artists, Jules Sandeau (from whose name she acquired her pseudonym), Prosper Mérimée and Chopin. Her work included both the political and the erotic, and some of the greatest books in French literature. (*Opposite*) Nine heroines from the novels of George Sand. From top left to bottom right: Pauline, Consuelo, Juliette, Noun, Naam, Marthe, Indiana, Giovana and Lavinia.

The new ideas that jostled one another in French politics and society released a stream of great literary works. Honoré de Balzac (*above, right and opposite*) came from Tours. He studied law at the Sorbonne, but, against his father's wishes, left to try his luck as an author in Paris. For ten years life was not easy, but he achieved his first success with the publication of *Le Dernier Chouan* in 1829. A succession of novels followed before Balzac conceived his grand scheme – a complete picture of human civilization. What followed was an amazing achievement, for he wrote eighty-five novels in twenty years.

Balzac worked regularly fifteen hours a day at the table in his study (*opposite, left*). When necessary, this was increased to eighteen hours a day, yet his income rarely exceeded 12,000 francs a year and he was plagued with money troubles all his life. He died in 1850 at the age of fifty-one.

Victor Marie Hugo was born in Besançon in 1802, the son of an army general. As a young man (*above, left*) he rapidly established himself as a poet and dramatist of extraordinary ability. After the *coup* of Napoléon III, Hugo fled to Guernsey and lived in Hauteville House (*left*). (*Above, right*) Hugo's mistress, the actress Juliette Drouet.

Hugo returned to France in 1870 but maintained a stormy relationship with the authorities for the rest of his life. (*Right*) A photograph of Hugo in 1877. (*Far right*) Quasimodo from *Notre-Dame de Paris*, Hugo's most famous creation. (*Below*) The funeral procession of Victor Hugo in 1885. He was buried in the Panthéon.

Opera was at the heart of French music in the early 19th century. The Théâtre de l'Ambigu in Paris (*above*) staged many of the works of Méhul, Auber, Berlioz, Adam and Ambroise Thomas. Daniel François Esprit Auber (*above, right*) first made his name as a composer of instrumental music shortly after the restoration of 1815. In his thirties he turned to opera, and it was during a performance of his *Masaniello* in 1830 in Brussels that the audience erupted and began the rebellion that led to Belgian independence. (*Right*) The title page of Louis Antoine Julien's *Lancers*, c. 1820. Julien made immense sums of money from his music, but died in poverty and completely insane.

(*Right*) A collage of composers whose music is associated with France during the early 19th century. From left to right (top row): Luigi Cherubini and Gaspare Spontini; (middle row) François-Adrien Boieldieu, Gioacchino Rossini and Daniel Auber; (bottom row) Ferdinando Paer, Henri Montan Berton and Giacomo Meyerbeer.

Jean Auguste Dominique Ingres (*above, right*) was a pupil of Jacques Louis David, master of the classical school. Ingres possessed superb draughtsmanship, but his motto – 'A thing well drawn is well enough painted'– attracted much criticism from the new Romantic school. Eugène Delacroix (*above, left*) was a Romantic. His style of drawing was loose. His choice of colour was vivid. His work was detested by Ingres, who loathed such paintings as Delacroix's *Liberty Leading the People.*

The career of Ingres see-sawed violently from success to failure and back again. His *Apotheosis of Homer* (on the ceiling of the Louvre) was well received, but his *Martyrdom of Saint Symphorian* was blasted by the critics. Late in life he re-established himself in the Paris art world, and he was awarded the *Légion d'Honneur*. (*Right*) *Madame de Senones*, a portrait painted by Ingres between 1814 and 1816.

Louis Jacques Mandé Daguerre (*above, left*) was originally a painter of scenery for the opera in Paris. In his late thirties, however, he formed a partnership with Joseph Nicéphore Niepce, a chemist from Chalon-sur-Saône. Together the two men experimented with the process of producing a photographic image on a metal plate – later to be known as the '*daguerréotype*'. (*Above, right*) A diorama constructed by Daguerre in 1830.

Credit for producing the world's first photographic image (*above*), however, goes to Niepce. It was taken from the window of his Le Gras estate at Saint-Loup-de-Varennes sometime in 1826. The picture was made by exposing a bitumen-coated pewter plate in a *camera obscura* for eight hours. The rest is history.

The British, in their habitually modest way, like to take credit for the invention of the railway. In so doing, they choose to ignore developments elsewhere that preceded their own efforts. (*Top, left*) Louis XIV's railway of 1714. It ran on rails, used a turntable, and was powered by servants pushing with their arms. (*Top, right*) The hydraulic railway of M. Girard. (*Above, from left to right*) Locomotive for a railway powered by atmospheric pressure; first-class carriages and passengers on an early French railway; and a hydraulically-powered railway.

More conventional early French railways. (*Above*) The benediction ritual at the opening of the Rouen–Le Havre railway in 1847. (*Right*) Crowds gather to celebrate the opening of the line.

François Pierre Guillaume Guizot (*left*), the occupant of seat No. 14 in the Chamber of Deputies, was responsible for an overhaul of the French education system in the 1830s. His law of 1833 established a primary school in every commune and did much to raise the country's literacy level. This had a knock-on effect politically (which Guizot may not have intended) enabling more people to read the pamphlets and tracts that poured from city printing presses.

Two views of French education – before and after the Guizot law. (*Above*) A scene of wild disorder as an aged teacher fails to control his boisterous pupils. Nemesis lurks behind the door. (*Right*) Well-behaved pupils take their instruction with looks of eager anticipation on their faces.

The 'Empire look', though largely flattering to men and women, had its more bizarre excesses of fashion. (*Above*) A Parisian caricature of *Les Invisibles en tête-à-tête* from *Le Suprême Bon Ton.* (*Left*) A British view of a Parisian gentleman attended by his barber and manicurist while taking a bath, from a drawing by George Cruikshank, c. 1824.

(*Above, left*) Fashions for French children in the 1820s. (*Above, right*) Family walking-out clothes from the mid-19th century, from *Le Lion*, a magazine devoted to fashion for men and women. (*Right*) The latest Paris fashions of 1868 – the parrot was recommended as an accessory but was not obligatory. By the beginning of the century Paris had already established itself as the centre of the world's fashion industry. Throughout Europe and the United States, those who could afford to bought their clothes personally or by mail order from the French capital.

15
TORN APART
1848–1871

In 1870, the French army was better equipped and better trained for crushing internal subversion than for fighting a war against a foreign power. When Napoléon III finally blundered into the Franco-Prussian War, defeat was inevitable. From September 1870 to March 1871 Paris was under siege. The rising known as the Commune flared and, with French official connivance, the Prussian army marched into the city on 1 March 1871 to suppress this most dangerous of insurrections (*right*). In many ways the Prussians did all they could to kindle a new spirit of united resolve among the French. Their occupation of France provoked bitter feelings and paved the way for future bloodshed.

Introduction

France hurried through the 19th century in a frenzy of activity – cultural, industrial, commercial, fashionable and suicidal. Paris was replanned and rebuilt. Biarritz became the chosen pleasure ground of the new Emperor Napoléon III. A young girl claimed that the Virgin Mary had spoken to her in a grotto near Lourdes. Au Bon Marché opened the world's first department store in 1852. It remained the biggest in the world until 1918. There were booms in the production of cotton and wine: the warm soil of Languedoc yielded the largest alcoholic harvest in the world. *Le Petit Journal* became the world's first tabloid-style newspaper. In 1869 the Suez Canal was opened – an engineering triumph for Ferdinand de Lesseps.

In concert halls and opera-houses well-dressed audiences delighted in the music of Berlioz and Gounod. The well-read rushed to buy the latest works of Alexandre Dumas *père*,

Flaubert and Baudelaire. The bourgeoisie insisted that their sons and daughters apply themselves to the newly-acquired family piano. Railways whisked all who could afford it to the Universal Exhibitions of 1855 and 1867.

In the midst of such excitement, few people realised that France was heading for one of its greatest tragedies. Napoléon III was a man who relied too much on his own cunning for his country's good. His wily diplomacy gained Nice and Savoy for France at the expense of Austria, but also left France with few friends or allies on the international scene. Outmanoeuvred by Chancellor Bismarck, Napoléon was swept into a disastrous war with Prussia.

Courage and *élan* were no match for the well-trained and well-armed Prussian army. The French defeat was swift and comprehensive. While the French army struggled to defend eastern France, Paris broke out in open revolt. The Commune of 1871 was a short-lived, brave and ultimately tragic attempt to overthrow the empire and complete the work of the 1789 Revolution, but it was ill-timed. The war with Prussia was already lost, and the Prussian army besieging Paris waited patiently while the French slaughtered each other in the streets of the most glamorous city in the world.

When the lust for revenge had been sated and the bodies hastily buried, much of France was still occupied by the Kaiser's troops, awaiting the payment of 5 million francs in war indemnities. Alsace and Lorraine were annexed by the new German Empire.

It was perhaps better to pretend that it had all been a bad dream and to bury one's head in the latest science fiction work of Jules Verne – *20,000 Leagues Under the Sea*, published in 1870.

The Second Empire began in splendour and ended in misery. On 30 January 1853, Emperor Napoléon III married Princess Eugénie of Montijo (*opposite, below right*) in the Cathedral of Notre-Dame (*above, left*). The imperial Court was the epitome of fashion and brilliance. (*Below, left*) The Court at Fontainebleau, 1865 – Empress Eugénie is third from the left in the front row.

(*Above, right*) The emperor and empress before their marriage. (*Above, left*) The emperor with his son Eugène Louis Jean Joseph in 1856, when the Prince Imperial was fifteen years old. The poor prince was killed in 1879 while serving with British troops in the Zulu War. Napoléon III combined lofty ambition with ordinary ability. His role in the Franco-Prussian War was disastrous for France. Twelve years earlier he had remarked that he cared little for war: there was too much luck in it for his liking. In the war of 1870–71 that luck was always bad.

There was little to relieve the misery of France. Troops besieged in Paris retained their sense of style (*opposite, above left*), but little else. Surrender at Sedan (*opposite, above right*) was followed by the emperor's personal surrender to Wilhelm I of Prussia (*opposite, below left*). The people of Paris heroically withstood siege – shopping for dog or cat meat at the butcher's (*right*), hunting for rats (*below, left*), and sardonically recalling the spirit of 1815 (*below, right*). The end came on 26 February 1871, when Bismarck dictated his peace terms to Thiers and Favre (*opposite, below right*).

After his defeat and surrender at Sedan, Napoléon III never again set foot in France. His place as leader of the country's destiny was taken by Léon Michel Gambetta (*opposite, right*), one of those politicians who proclaimed the Third Republic on 4 September 1870. Gambetta became Minister of the Interior in the Government of National Defence, and was one of the organisers of resistance during the siege of Paris. When it became clear that relief of the city was impossible, Gambetta and other members of the government made their escape from Paris by balloon. (*Above*) The Gare d'Orléans, transformed into a workshop for Godard's Balloon Post during the siege of Paris.

A new government was established in Tours, and Gambetta became the virtual dictator of France for five months. He refused to admit defeat, assembling army after army and demanding that the war should never end while Prussian troops stood on French soil. Gambetta played no part in the suppression of the Commune, resisted the attempt to re-establish the monarchy, and was Prime Minister from 1881 to 1882. (*Above, left*) A cartoon of Gambetta dating from the mid-1870s.

In January 1871, Paris elected a municipal government known as 'the Commune'. It pursued a policy of war and radical social change. Citizens destroyed the old icons, including the column of Napoléon I in the Place Vendôme (*opposite, above*). Among those responsible was the artist Gustave Courbet (*above, left*). The photograph of Communards executing hostages in La Roquette prison (*opposite, below*) is almost certainly staged. Hortense David (*above, right*) was a leading female member of the Commune. Louis Adolphe Thiers (*right*) was an implacable enemy.

85

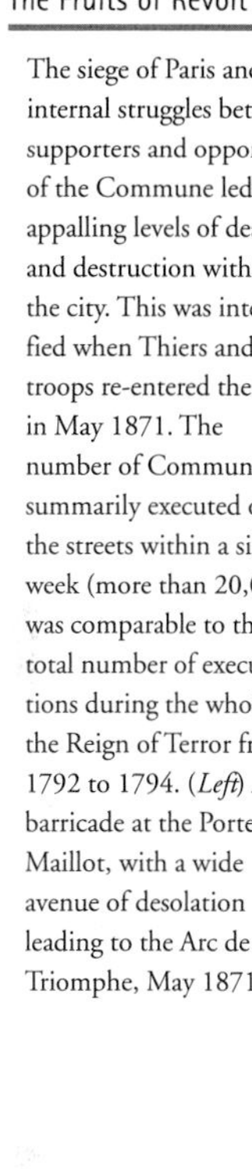

The siege of Paris and the internal struggles between supporters and opponents of the Commune led to appalling levels of death and destruction within the city. This was intensified when Thiers and his troops re-entered the city in May 1871. The number of Communards summarily executed on the streets within a single week (more than 20,000) was comparable to the total number of executions during the whole of the Reign of Terror from 1792 to 1794. (*Left*) A barricade at the Porte Maillot, with a wide avenue of desolation leading to the Arc de Triomphe, May 1871.

Alexandre Dumas (*left*) had a misspent youth and then transformed French drama with his plays *Henri III*, *Antony* and *Richard Darlington*. He is best known, however, for his historical novels: *Les Trois Mousquetaires*, *L'Homme au Masque de Fer* (*opposite, below right*), and *Le Comte de Monte-Cristo* (*opposite, below left*). (*Opposite, above*) The house in Villers-Cotterets where Dumas *père* was born.

Charles Baudelaire (*left*) quarrelled with his step-father, left for India, and met Jeanne Duval on the way. She became his inspiration. His poetic masterpiece – *Les Fleurs du mal* – led to prosecution, but inspired poets well into the 20th century. Gustave Flaubert (*opposite, left*) was a novelist and friend of Victor Hugo. His greatest work, *Madame Bovary*, achieved a *succès de scandal* in 1857. (*Opposite, above right*) Flaubert's study in Croisset. (*Opposite, below right*) A statue of Madame Bovary in the museum at Croisset.

In 1858 a girl named Bernadette Soubirous (*left*) claimed to have seen eighteen apparitions of the Virgin Mary in a cave near Lourdes in south-west France (*opposite, below right*). Crowds gathered to witness her repeat this experience (*opposite, below left*). (*Opposite, above*) The house in Lourdes inhabited by Bernadette. She died in 1879, was beatified in 1925 and canonized in 1933.

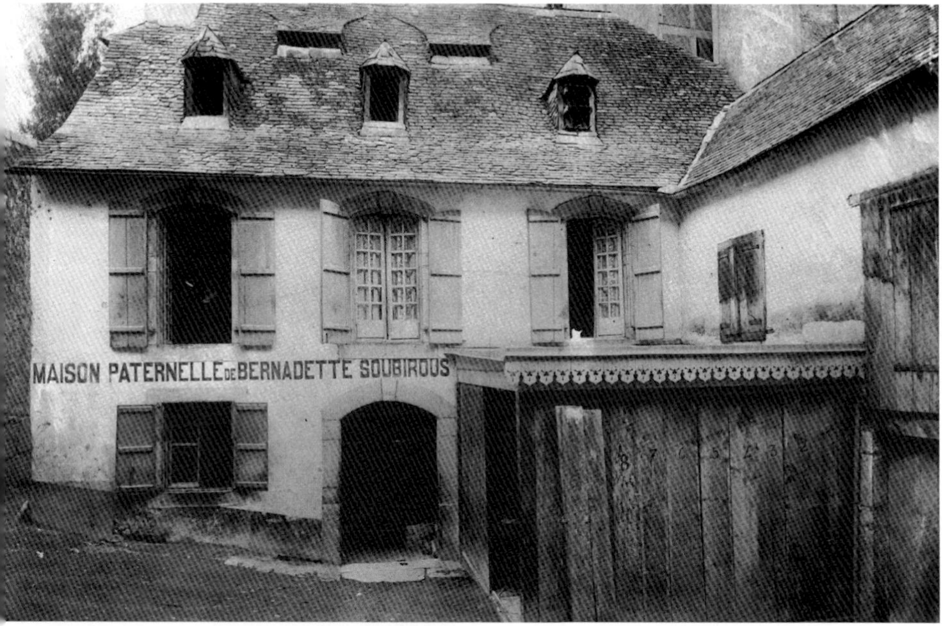

The music of Hector Berlioz (*left*) was swaggering, triumphant, tragic, tender and vivacious, forged in a long struggle with his family to allow him a musical career. With Hugo and Delacroix, he completes the trio at the heart of French Romanticism. The unrequited love of his life was an English actress named Harriet Constance Smithson (*opposite, above left*).

(*Above, right*) A caricature of Berlioz by Cham from *Charivari*. Wagner's *Tannhäuser* (a success) asks to see his infant relative *Les Troyens* – one of Berlioz's failures. (*Right*) A letter from Berlioz, with musical inscription, dated 1850.

Je vous remercie, monsieur, d'avoir bien
voulu vous donner la peine de retraduire
en vers le Chœur des Bergers de mon
opuscule Biblique. Je regrette bien plus
que vous de recevoir votre travail Post
festum (comme vous le dites) et c'est
une singulière fête que celle dont mes
traducteurs m'ont honoré jusqu'à présent.
Puisque vous m'offrez si gracieusement
votre appui contre eux, je prendrai la
liberté de vous envoyer de Paris une
dernière épreuve de ~~Faust~~ et de
vous demander de la revoir. Vous
m'obligerez beaucoup de la corriger sévèrement.
Mille amitiés à Liszt; le concert
~~tient~~ toujours pour samedi, nous
répétons ce soir et demain.
Je serre la main à Reményi, qui se met,
dit-il, à mes genoux; et pour qu'il se relève
au plus vite je lui envoie une bordée de
cuivre sur son Hony thème:

Votre tout dévoué

Hector Berlioz

Leipzig 6 Décembre 1850

Fac-simile of a Letter from Hector Berlioz.
(From the Autograph Collection of Hermann Scholtz of Dresden.)

38

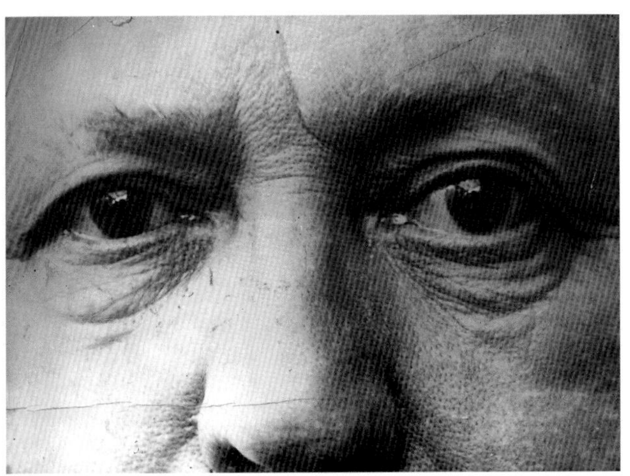

(*Opposite*) Four views of Charles François Gounod. (*Clockwise, from top left*) Gounod as a young man; the composer late in life; a caricature from the English magazine *Vanity Fair*, and a portrait of Gounod's eyes by Nadar – note the reflection of the photographer and the camera. (*Above, left*) The music library at the *Conservatoire des Arts et Métiers* in Paris. The room was used by many French composers, including Gounod. (*Above, right*) The cover of a piano selection of many of the arias and themes from Gounod's most famous and popular work, the opera *Faust*.

Though born in Cologne, Jacques Offenbach spent most of his life as a working composer in Paris, where he was *chef d'orchestre* at the Théatre-Français and manager of the *Bouffes parisiennes*. (*Opposite*) A music cover for Offenbach's *La Fille du Tambour Major*. Many of the comic operas of Adolphe Charles Adam (*above, left*) were produced at the Théâtre des Nouveautés in Paris (*above, right*), but he is best known today as the composer of music for the ballet *Giselle*. (*Right*) The interior of the *Comédie-française*, where many of the works of Berlioz, Adam, Ambroise Thomas, Auber, and Etienne-Nicolas Méhul were performed.

On the evening of 17 November 1869, 10,000 lanterns blazed in the new city of Ismailia to mark the opening of the Suez Canal. At Port Said, 70 kilometres away, ships queued (*opposite, above*) to enter the new waterway that connected the Mediterranean and the Red Sea. The Canal took nine years to complete, was dug by tens of thousands of workers (*opposite, below*), and was the engineering brainchild of Ferdinand de Lesseps (*above, left*). (*Below, left*) De Lesseps (second from right) and some of his colleagues, 1865.

It took surprisingly little time for the streets and buildings of Paris to recover from the trauma of the Commune and its suppression. Life returned to what passed for normal in the pleasure capital of Europe. Many of the old landmarks had been destroyed – among them the Tuileries and the Hôtel de Ville – but others survived. No insurrection could destroy the Bois de Boulogne with its Hôtel de la Cascade (*above*).

In the Bois de Boulogne and the Bois de Vincennes, the middle classes took their evening stroll, met their friends, exchanged the gossip of the day, exercised their dogs, and turned their eyeglasses and pince-nez on the latest fashions. (*Above*) An elegant young couple of newly-weds set out for their wedding reception in the Bois de Boulogne, 11 July 1874. A light dinner under the trees would follow, and then...ah, a night of wedded bliss.

Contemporary opinion was divided as to the strategy behind the rebuilding of Paris. Some saw it as the destruction of the working-class hovels that had bred generations of radicals and *sans-culottes*, to provide smart boulevards for the bourgeoisie. Such broad thoroughfares would be too wide for rebels to barricade. Those who approved the new plans applauded Baron Georges Eugène Haussmann (*opposite, above right*), prefect of the Seine *département*. (*Opposite, above left*) Haussmann and his wife. (*Opposite, below*) Two examples of Haussmann's town-planning – the Boulevard des Italiens (*left*) and the Rue de Rivoli (*right*). (*Above*) The new Hôtel de la Paix begins to take shape, c. 1860.

Paris set the pace for all other cities in the 1860s. It became the hub of a national transport system, and the economic heart of the country. With the new hotels and new boulevards came new shopping centres, new parks and new galleries. The emperor declared Paris to be the heart of France and encouraged its citizens to put all their efforts into embellishing it, to open new roads, make populous neighbourhoods more healthy and to let 'benevolent light' penetrate everywhere. (*Above*) The new city market at Les Halles.

The old pattern of class strata changed. Previously, the first and second floors above shops had been occupied by the middle classes, the tops and garrets by the poor. Now Paris was geographically divided into rich, middle class and poor districts. The rapidly increasing bourgeoisie had their own *arrondissements* – and a brand new shopping experience. Au Bon Marché (*above, top and bottom*), founded by Aristide Boucicaut, was the world's first department store.

The new telegraph turned the world on its head. Within minutes messages could be sent by wire across countries, oceans, continents. Relays of horses to deliver military orders, government commands, news of triumphs and disasters became as obsolete as the stagecoach. For a franc or two a dealer in Bordeaux could keep in touch with prices on the Paris stock exchange, a fish merchant in Marseilles could pick up orders from a restaurateur in Lyons, an agent in Nantes could seek instructions from his principal in Nancy.

The first submarine telegraph cable was laid between England and France along the bed of the Channel in 1851 (*above*). The telephone system followed soon after. (*Opposite*) Women switchboard workers at a telephone exchange in the early 1870s. (*Right*) A telegraph worker reads the message from her ticker-tape roll.

Galop chromatique

No truly bourgeois home was complete without its piano (*right*). Though Italy long claimed to be the birthplace of this most comprehensive of instruments, there were rival French claims – Maurius submitted a prototype piano to the French Academy in 1716. (*Opposite, above*) A family gathers round the piano, c. 1850. (*Opposite, below left*) An illustration on the cover of piano music, c. 1840. (*Opposite, below right*) Henri Lehmann's drawing of Liszt pounding the piano, while Lablanch conducts and Louis-Philippe beats time.

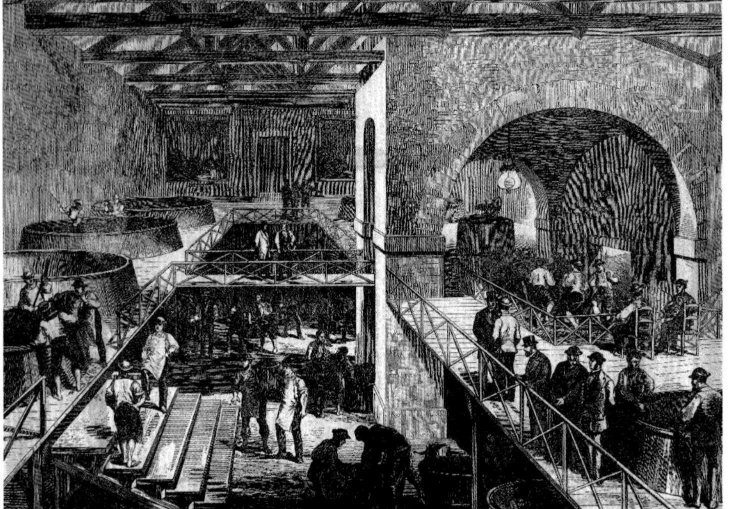

After experiencing a boom in production and a huge increase in sales, wine-growers went through a desperate crisis in the 1870s. An epidemic of phylloxera ravaged the vineyards of France. Entire vintages were wiped out, whole regions were depressed, agrarian economies were shattered.

Where possible, however, the old ways of tending the vines and making the wine were maintained. In the Médoc, hundreds of villagers gathered the grapes on estates such as that at Château-Lafite (*opposite, above*). (*Opposite, below*) The *cuivier,* or pressing house, at Château d'Estournel. And when all the work was done, there were always those ready to sample the new vintage and drink to its success (*above*).

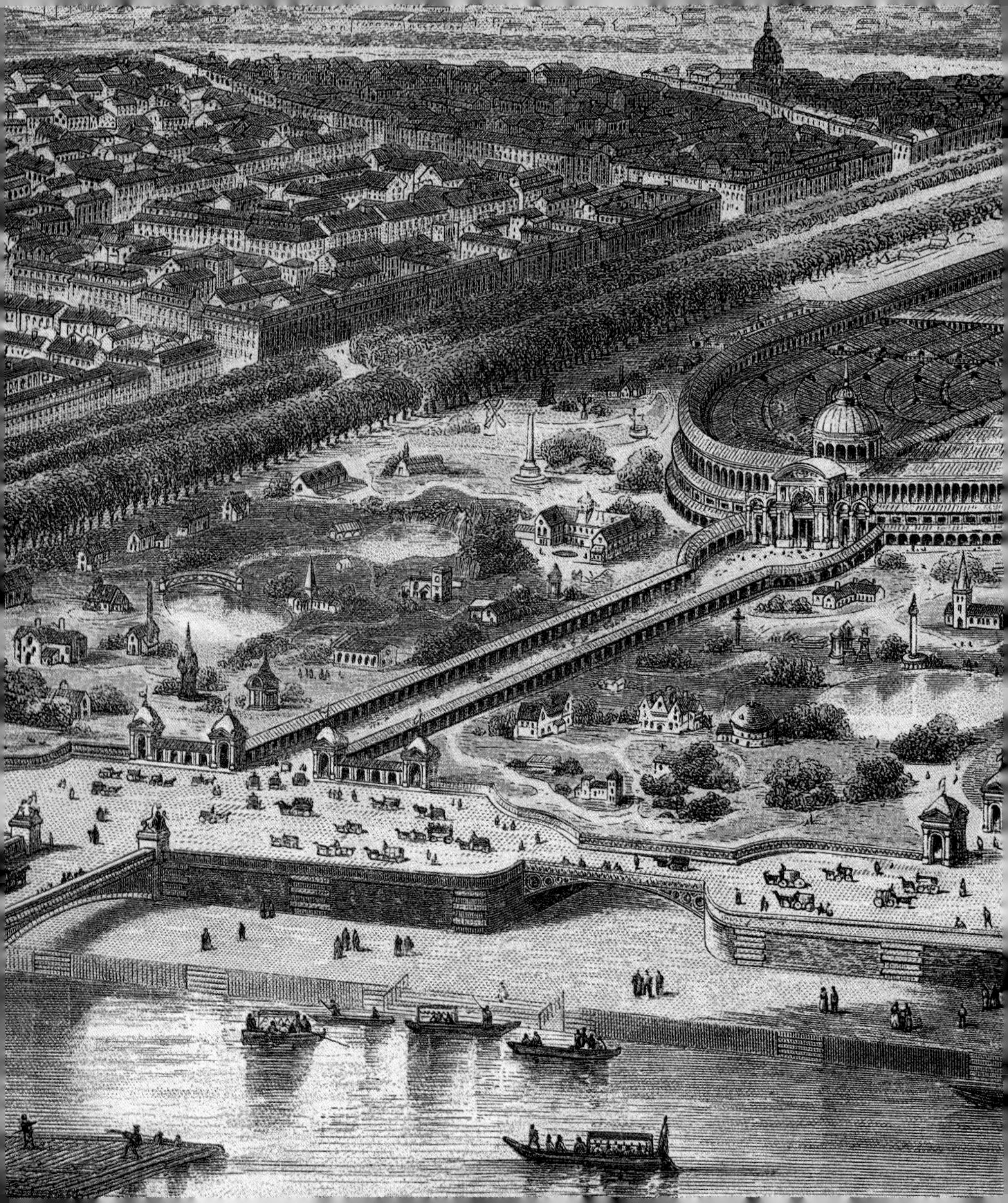

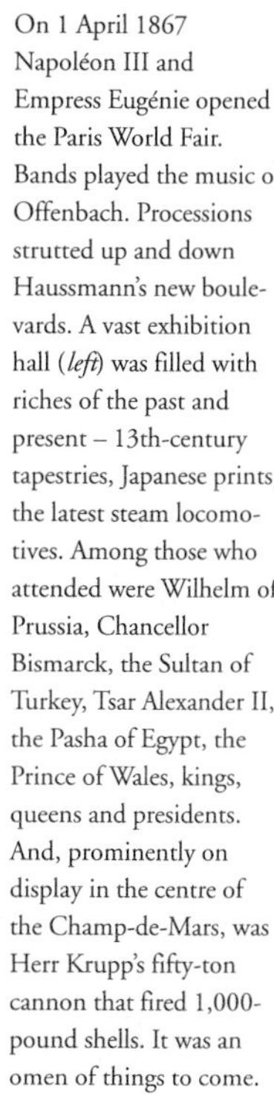

On 1 April 1867 Napoléon III and Empress Eugénie opened the Paris World Fair. Bands played the music of Offenbach. Processions strutted up and down Haussmann's new boulevards. A vast exhibition hall (*left*) was filled with riches of the past and present – 13th-century tapestries, Japanese prints, the latest steam locomotives. Among those who attended were Wilhelm of Prussia, Chancellor Bismarck, the Sultan of Turkey, Tsar Alexander II, the Pasha of Egypt, the Prince of Wales, kings, queens and presidents. And, prominently on display in the centre of the Champ-de-Mars, was Herr Krupp's fifty-ton cannon that fired 1,000-pound shells. It was an omen of things to come.

16
ARTISTIC IMPRESSIONS 1871–1890

In 1863 Edouard Manet entered his painting *Le Déjeuner sur l'herbe* (*right*) for exhibition at the Paris Salon. It was rejected, members of the jury being scandalised by the juxtaposition of a nude female with clothed males. The critic Théophile Thore was moved to comment that, while the public accepted monsters with goats' feet who carried off completely naked, fat ladies, it did not want to see the garters of the girls of the Seine. But art conquers all. Within a few years, Manet and the Impressionists had produced a revolution in painting. A new age had found a new identity.

Introduction

The soul of France recovered in the best way possible. The late 19th century was one long French artistic triumph. It was as though France had discovered the secret of living – how to eat, dance, paint, write, frolic, and enjoy the abundant pleasures created by God, nature or human ingenuity, especially French ingenuity. Patriotic pride was restored with the adoption of the *Marseillaise* as the national anthem in 1879, and the adoption once more of Bastille Day as an annual national holiday in 1880. Every town hall in the land was graced with a bust of Marianne, the female symbol of the Republic since 1790 and a figure expressing much-needed unity.

Over a period of five years between 1881 and 1886, the educationalist and politician Jules Ferry established a State system of primary schools, much to the horror of the Church, who saw this move as further evidence that Protestants and Freemasons were now running the country. The ensuing struggle between village schoolteacher and *curé* for supremacy over the culture of rural France was won by the former. The ardour with which teachers embraced the Third Republic was later to cost them dear. A greater proportion of teachers (20 per cent) than any other social group died in the trenches of the First World War.

In Paris and the other major cities of France, culture exploded in a brilliant display of writing, music, and painting. Verlaine, Rimbaud and Mallarmé produced some of the finest French poetry of all time. The short stories of Maupassant and the novels of Dumas *fils* sold in their thousands of copies. Crowds flocked to hear the music of Saint-Saëns, Debussy, Delibes and Bizet. The Impressionists freed themselves from academic restrictions, bursting out in sunlit glory with the paintings of Cézanne, Monet, Gauguin and Toulouse-Lautrec.

The heart of Paris offered further joys to citizens and tourists alike. The day could be spent sauntering through newly-developed Montmartre, admiring the dazzling pink splendour of the Sacré-Cœur, or strolling down to the Seine to climb M. Eiffel's new tower (the tallest structure in the world). In the evening, the rich dined at Maxim's, or any one of a dozen restaurants where their palates would be seduced by the creations of Escoffier and other *chefs* of *grande cuisine*. After dinner (or before supper), there were other delights to be savoured at the Casino de Paris or the Moulin Rouge, where the can-can first erupted on stage during a wild night in 1889.

And all the while, new wealth was being created by new industries. René Panhard developed the French internal combustion engine and began manufacturing automobiles. Michelin became an early and permanent leader in the production of tyres. There was a huge increase in the amount of electricity generated. The canal network increased. Railways boomed again.

Was it possible that life could get any better?

From 1887 to 1889 the Eiffel Tower slowly rose from the Champ-de-Mars (*left*). It became the centrepiece of the World Exhibition of 1889 and the most talked about building in the world. It was a staggering achievement, a masterpiece of metal, literally the high point of the 19th-century industrial age, and it remained the tallest structure in the world until 1930. (*Opposite*) The tower completed.

Gustave Eiffel (*above, right*) had gained a moderate reputation as a designer of bridges and viaducts before he submitted the plans for his tower. It made him famous. The cost of building was £260,000 – which worked out at roughly £260 per foot, for the completed tower was 985 feet high (325 metres). (*Above, left*) M. Eiffel – in top hat – poses near the top of the tower, April 1889.

(*Above, right*) Workmen and the elevator at the first level of the tower, during its construction. Well over a hundred years later, the elevator is still used to carry visitors to the higher floors. (*Above, left*) One of the favourite sports of Parisians in the early days of the tower was to release toy balloons from the top and watch them float over the rooftops of the city. It was also the chosen point of departure for many would-be suicides, and for those sad eccentrics who believed that they could fly.

By the 1870s railways had come of age: they were swift, reliable, comfortable and frequently crowded. (*Left*) A typical scene at a French railway station on a Sunday morning in 1874. The 'crack' expresses offered a service that was second to none – including sleeping-cars, observation coaches and dining-cars.

(*Above*) The dining-car on the *train de luxe* that ran from Paris to the south. Passengers could enjoy *haute cuisine*, fine wines and champagnes, crisp table linen...

The friendship between the French and American peoples, forged in the early days of the struggle for American independence, was given a new lease of life in the 1870s. High above the streets of Paris appeared a vast statue of the figure of Liberty. It was the work of Frédéric Auguste Bartholdi (*left*), a French sculptor born in Colmar, Alsace, in 1834.

The complete statue took ten years to make, and was shipped in pieces across the Atlantic to New York, where it was placed on Bedloe's Island in 1886. Its small sister (the prototype) remained in Paris, on the Pont de Grenelle over the River Seine.

In the 1870s Montmartre still maintained an air of semi-rural calm and repose. There were windmills (*opposite, above*) on the ridge of the hill overlooking Paris, carts parked on the cobbled streets (*right*), and wooden verandahs fronting the old houses (*opposite, below*).

Changes were in the air all over Paris. In the Champs-Elysées, a new pleasure dome known as the Cirque de l'Impératrice blazed with light as it called young and old to stroll in and try its wares. Montmartre's time to change was not far away. For a while it slept on, but Paris in the late 19th century was no place for peace and calm.

Trains rattled across the length and breadth of France, bringing workers and produce to the cities, whisking the holidaymaker away for a day in the country, or at the seaside, and transporting the rich to far-flung destinations. One of the most popular was Monte-Carlo, on the Mediterranean. Here was a fine new casino, where fortunes could be won on the spin of the roulette wheel, the turn of a card, the throw of a dice. Visitors were more likely to lose and be ignominiously escorted from the premises (*above*), but the casino's publicity suggested otherwise (*above, right*).

When the doors were opened for an afternoon or evening session, gamblers raced (and sometimes fought) to gain their own 'lucky' seat (*above, right*). The opulent surroundings reeked of wealth – few visitors stopped to think how such wealth had been accumulated. (*Below, right*) The odds offered on the roulette wheel at the Monte-Carlo Casino.

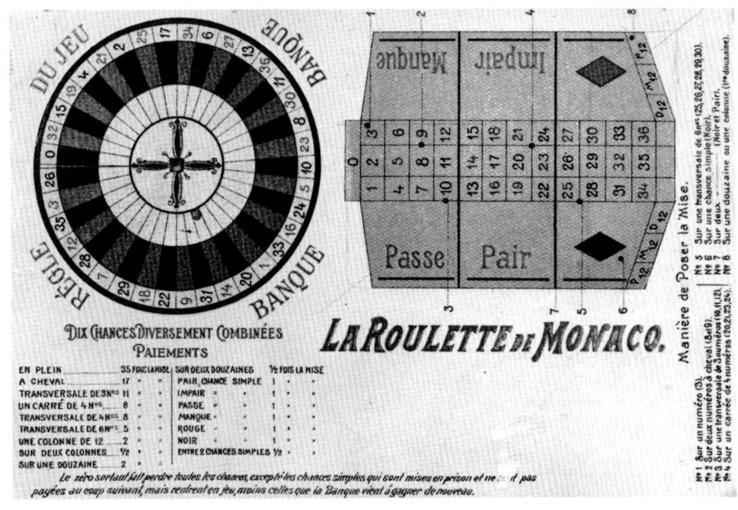

Georges Bizet (*below, left*) struggled to make his reputation as a composer. Not until after his death did *Carmen* become hugely successful. (*Far left*) The French soprano Emma Calve as Carmen. Emmy Soldene – one of the earliest performers of Carmen – smoking (*left*) and dying (*below, right*).

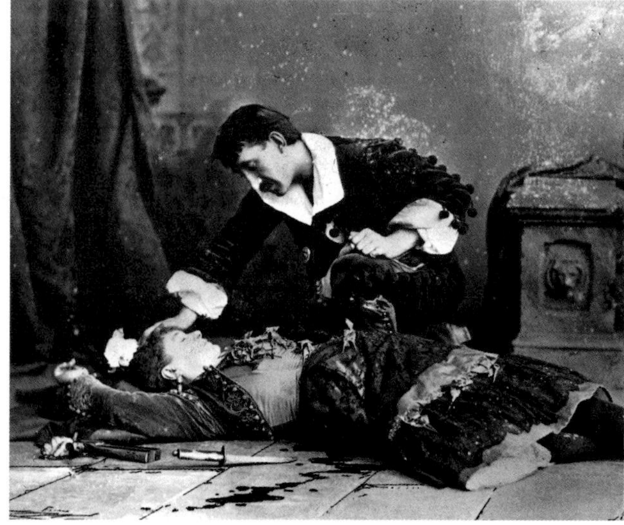

Once again, Paris had a brand new opera-house (*right*). It was grand, it was magnificent, it was the most fashionable place to be seen. (*Above, right*) Crowds leaving the Opéra after a performance, 1888. (*Above, left*) The painter Paul Jacques Aimé Bauldry, whose series of murals illustrating music and dancing decorated the foyer of the new Opéra.

REUTLINGER
Photo

French music was rich in talent in the late 19th century. (*Opposite, clockwise from top left*) Charles Camille Saint-Saëns; Claude Debussy; Gabriel Fauré; Vincent d'Indy; and Jacques Offenbach. (*Right, clockwise from top left*) Jules Massenet; Léo Delibes; Cécile Chaminade, pianist and composer; and César Franck.

The high-kicking, petticoat-waving, leg-revealing can-can delighted many, disgusted some, and completely changed the character of Montmartre. The dancers themselves (*left and right and below, left*) were a mixture of cabaret artists, ballet dancers and natural acrobats.

The venues were newly converted or newly (and hastily) built. Most famous among them were the Folies Bergère (*opposite, below right*), a purpose-built music-hall, and the Moulin Rouge (*above, left*), a revamped windmill. Every age believes it has invented new and daring ways of enjoying itself. The *Belle Epoque* was one of the few that really did. The pace of life quickened, night-life became exciting, brash and exuberant. (*Above, right*) A poster for the Elysée Montmartre, Paris, at the turn of the century.

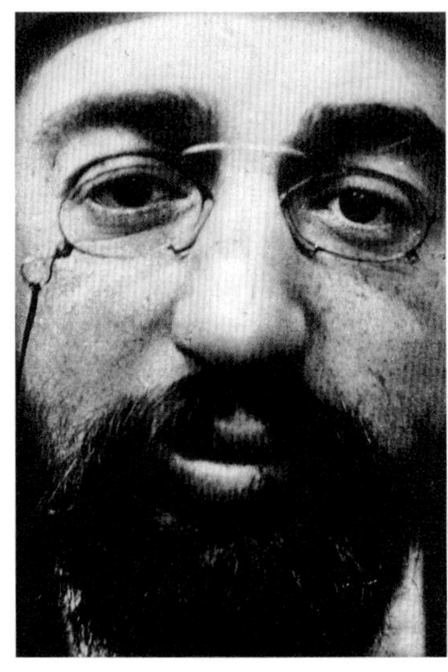

The artist who caught the character and flavour of Montmartre and the excitement of the can-can was Henri Marie de Toulouse-Lautrec (*above, right and below, left*). Toulouse-Lautrec came from an aristocratic family and was encouraged to train as an athlete, but at the age of fourteen he broke both his legs (in a riding accident), which then ceased to grow. He turned to painting, and his brilliant posters remain the most revealing portraits of the age. (*Opposite*) Lautrec's poster the *Divan japonais.* (*Above, left*) Lautrec and Tremolada, director of the Moulin Rouge, with one of Lautrec's posters for the club.

Divan Japonais
75 rue des Martyrs
Ed Fournier

Paul Verlaine (*above, left*) was one of the most brilliant poets of the 19th century. He was a man of passion and politics – he served as press officer for the Communards. His marriage was an understandably fraught affair, for in 1872 he embarked on a homosexual romance with the young poet Arthur Rimbaud (*above, right*). Rimbaud threatened to leave Verlaine, who retaliated by wounding him with a knife. Less emotional was the Symbolist poet Stéphane Mallarmé (*opposite*), author of *vers libre* and word music. His most famous poem was *L'Après-midi d'un faune.*

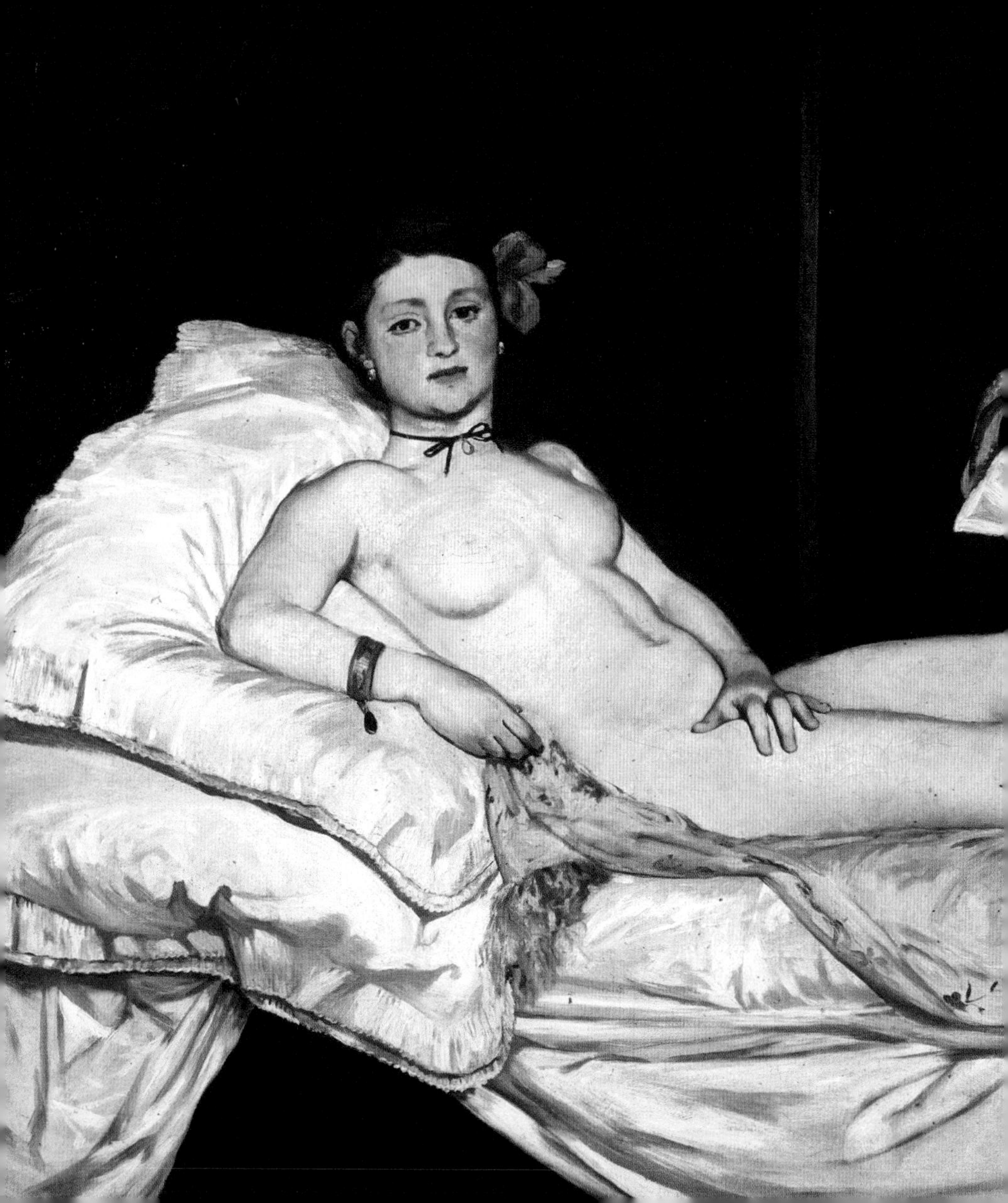

After the scandal of *Le Déjeuner sur l'herbe*, Edouard Manet (*above*) produced a full-length nude study that owed much to the earlier works of Titian and Goya. The problem was that the art world realised that the subject for his 1865 *Olympia* was a prostitute (she had dirty feet). The Salon, the bourgeoisie and the old guard were once again appalled. Manet moved away from conventional painting, but never fully committed himself to the Impressionist cause.

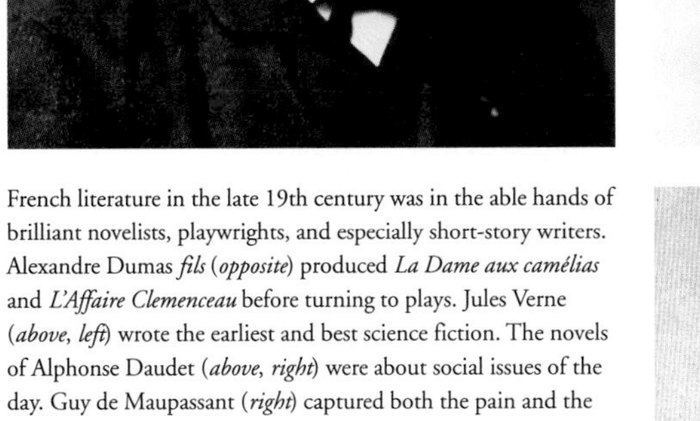

French literature in the late 19th century was in the able hands of brilliant novelists, playwrights, and especially short-story writers. Alexandre Dumas *fils* (*opposite*) produced *La Dame aux camélias* and *L'Affaire Clemenceau* before turning to plays. Jules Verne (*above, left*) wrote the earliest and best science fiction. The novels of Alphonse Daudet (*above, right*) were about social issues of the day. Guy de Maupassant (*right*) captured both the pain and the humour of the age.

Paul Cézanne (*left*) declared that one of his artistic aims was 'to make Impressionism something solid and endurable, like the art of the Old Masters'. By emphasising the underlying forms of nature – the cone, the cylinder and the sphere – he was also one of the forerunners of Cubism. He was a man who loved the act of painting, rather than the finished products. His wife, Hortense Fiquet, faced the task of collecting his works, which he abandoned as soon as he completed them.

(Above, right) Still Life with Bread, painted by Cézanne sometime between 1888 and 1890. *(Below, right) Mer à l'Estaque, with a View of the Gulf of Marseilles,* painted in 1879. Despite his enormous influence on other artists and his considerable popularity in more modern times, Cézanne received little recognition for his work during his lifetime. Not until the exhibitions held by Vollard in 1895 and 1899 did critics come to respect his brilliant use of colour and form, and the inspiring quality of his canvases.

Before he became an artist, Paul Gauguin (*above*) was a successful stockbroker and collector of Impressionist paintings. With the help of his friend Camille Pissarro he arranged the first exhibition of his work in 1883. From 1891 to 1901, Gauguin lived in the French colony of Tahiti and the Iles Marquises, where he produced some of his most famous works. (*Right*) *Arearea* or *Le Chien rouge*, painted in 1892 while Gauguin was living and working in Tahiti.

ARCAREA

Auguste Rodin (*below, left*) made three unsuccessful attempts to gain admission to the Ecole des Beaux-Arts. After these rejections he travelled extensively in Europe, studying the work of the Old Masters and the ancient Greeks.

(*Opposite, above*) Rodin in his studio at Meudon. Rodin's output was astonishing. The figures he carved and sculpted owed much to the Romantic movement, of which he wholeheartedly approved. (*Opposite, below right*) *Le Penseur*, a late work, dating from 1904. (*Above, left*) *Eternelle Idol*, sculpted c. 1889. (*Above, right*) Perhaps the most famous of all Rodin's figures – *Le Baiser* (1898).

(*Left*) Bathing at Trouville, 1879. 'In this sketch,' wrote an English commentator, 'may be seen how the French lounge on the sands, how they attire themselves for what is often not more than a paddle, and how they contrive to render dignified and becoming dresses and garments in which most English men and women would appear ridiculous.'

Paris maintained its lead in the fashion world. The French still set the style for others to follow. (*Opposite, below left*) More beach fashion from the *Journal des Demoiselles*, August 1892. (*Opposite, below right*) Paris dresses from the mid-1870s. (*Right*) Youth, serenity, romance, a picnic hamper – and the latest clothes from France. An English couple pass an afternoon of summer bliss by the river.

Paris fashion houses exported their finest designs to England. French music-hall comedians imported the latest English fashions as costumes for their acts. (*Left*) Potier (left) and Brunet play the parts of comic Englishwomen in a sketch entitled *Des Anglaises Pour Rire,* c. 1890.

(*Right*) Rosa Bonheur, well-known painter of animal studies during the second half of the 19th century. She exhibited at the Salon at the age of nineteen. She was also given permission by the government to wear men's clothing for her work as an agricultural inspector – cross-dressing was illegal at the time. She was the first woman to be awarded the Grand Cross of the *Légion d'Honneur*.

Gaspard-Félix Tournachon (*above, left*) was one of the greatest photographers of the 19th century. He used the professional name Nadar, and was a pioneer of aerial photography – flying over Paris in a small balloon. (*Above, right*) Nadar poses in a balloon basket in his Paris studio. (*Left*) A photograph taken by Nadar in 1890 of the vine planted three hundred years earlier by the poet and dramatist Racine in the Rue de Marais, Saint-Germain. (*Opposite*) The first aerial photograph taken of Paris, from a hot air balloon. Nadar took the picture in 1858, some 520 metres above the city. A rustic Montmartre may be seen in the background.

TERNES
du Bois

In 1884 France was hit by an appalling outbreak of cholera. The disease was believed to have arrived by boat from Egypt. (*Opposite, below*) Fleeing by train from the south of France. (*Opposite, above left*) Passengers from Marseilles are fumigated with carbolic acid at Avignon, and (*opposite, above right*) fumigating a ship. (*Above*) The Hôpital des Mariniers at Montrouge, built to house cholera victims. (*Right*) A quarantine camp on the Franco-Italian border.

Although the Scottish engineer John Dunlop is credited with the invention of the world's first pneumatic tyre, it was Edouard Michelin (*left*) who realised and exploited its commercial potential. (*Above*) An early advertisement for Michelin's non-skid and square-thread rubber tyres. The inflated figure of M. Bibendum was an early mascot for the company.

René Panhard and Emile Levassor were early pioneers of the motor car. Panhard was the first engineer and designer to mount an internal combustion engine on a chassis. (*Above, left*) An 8hp Panhard-Levassor of 1898, with the British motor engineer Charles Stuart Rolls at the controls. (*Right*) The first Panhard-Levassor car. Levassor holds the steering tiller, beside him is M. Playade. Seated in the rear are Mme Levassor and Panhard himself. (*Above, right*) An early advertisement for the Daimler powered Panhard-Levassor car, c. 1890.

In 1883 the brothers Tissandier invented a dirigible balloon, powered by electricity. (*Opposite*) Albert Tissandier (left) and his brother Gaston had already founded the Paris Balloon Post, back in 1870, when they took this bold step (*above, left*). (*Below, left*) An earlier flight by hot air balloon, 1875. In the foreground Gaston Tissandier drops a line over the side. The balloon later crashed, killing Croce-Spinelli and Sivel. Gaston survived.

17
BELLE EPOQUE
1890–1900

Zola the novelist could not have invented a more dramatic story; Zola the journalist could not have found a more exciting subject; Zola the radical could not have campaigned for a worthier cause. When Captain Alfred Dreyfus was court-martialled, cashiered and imprisoned in 1894, France was divided into two sides. Conservatives and anti-Semites bellowed for harsher punishments, stricter laws. Socialists and anti-clerics bellowed that a grave injustice had been done. The nation suffered almost irreparably. (*Right*) Journalists gather in their room during the Dreyfus court-martial at Rennes.

Introduction

Life could get better – and did. Renault and Citroën established the French automobile industry. Louis Pasteur and Marie Curie received international recognition for their scientific work. Hot on the heels of the successful Suez venture, de Lesseps floated the Panama Company. The Lumière brothers staggered even sophisticated audiences with the projection on screen of *La Sortie des usines Lumière* and the image of an ordinary train arriving at an ordinary station. Real trams appeared on real city streets. Cyclists explored the rural byways of France.

Seaside towns rivalled each other in a spate of casino building. Deauville, Enghien-les-Bains and Le Touquet became playgrounds of the north, the Côte d'Azur offered a warmer welcome and some of the finest hotels in Europe. Domestic servants were cheap, waiters were in plentiful supply. Wine was good, and could be followed by any one of the colourful *digestifs* that enriched the shelves of bars and cafés – yellow and green Chartreuse, Bénédictine, Cointreau, the pinks and purples of numerous *eaux de vie*, and the heavy brown beauty of Cognac. If all else failed, there was always absinthe.

The brushes and palettes of the Impressionists still sizzled with colour. Degas and Renoir joined their number and new masterpieces blazed on their canvases. Paul Dukas composed *L'Apprenti Sorcier* and *Ariane et Barbe-Bleue*. Auguste Rodin carved and cast *The Burghers of Calais*. Edmond Rostand wrote *Cyrano de Bergerac*.

Baron Pierre de Coubertin founded the modern Olympic Games in 1896, and much was made of the new international spirit of sport – the 'taking part' as opposed to winning – though Coubertin's main aim was to 'show the Boches' (i.e. the Germans) that France was at least one hop, step and jump ahead on the sports field, if not the battlefield.

There was a darker side to the *Belle Epoque*, however. In 1892, Captain Alfred Dreyfus was assigned to the general staff of the French army. Two years later he was accused of passing classified information to the Germans. He was stripped of his rank, dismissed from the army and sent to Devil's Island in Guiana. Dreyfus was a Jew, and there is no doubt that anti-Semitism played a large part in his false conviction.

France was torn apart by the Dreyfus affair. Emile Zola sprang to his defence. Right-wing newspapers and pro-Church politicians snarled their condemnation. Both sides hurled the same slogans at each other: *Vive la France*, *Vive la République*, *Vive l'Armée*, *à bas les Traitres*. After four years Dreyfus was brought home, but the split in French society and the French army did not heal. The Dreyfus affair smouldered on, playing its part in the military *débâcle* of the First World War.

Dreyfus (*above, left*) was a competent officer and a Jew. He was charged with passing military information to a foreign government, and tried at Rennes (*opposite*). (*Above, right*) Dreyfus at the time of his trial. (*Below, left*) Dreyfus and his family shortly before charges were brought against him. (*Below, right*) Charles Maurras, a right-wing journalist and critic, who denounced the Republic when Dreyfus was subsequently pardoned.

Emile Zola (*left*) was first and foremost a novelist, a writer whose works reveal the pain, suffering and humanity of the working classes in the late 19th century. Among the most famous are *Germinal, La Terre* and *L'Assommoir*. He was a man of great compassion, a student of the life he witnessed around him, and a champion of those he considered oppressed.

He was also a man moved to almost uncontrollable wrath by the injustice meted out to Dreyfus. He accused the authorities who had sentenced Dreyfus of bigotry, perjury and treachery. For this he was sentenced to a year's imprisonment, but he escaped to Britain. (*Above*) Zola with his family at their home in Verneuil-sur-Seine – (left to right) Jacques, Zola's wife Jeanne, Denise and Zola. (*Right*) Zola's ringing pronouncement during the Dreyfus affair – '*La verité est en marche et rien ne l'arrêterá*' ('Truth is on the march and nothing will stop it').

La vérité est en marche et rien ne l'arrêtera.

Emile Zola

Republicanism limped along through the 1870s and 1880s under Thiers and Jules Favre (*above, right*) as the regime 'that divides us the least'. Monarchists linked their cause to that of the Catholic Church, which increasingly moved to the right. Alfred Capus (*above, left*) one of the founders of *Le Figaro,* wrote a handful of novels and is best remembered as the author of the highly successful bourgeois comedy *La Viene.*

Socialism gained followers but provoked bitter opposition. Léon Victor Auguste Bourgeois (*above, left*) was one of the more successful socialist politicians, and was Prime Minister of France from 1895 to 1896. On the royalist side, there were several who clung to the hope that they would one day sit on the defunct throne of France, among them the Duc d'Orléans (*above, right*), here wearing a sign labelled '1'. His dreams never came true.

The French economy grew, especially in the iron, chemical and automobile industries, but the growth was slow, and by the beginning of the 20th century France had slipped from second to fourth greatest industrial power in the world. There was more slack in the system for many, however. The rich and the bourgeois had money to invest on the stock exchange, with La Bourse (*above*) as its classical headquarters. The building was designed by Alexandre-Théodore Brongniart.

More people opened bank accounts, and branches of the leading banks opened in country towns as well as the principal French cities. In the last twenty years before the First World War, real wages rose by over 50 per cent, and the number of banks quintupled. (*Above, left*) Gold reserves are placed in the vaults of the Bank of France, 1898. (*Above, right*) Brisk business in the main hall of the Bank of France.

The fecundity of the Vicomte Ferdinand de Lesseps and his wife (*above, left*) was never in doubt. What were questioned were the financial dealings attached to his attempt to construct a canal through the isthmus of Panama to link the Atlantic and Pacific Oceans in the 1880s (*opposite*). At first all went well, and de Lesseps was given a triumphant welcome to Panama City in May 1886 (*below, left*). Among those implicated in the Panama Company scandal was Georges Clemenceau (*above, right*), then a young left-wing politician.

As ever, there was much to worry the middle classes during the *Belle Epoque*. There was the music hall, with its sense of frivolity and lack of respect. There was socialism, anti-clericalism, alcoholism, and 'modern' thought. Academics and social scientists began to study society, to produce statistics relating to standards of living, life expectancy, population growth – always a cause of concern to France – and, above all, crime rates.

New ways were sought to combat crime and the criminal. Among them were the use of photography and the science of antropometry (*opposite*). Measurements were taken as part of an identity card process; the term '*physiognomie*' was given to the science of depicting a criminal by looking at his or her features. New criminals, new gaols, new police forces needed new waggons to take those arrested from police station to court, and from court to gaol. (*Above*) A line of Black Marias waits for business at Fresnes.

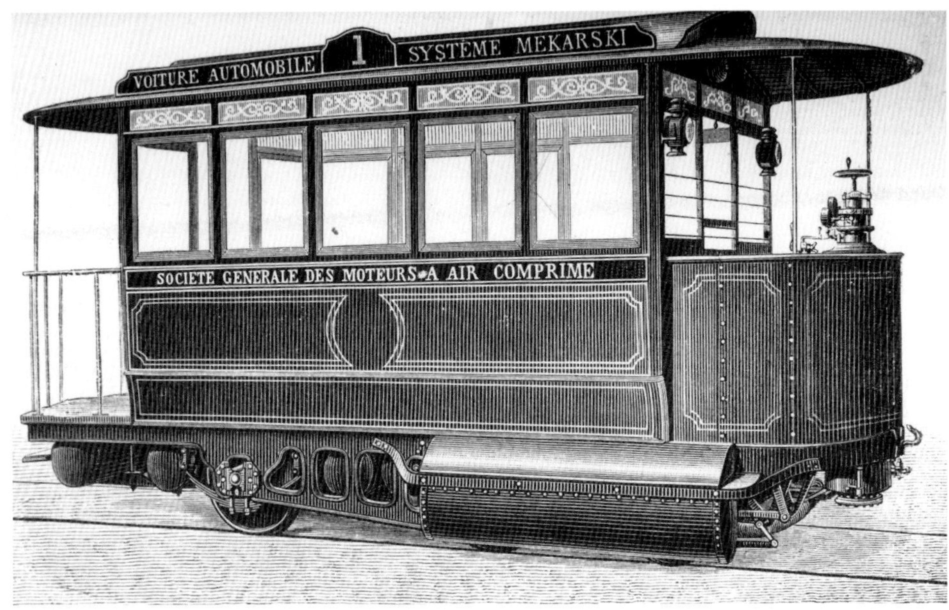

A happier way of travelling around Paris or any other large city was the tram. The newest and most stylish models were those of the *Système Mekarski* (*above*) powered by compressed air. In the last years of the 19th century, before the development of the Métro, such vehicles provided cheap, clean and relatively comfortable travel for thousands of Parisians.

The wide boulevards created by Baron Haussmann provided the ideal location for tramlines, and gave shoppers the chance to cover the whole city centre within a day. Customers crowded into the new stores and markets, shops and boutiques. (*Above*) Shoppers throng the Boulevard de Strasbourg in Paris during the winter of 1890.

CHALETS DU CYCLE

As well as being the quickest method of crossing the city, the bicycle offered healthy days out in the country-side. (*Below*) A ladies' cycling party pauses for refreshment on the outskirts of Paris. (*Opposite*) The Comtesse Liane de Pougy and La Belle Otero (front row, left and right) lead a group of young aristocrats through the Bois de Boulogne, c. 1890. (*Left*) Madame du Gast in her *costume de balon*, the last word in cycling fashion.

JE
V
OUS
AI

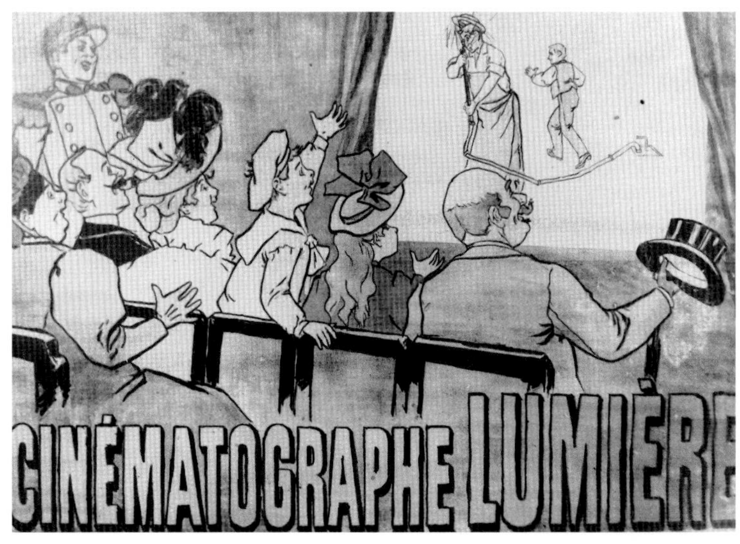

Credit for the invention of cinematography is usually given to Auguste and Louis Lumière, but many Frenchmen worked on the same idea. (*Opposite, below left*) Louis Aimé Augustin le Prince, a fellow pioneer. (*Opposite, above*) Chronophotograph of a fencer by Etienne Jules Marey, c. 1890. (*Opposite, below right*) A series of images by Demeny, showing a man saying '*Je vous aime*'. (*Above*) One of the first Lumière projectors. (*Above, right*) A poster for *L'Arroseur arrosé*. (*Below, right*) The first moving picture – *La Sortie des usines Lumière.*

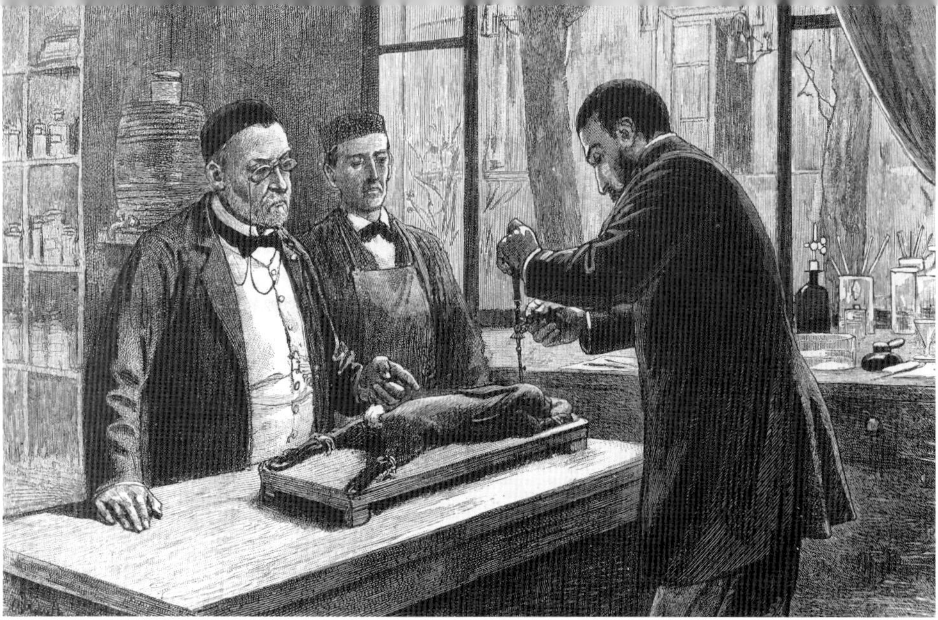

Louis Pasteur (*opposite, below*) was the father of modern bacteriology and one of the most influential scientists of the modern age. The range of his work was enormous – he investigated fermentation, putrefaction, diseases in poultry and cattle, as well as a host of human diseases. (*Left*) The apparatus used by Pasteur for cooling and fermenting beer during his experiments with micro-organisms at the Sorbonne, c. 1870.

Much of Pasteur's later work was into diphtheria, tubercular disease, cholera, yellow fever and hydrophobia. (*Opposite, above*) Pasteur experiments on a chloroformed rabbit during his research into hydrophobia, c. 1885. In 1888 the Institut Pasteur was founded for the treatment of hydrophobia. Pasteur became the first director. (*Above*) Pasteur stands in one of the main laboratories of the institute named after him, 1890.

Marie Sklodowska (*above, left*) graduated from the Sorbonne and married Pierre Curie (*above, right*) in 1895. Together they worked on magnetism and radioactivity – the latter being a term invented by Marie Curie. For their work in isolating radium and polonium, the Curies were jointly awarded the Nobel Prize for Chemistry in 1903 with Henri Becquerel. Three years later Pierre Curie was killed when he was knocked down by a tram. Marie worked on as director of research at the Radium Institute in Paris. (*Opposite*) The Curies at work, 1902.

She was divine, she was incomparable, she was the most famous actress of her age. Rosine Bernhardt, known to the world as Sarah (*opposite*), made her debut as Iphigénie at the Théâtre Français in 1862, at the age of eighteen. For more than sixty years she continued to perform, even after the amputation of a leg in 1915. She was certainly the most popular and probably the most versatile actress of all time. (*Right, clockwise from top left*) A portrait of Bernhardt by Sarony; a poster by Alphonse Mucha; art nouveau combs and jewellery designed for Sarah Bernhardt; and Bernhardt in dramatic mode.

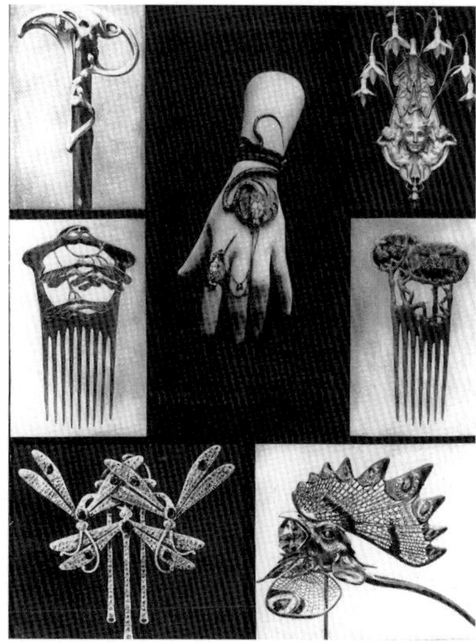

It was daring, exciting, enticing – and at times squalid and bizarre. Thousands flocked to the cabaret venues that opened in Paris and other cities during the *Belle Epoque*. The most famous venue was the Moulin Rouge (*opposite, above*). (*Opposite, below from left to right*) Mistinguett (Jeanne Marie Bourgeois), a top cabaret artist; an unknown cabaret dancer; the Parisian performer Dorgere; and Elise de Vere as Cupid. (*Right*) A stirring (though somewhat higgledy-piggledy) tableau of semi-naked women and men dressed as devils at *Le Cirque* music-hall in Paris, 1900.

Edgar Degas (*above, right*) studied at the Beaux-Arts under Lamothe, before joining the Impressionists. He visited New Orleans in the 1870s, where he liked to drink at the Old Absinthe House (*above, left*). Many of his paintings and sculptures centred on dancers, including the beautiful *Orchestre de l'Opéra* (*opposite*). As his sight began to fail, Degas turned increasingly to sculpture. (*Below, right*) Degas surrounded by worshipping fans, c. 1900.

Claude Monet (*opposite, below left*), with Renoir, Pissarro and Sisley, was one of the artists who submitted work to the first Impressionist Exhibition in 1874. He painted mainly in the open air, and *Les Coquelicots* (*opposite, above*) is typical of his response to landscape. (*Opposite, below right*) Auguste Renoir with his family in the garden at Les Collettes, Cagnes. On Renoir's left is his model, Gabrielle. (*Right*) Renoir's *La Balançoire.*

Edmond Rostand (*above, left*) was born in Marseilles in 1868. He was a poet and dramatist who first achieved success with *La Samaritaine,* largely thanks to Sarah Bernhardt. His international reputation was made with his verse play *Cyrano de Bergerac,* first performed in 1897. Theatregoers throughout the world loved the swaggering, warm-hearted, courageous hero, and Rostand's name was made. (*Above, right and opposite, left and right*) Three portrayals of Cyrano in late 19th-century productions.

The great outdoors beckoned. Rail travel brought the far-flung wildernesses of France within reach of those who wished to explore caves, lakes, forests and mountains. The cult of athleticism attracted tens of thousands of men and women. It was the age of the talented amateur, the part-timers who looked forward to the few days in the year when they could exchange offices, class-rooms, laboratories and banks for the joys of the open air. (*Left*) French climbers pause to collect their breath as they fight their way to the summit of Mont Blanc, 1895.

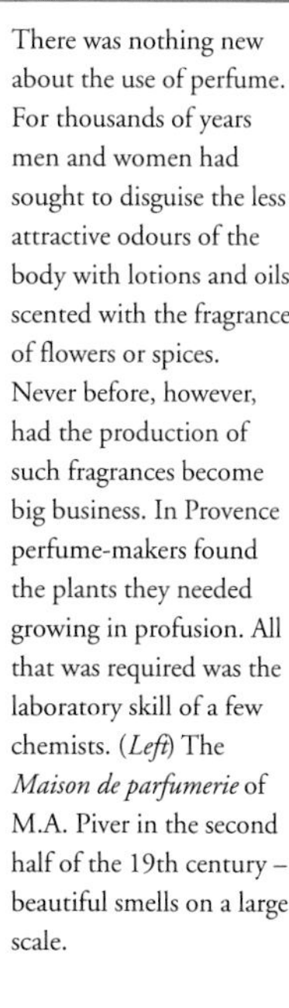

There was nothing new about the use of perfume. For thousands of years men and women had sought to disguise the less attractive odours of the body with lotions and oils scented with the fragrance of flowers or spices. Never before, however, had the production of such fragrances become big business. In Provence perfume-makers found the plants they needed growing in profusion. All that was required was the laboratory skill of a few chemists. (*Left*) The *Maison de parfumerie* of M.A. Piver in the second half of the 19th century – beautiful smells on a large scale.

The French automobile industry got off to a flying start. Few countries could rival the variety and reliability of early French cars. (*Above*) The steam-powered car of the Comte de Dion, Paris, 1895. (*Left*) Vis-à-vis built by Peugeot in the same year.

(*Above, left*) Another early De Dion model with a proud family off for a 'spin'. (*Above, right*) The first Renault model to provide enclosed comfort for the driver. (*Right*) Jamais Contente, the electric-powered car with which the Belgian Camille Jenatzy (in driver's seat) became the first motorist to exceed 100kph (62mph), Achères, 1 May 1899.

To the horror of some, women of the *Belle Epoque* began to flex their social muscles and to invade what had previously been seen as 'the man's world'. The bride (*top, right*) was still expected to stay at home and look after her husband, but there were other things to do.

(*Opposite, above left*) A woman taxi-driver in Paris, c. 1900. (*Opposite, below left*) Women workers in Champagne protect young vines from frost. (*Above*) A woman uses a telephone, September 1882. Improved communications were a boon to many women. (*Right*) An advertisement for Job cigarettes, c. 1889. Though many frowned on women who smoked in public, there was little they could do to prevent it. (*Opposite, below right*) Sticking to the old ways – a well-corseted woman performs her 'toilette', and all to please her beau.

PAPIER A CIGARETTES
JOB
Hors Concours
PARIS 1889

18
SWEETLY TO THE ABYSS
1900–1914

On 25 July 1909, at five in the morning, Louis Blériot (*right*) set off in a monoplane powered by a three-cylinder engine from Baraques on the French coast. He had waited three days for the right weather conditions. In thirty-seven minutes he covered the 21 miles across the Channel to the white cliffs of Dover, thus winning the £1,000 prize offered by the British *Daily Mail* to the first aviator to fly from France to England. Blériot became a national hero. History has forgotten the two other aviators whose planes suffered mechanical damage and who were left behind in the Pas-de-Calais. They were the Comte de Lambert and Hubert Latham.

Introduction

France swaggered, bustled and fought its way into the 20th century. Jean Jaurès helped to mould socialist factions into a recognisable and effective left-wing force. The Confédération Générale du Travail scorned parliamentary means of advancing the cause of the workers. Clemenceau and his fellow politicians struggled against Marxists, socialists and anarchists, offering reforms in welfare, programmes of social insurance, a ten-hour working day and a mandatory weekly day of rest in return for industrial peace and quiet. The arrival of phylloxera to wipe out whole vineyards in 1907 sparked further trouble. Cheap Algerian wine was imported to replace that lost in the Midi, and French wine-growers broke out in open revolt.

Away from politics, France continued to flourish, seizing on modern technology with verve and dash. In 1909 Louis Blériot became the first aviator to fly the Channel in a powered machine, and France established the world's first air mail service in 1911. The annual Tour de France was inaugurated in 1903. Peugeot and de Dion Bouton joined the early giants of the French motor industry.

Following the pioneer work of the Lumière brothers, Georges Méliès created the first sci-fi movies. Charles Pathé released the first newsreel in 1909, and Léon Gaumont produced the first talking picture in 1910 – nearly twenty years before Warner Brothers released *The Jazz Singer*. The Métro raced beneath the boulevards of Paris, its art nouveau signs and station entrances bringing 20th-century style to a 19th-century city.

The harsher side of French life revealed itself. The oppressed were becoming impatient – among them women, who perhaps had more to complain about than any other group in French society. They could not vote, hold public office, serve as jurors, manage their own property, or even accept a job without their husband's consent. If adultery took place, the woman was guilty of a crime, the man of a misdemeanour. And yet, on the eve of the First World War, almost 40 per cent of French women had jobs outside the home, a higher proportion than in any other European country.

France plunged into a series of treaties and conventions with its neighbours. The Entente Cordiale with Britain of 1904 was followed a year later by an Anglo-French military convention. There were agreements with Germany over the future of Morocco and the Congo, and Franco-Russian military and naval conventions in 1911 and 1912. Desperate diplomacy did what it could to reverse the drift towards war, but there were already too many ships, guns, soldiers, generals and unsettled scores. On 7 August 1913 the French Army Bill became law, lengthening the period of compulsory military service for all young men to three years.

They became the backbone of the French army that went to war less than a year later.

Some worked for peace, others were hungry for war. Paul Deroulede (*left* – top hat raised) was a nationalist politician and poet who called for revenge on Germany for the wrongs of 1871. He was exiled for ten years in 1900 for sedition, but returned to France in 1905, and died on the eve of the First World War.

(*Above, right*) Members of the French delegation to the Franco-German International Socialist Conference, held at Basle in 1910. (Front row, left to right) M. Sembat, M. Lidebourg, Albert Thomas (later to work for the League of Nations), and M. Dugagueur. Three years later, French Socialists made another attempt to avoid war – this time at Berne University. (*Below, right*) Among the members of the delegation is Jean Jaurès (fifth from the left).

Being in charge of the destiny of France was no easy matter in the early 20th century. The battle between Church and State for the control of education still raged, and the establishment remained torn apart by the Dreyfus affair. But France was well served by a handful of politicians. Raymond Nicolas Landry Poincaré (*opposite, above* – in top hat) was Prime Minister from 1911 to 1913. Théophile Delcassé (*opposite, below left*) forged the Entente Cordiale. Aristide Briand (*opposite, below right*) led the French Socialists. The father figure of French politics was Georges Clemenceau (*right*). (*Above*) Clemenceau with President Armand Fallières leaving Longchamps racecourse, 14 July 1907.

The Paris Exhibition of 1900 was the biggest of its kind ever held in Europe. The nations of the world showed off their treasures in a host of pavilions along the Quai d'Orsay. (*Above, left*) A general view of one of the main exhibition areas. (*Below, left*) The Horticultural Pavilion.

(*Above, right*) Crowds visiting the Grand Palais (left) and the Petit Palais, June 1900. (*Below, right*) The Château d'Eau, brilliantly lit by electricity and one of the greatest successes of the Exhibition. (*Below, left*) Twentieth-century technology at its most daring – the huge wheel from which visitors had spectacular views over Paris.

At a City Council meeting in 1896 an alderman of Paris glumly forecast that the planned new underground railway would be a total failure, fearing that no one would use 'this new *métropolitain*'. The Métro opened four years later on 19 July 1900. There were no fanfares or speeches, and a single passenger made the journey from Porte Maillot to the Porte de Vincennes. Nevertheless, the alderman was totally wrong in predicting failure.

The Métro was an enormous success. Within the first six months of its existence millions of Parisians passed through the art nouveau entrances to its stations (*opposite and above*), to buy their tickets and be whisked across town. The stations themselves became features of the city, though many of them were rebuilt in the 1960s.

In the cities women challenged the traditional restrictions on their lives. In rural areas the old ways lingered. Women were brought up to be cooks and housekeepers, to serve and obey their husbands, and to be mothers of large families. (*Above*) A cookery class in a French school, c. 1908. (*Left*) Villagers wear traditional dress for a christening in a Breton house, 26 June 1909.

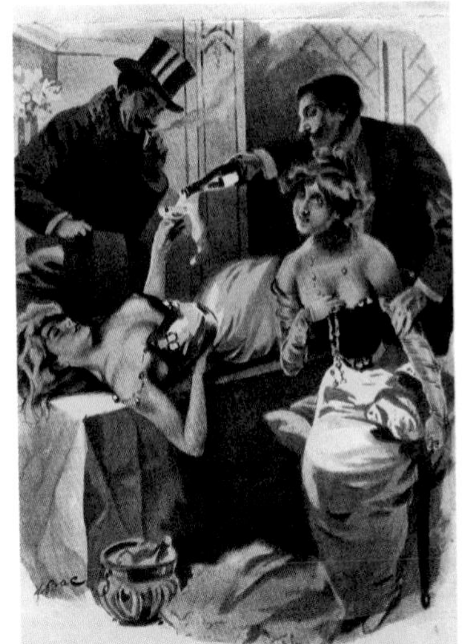

Mixed opportunities for women in French towns at the beginning of the 20th century. (*Above, left*) Two prostitutes are plied with wine by clients in a brothel. (*Above, right*) A woman taxi-driver climbs into her horse-drawn cab, c. 1910. (*Below*) The French suffragette Charlotte Despard addresses a crowd, 1913. Not until the 1940s were women given the right to vote in France.

Sidonie Gabrielle Colette (*above*) was born in 1873. Her first novels were published under her husband's name, but that unhappy arrangement ceased after their divorce in 1906. Colette worked as a dancer and mime artist in the music-halls, and published her first title under her own name in 1913 – *L'Envers du music-hall.* She continued writing into the 1950s.

After the death of his mother in 1905, Marcel Proust (*above, left*) withdrew from society and retired to a sound-proof flat. Here he wrote one of the most famous novels of all time, the sixteen-volume *A la recherche du temps perdu.* It took him the best part of seventeen years, and he died just after it was completed. Jacques Anatole François Thibault (*above, right*) was better known as Anatole France. He was a novelist and satirist, whose principal works include *Le Livre de mon ami* and *Les Opinions de Jérôme Coignard.* Like Zola, France was appalled by the injustice of the Dreyfus affair.

The Entente Cordiale of 1904 was part of the new French foreign policy in the early 20th century. With the exception of the Socialists, most politicians believed that war was almost inevitable; it was simply a question of how soon it would come. When it came, it would involve hostilities with Germany. The task, therefore, was to forge new alliances. France turned to Russia and Britain. (*Above*) A cartoon in which the Entente Cordiale is illustrated as France and Britain shaking hands beneath the waters of the Channel.

There were plenty of incidents that almost led to war. In 1905 France and Germany clashed over Morocco. A visit by the Kaiser to Tangier provoked months of sabre-rattling before agreement was reached between the two nations at the Algeciras Conference in March 1906. (*Above*) Théophile Delcassé of France, Edward VII of Britain and Wilhelm II of Germany are portrayed as 'three thieves', toying with Morocco as a cat toys with a mouse.

French cars and French drivers were among the finest in the world. Crowds lined the routes of cross-country and transcontinental races. The first French Grand Prix, held in 1906, was won by Renault. (*Left*) Boillot in a Peugeot speeds through Moreuil during the Grand Prix of 1913. (*Below*) In the same town, and the same race, Champoiseau rattles round a corner, 12 July 1913.

One of the most popular of the early competitions was the annual Paris–Madrid race. In May 1903, a series of disasters turned the race into a tragedy. In all, eight people were killed, among them Marcel Renault. (*Right*) Renault and his co-driver Lorraine Barrows near Saint-Maure, shortly before the fatal crash. (*Below, right*) The remains of the car after the crash. (*Below, left*) Louis Renault arrives at Bordeaux, to be told of his brother's death.

French pilots were among the most daring and successful in Europe during the early days of aviation. The most famous was Louis Blériot, seen here (*left*) crossing the Channel in his Blériot XI on 25 July 1909. Another pioneer was the Brazilian Alberto Santos-Dumont, who built the world's first airship station, at Neuilly in 1903. (*Below*) Santos-Dumont with his 1909 Demoiselle, one of the first monoplanes.

A few of the giants of early French aviation. (*Clockwise, from top left*) Jean Bécu at the controls of Henri Fabre's *Canard*, near Marseilles, 21 April 1911; Hélene Dutrieu, one of the first women pilots, wearing a *jupe aviatrice*, July 1910; Henri Farman (left), whose factory at Boulogne-sur-Seine produced the world's first long-distance passenger plane (the *Goliath*), with his partner Gabriel Voisin; and Roland Garros in a Santos-Dumont Demoiselle, 22 May 1911.

In an age of piano virtuosi, one of the most brilliant was Alfred Cortot (*above*). He was renowned as an interpreter of Beethoven's piano concertos, and with Jacques Thibaud and the cellist Pablo Casals founded the greatest chamber music trio of all time. (*Opposite, clockwise from top left*) A quartet of French composers: Maurice Ravel, best known for the *Boléro*, which he described as fifteen minutes of orchestra without music; the composer and organist Charles-Marie Widor; the witty and eccentric opponent of orthodoxy, Erik Satie; and the opera composer Gustave Charpentier.

In an age which knew nothing of safety goggles or even dark glasses, French men and women from the Paris suburb of Saint Germain-en-Laye gaze up at a total eclipse of the sun, 17 April 1912 (*right*). The eclipse was visible across the whole of Western Europe, providing wonderful opportunities for astronomers and photographers. In so sophisticated an age, few sought to read portents of evil or disaster in such an event. But evil and disaster on a hitherto unknown scale were not far away...

19
WAR AND DEPRESSION
1914–1930

No one knows how many French men and women were killed in the First World War. The approximate figure of those killed in battle is put at 1,350,000, but another 35,000 may be added to that. Not a village escaped. The war memorials that were erected throughout France in the years that followed the war bear the names of fathers and sons, brothers and uncles – terrifying testimony to the sacrifice made by entire families. (*Right*) A soldier's grave is marked by his rifle and helmet, somewhere on the battlefield of Verdun, 1916.

Introduction

'Soldiers! Your country's survival waits upon the outcome of this battle,' declared General Joffre on the eve of the Battle of the Marne in September 1914. 'Retreat would be unforgivable!' It was a speech that could have been repeated at weekly intervals during the next four years. A line of mud and men extending from the North Sea to the Swiss border was all that protected France for the rest of the First World War. Every battle was critical. Retreat was always unthinkable. Every speech was an impassioned call to death.

Over a million Frenchmen died to make sure that '*ils ne passeront pas*' at Verdun, Soissons, the Argonne, the Meuse, the Woevre Plain, Champagne, the Chemin des Dames... Troops were driven to despair, madness and mutiny. In newspapers back home, the French *poilu* was painted as rugged, cheerful, uncomplaining and wryly good-humoured. 'Men looked forward to the offensive as to a holiday,' wrote one journalist. 'They were so happy, they laughed, they joked.' Reality was a nightmare world away.

All bad things come to an end. The fighting stopped in November 1918, and France embarked on the bitter and exhausting process of returning to some sort of normality. Through the 1920s, governments arrived and departed almost as often as the *Train bleu* that plied between Paris and the Côte d'Azur. There were seven premiers within ten years: Briand, Poincaré, Herriot, Painlevé, Poincaré again, Briand again, and finally Tardieu. The right-wing *Croix de Feu* was founded in 1927, the French Communist Party a few years earlier. There were those who looked for a new idealistic internationalism, those who wished only to settle old scores, those who merely wanted a job and somewhere to live.

French creativity recreated itself with the Surrealist manifesto of 1924, the work of Dali and Breton as well as Ernst. Dufy, Matisse and Braque stretched the boundaries of art in newly colourful and geometrically angular ways. Claude Monteux conducted the Orchestre de Paris to international recognition. Josephine Baker brought shock and delight in equal quantities to her adopted home with the *Revue Nègre* in 1925.

Suzanne Lenglen volleyed and drove her opponents from the tennis courts of Europe, and French motor aces such as Louis Chiron, Philippe Etancelin, René Dreyfus and Marcel Lehaux roared to victory around continental racing circuits.

Life never returned to normal, for there was no such thing as normality.

Enthusiasm that bordered on joy greeted the First World War in August 1914. The initial German advance was halted by the French at the Battle of the Marne. (*Opposite, above*) A highly posed picture of the battle. (*Opposite, below*) French soldiers with captured German equipment, 9 September 1914. (*Above, right*) The French and Belgian medals of General Grosetti, hero of the Marne, are displayed at his funeral in 1918. (*Below, right*) A 1910 Charron taxicab, one of the thousands used to take French and British soldiers from Paris to the front during the Battle of the Marne.

Within a year, two lines of trenches wormed their way from the Swiss border to the Channel. French and German troops faced each other from distances that were in places down to less than 30 metres. (*Opposite*) French soldiers remove corpses from a section of trench near Bagatelle in the Argonne, 30 June 1915. (*Above*) A well-constructed and defended dugout for officers. Junior officers suffered the worst casualties. Senior officers enjoyed the best conditions.

All the combatants made use of the camera for propaganda purposes. (*Above*) French reservists march to headquarters at the beginning of the war. Pictures such as this were given enormous publicity, to encourage many to join the army, and to shame others. (*Left*) A War Loan poster from October 1918. The end of the war was only four weeks away, but a 'supreme effort' was nonetheless called for.

Two postcards playing on the heartstrings and stiffening a nation's resolve for further sacrifice. (*Above, left*) A nurse (with bayonet fixed) stands guard over two young soldiers. The caption reads: '*Pour la patrie. Reposez, camarades*' ('For your country. Rest, comrades'). (*Above, right*) Marianne appears with the tricolour once more to rally the nation in its hour of need. The caption here reads: '*Salvons ces oiseaux français, délicieux gages de la paix*' ('Welcome to these birds of France, sweet harbingers of peace...').

Primarily, the First World War was a struggle of attrition, not a war of movement. Only in the autumn of 1914 and the spring of 1918 were armies on the march. The Ludendorff offensive of March and April 1918 led to considerable German advances to the north and east of Paris. Once again French refugees crowded the roads and lanes, struggling westwards with a few possessions, leaving behind land and livelihood as they fled the horrors of war.

(*Opposite and above*) French refugees gather at the Gare du Nord, Paris, in the spring of 1918. Many of them had farmed their land for four years within the sound of gunfire. None knew what they would find when they were able to return to their farms, but they were lucky enough to have escaped with their lives. Their numbers were composed of women and children, and men too old for military service. Somewhere, in the war-tossed land that they had left, a whole generation of young men had died.

By March 1918 Field Marshal Ferdinand Foch (*left*) had worked his way to becoming commander-in-chief of the Allied Forces. He was a man of indomitable spirit, as revealed in a despatch he sent during the battle of the Marne: '*Mon centre cède, ma droite recule; situation excellente. J'attaque!*' ('My centre is giving way, my right is retreating; situation excellent. I shall attack!')

Joseph Jacques Césaire Joffre (*above, left*) resigned his post as commander-in-chief of the French army after the Battle of Verdun in 1916. Albert Lebrun (*above, right*) was the Minister for Blockade and the Liberated Regions during the First World War. (*Below, left to right*) André Tardieu, President of the Republic between the wars; Léon Blum, the first Socialist Prime Minister of France since 1870; and Edouard Herriot, Premier from 1924 to 1925, in 1926 (for two days) and in 1932.

It was difficult to distinguish heroes in armies that numbered 3 million men, but the fledgling air forces of Germany, France, Britain and the United States supplied plenty. The Germans had Manfred von Richthofen; the Allies had the Frenchman Captain René Fonck (*above, left*). Fonck was credited with seventy-five kills, six in one day, and three in a ten-second burst of gunfire. Unlike von Richthofen, Fonck survived the war. (*Above, right*) France's third-highest-scoring air ace in the First World War, Lieutenant Charles Nungesser. He destroyed forty-five German planes.

(*Right*) Captain Georges Guynemer prepares to take off on one of his last flights. By the time he disappeared in action in September 1917, he had been credited with fifty-four kills. (*Above*) Henri Marchal, another leading French pilot in the First World War. The plane revolutionised reconnaissance work in war. From a few hundred metres in the air, a pilot could assess the relative strength of any section of the enemy's line as well as detect movement of troops.

When the guns at last ceased firing and the nations gathered round the conference tables at Versailles in 1919, high on the French agenda was Alsace-Lorraine, the provinces that had been taken by Germany after the débâcle of 1871. (*Above*) Patriots from Alsace-Lorraine take part in a pro-war procession after the sinking of the *Lusitania*, April 1916. (*Opposite, above*) French mounted troops proudly display the tricolour as they ride into Alsace-Lorraine at the end of the war. (*Opposite, below*) A rash of French flags in an Alsatian village, 1919. It was the village's fourth change of nationality in barely fifty years.

War is an expensive business. When men went off to the Front, many women were given an inadequate income with which to bring up a family. The new ordnance and munitions factories offered good wages as well as a chance to contribute to the war effort. (*Above, left*) Women workers in a munitions factory 'somewhere in France', 1916. (*Below, left*) Women examine bomb fuses, January 1916. It was generally accepted that they were better at this sort of work than men.

(*Above, right*) Women work on shell cases in a factory near Paris. (*Below, right*) A French woman welder at work in an armaments factory, c. 1915. When the heroes returned from the war they wanted their jobs back. Many women had enjoyed working in factories and were loath to return to the grind and poverty of housekeeping. A new friction entered the labour market. In the boom years immediately after the war, when there was full employment, the problem was contained. In the depression that followed, social and economic unrest reached critical levels in France.

The old order had been destroyed. The traditional values of family life no longer applied. Neighbourhoods had been shattered. There was an appalling shortage of young men – the best of a generation had been wiped out. Society had lost its way. The routines of the past no longer offered their comforting familiarity. Courtship was now a business, a matter of posting a notice in a marriage bureau. (*Right*) A woman consults the menu in a marriage bureau, 1920. Most of the advertisers are men. One of the traditions that had not yet died was that men should take the first step.

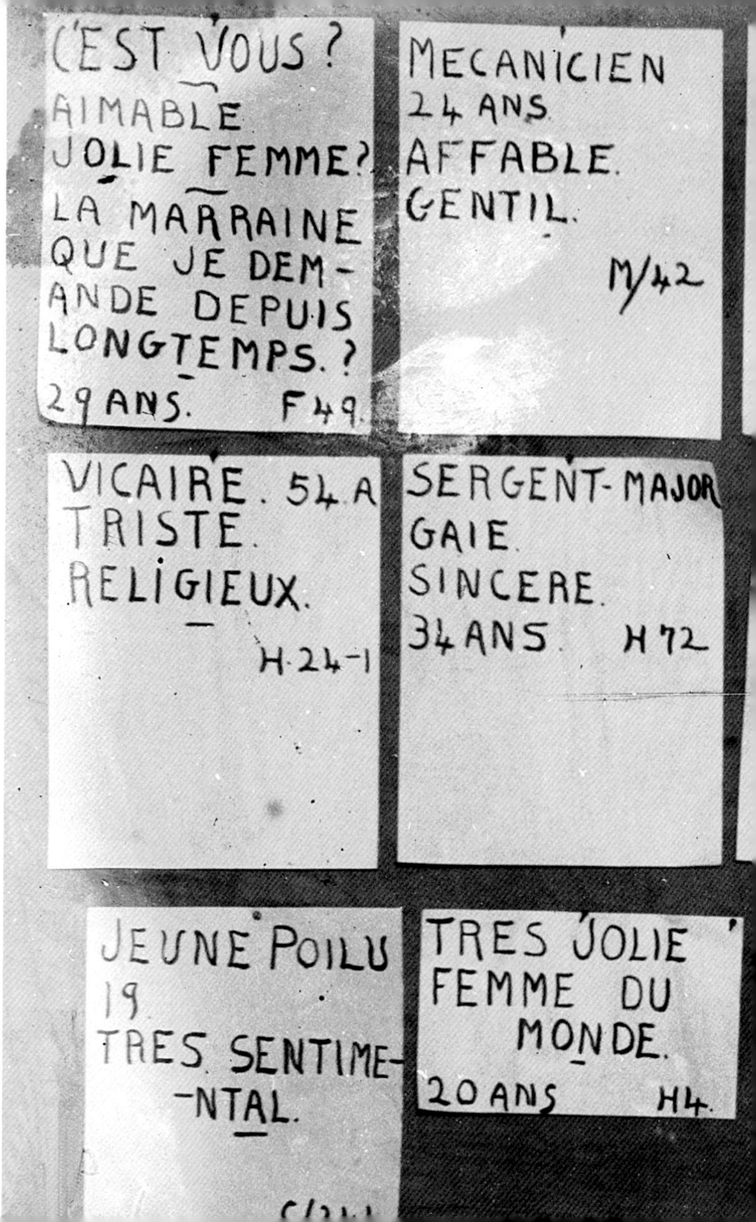

BESOIN
NE
IE
LE.
ABLE
TINGUÉE.
24 ANS.
HM4.
LIEUT. 23 ANS.
DÉSIRE MARRAINE
JEUNE, JOLIE ET
DISTING FEMME
DU MONDE.
ETUDIANT
41 ANS
TAINE (34)
IL ET TRES
TIMENTAL.
B434.
N'HESI
PLUS!
JEUNE
OFFICIER.
21 ANS
AFFECTUE
F424.

The brave new world was a bright and busy place. The world was shrinking, and 'getting around' had never been so easy. The motor car had not yet gained its awesome predominance, but the threat was there. (*Above, left*) Trams, cars and buses jostle for supremacy at a busy road junction in Paris, 1929. (*Below, left*) A man helps himself from a ticket dispenser at a bus stop in Paris, 1929.

(*Above, right*) Crowds mingle on the concourse of the Gare du Nord, 1929. (*Below, left*) A passenger aircraft, one of the *Rayon d'Or* fleet that operated between Paris and London, waits on the runway at Le Bourget airport, Paris. (*Below, right*) On board the *Rayon d'Or* a waiter serves champagne to passengers. The flight was celebrating the tenth anniversary of the Paris–London service, April 1929.

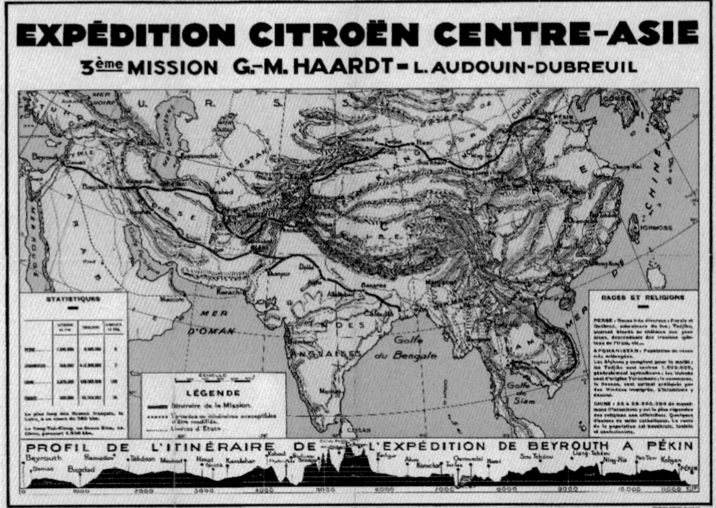

By the 1920s Citroën had taken the lead in French car production. The Citroën 10hp Type A (*opposite, above left*) was the first mass-produced European car, and one of the first to gain a national reputation for reliability. In 1925 Citroën organised a trans-Asiatic expedition (*left*) as part of a publicity campaign. (*Below*) The expedition pauses on the shores of Lake Kara-Kul, Tadzhik-istan, USSR.

The founder of the great automobile empire was André Citroën (*right*). He had been responsible for the mass production of armaments in the First World War, and used the same methods and principles to produce low-priced cars. In 1934 Citroën became bankrupt and lost control of the company he had founded. In happier days (*above, right*). The art deco garage of Le Marbeuf in Paris, January 1930. The building was designed for Citroën by the architects Albert Laprade and L.E. Bazin.

Music-hall prospered in the 1920s and 1930s. Venues became more stylish, stars more glamorous, productions more lavish. Mlle Ledue (*above*) was one of dozens of performers at the Folies Bergère to attract the attentions of the rich and infamous. Early in her career she was lent the Hope Diamond by Prince Kanitovsky, who then shot her the first time she wore it on stage. Mlle Ledue survived. The prince was killed in the Russian Revolution. (*Opposite, above*) The Folies Bergère on 1 February 1929. (*Opposite, below*) The Moulin Rouge at night, 1929. Mistinguett was a top cabaret star between the wars.

FOLIES BERGERE

MISTINGUETT
SPADARO
MUSIC HALL
PARIS QUI TOURNE
TERRASSE & JARDIN
ENTREE
TERRASS
BAL

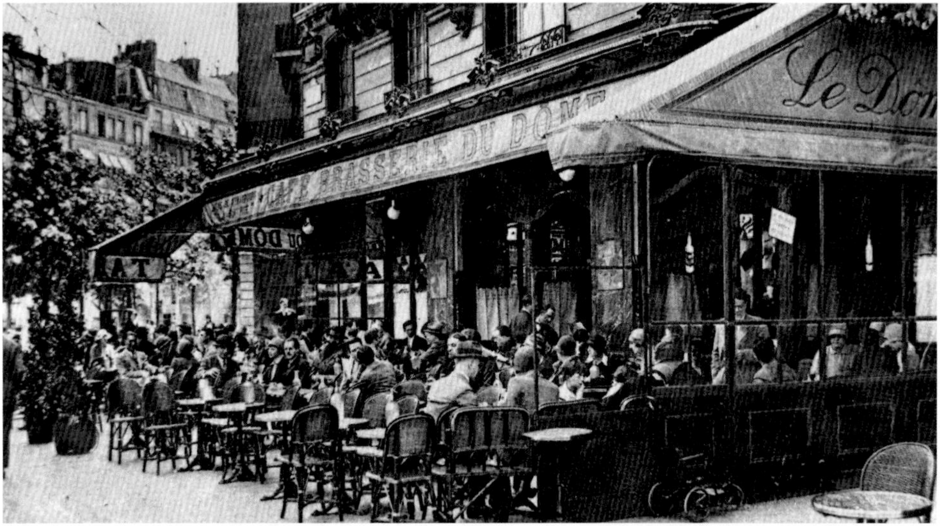
Le Dôme
CAFE BRASSERIE DU DOME

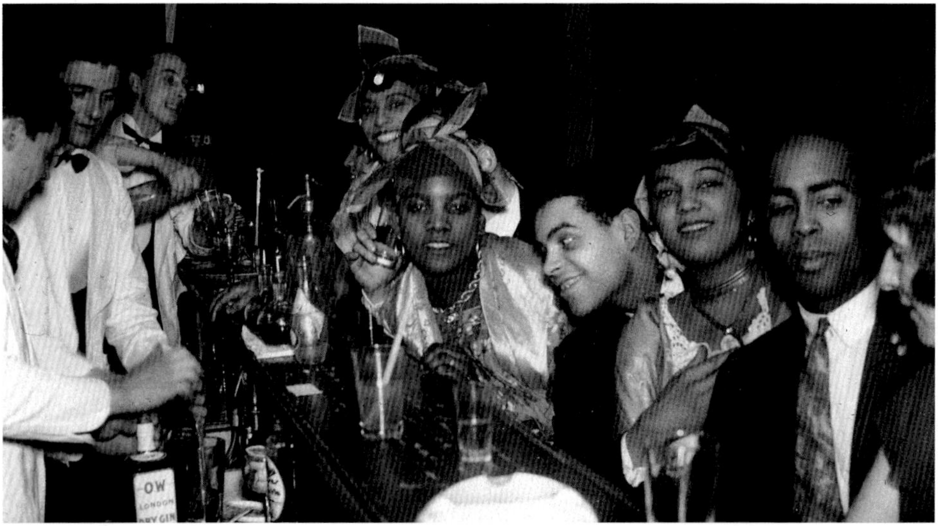
LONDON
DRY GIN

For those with money, Paris was still the pleasure capital of the world. (*Opposite, above*) The Café Brasserie du Dôme, Montparnasse, c. 1920. (*Opposite, below*) La Boule Blanche, a popular Paris nightclub, c. 1930. (*Above, right*) A plethora of waiters attend customers at a Paris street café in the late 1920s. (*Below, right*) The Lido of the Champs-Elysées, designed by René Berger, c. 1925.

Where to be seen, and what to be seen in? Questions that plagued the bright not-so-young things in the 1920s. (*Above, left*) Fashion stalks the boardwalk of Deauville, 15 August 1927. (*Below, right*) A dress of silver-grey georgette with fur-trimmed embroidered jacket by Lucien Lelong, 1925. (*Below, left*) Another Deauville beauty, October 1923. (*Opposite, left*) The favourite to win the fashion stakes at Longchamps, 5 May 1925. (*Opposite, right*) *Honi soit qui mal y pense...* a metal garter from 1930.

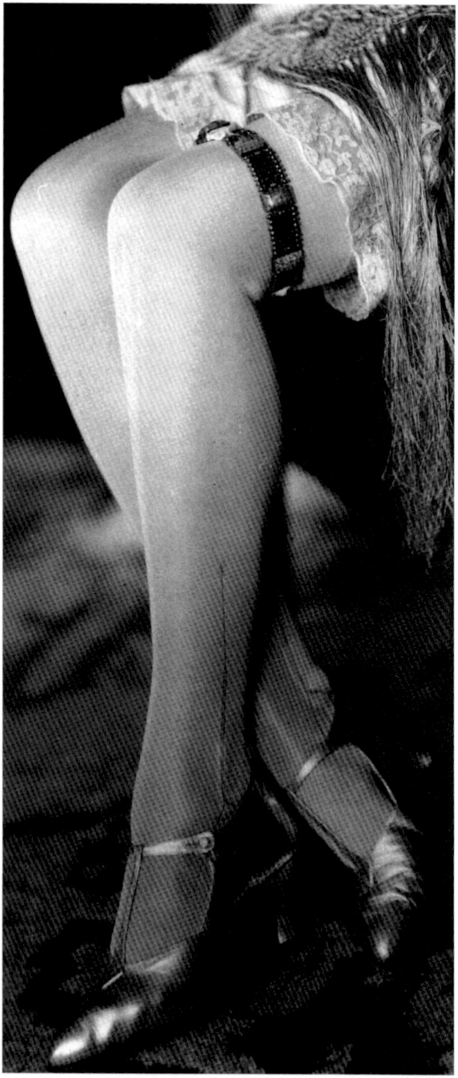

In 1919 levels of agricultural and industrial production were around 45 per cent of those of 1913. Swathes of the best agricultural land in France had been devastated by the war. Economic refugees limped their way from north to south. Later, both agriculture and industry revived. But the early 1920s were times of hardship, distress and bitterness. Strikes and lockouts hinted at a class war to replace the military conflict. (*Right*) Poor line the streets of a Paris suburb in February 1923. They are waiting for a delivery of coal from the Ruhr, occupied by the French as part of the war reparations.

With the return to peace came a return to sport. The Olympic Games were staged in Paris in 1924, with France winning a fair share of the medals – especially in the combatant sports (rifle-shooting, fencing and boxing). Internationally, however, it was French tennis players who won the most laurels in the 1920s. One of the best was Henri Cochet (*above*), seen here on his way to winning the men's singles title at Wimbledon in 1929.

Two years earlier the men's singles final had been an all-French affair. Jean Borotra (left) and Cochet battled it out on the Centre Court on 2 July 1927 (*above, right*). Cochet won. The greatest of them all was Suzanne Lenglen. She was the ladies' champion of France from 1919 to 1923 and from 1925 to 1926, the Wimbledon champion from 1919 to 1923 and in 1925, and the Olympic champion in 1920. (*Below, right*) Lenglen with René Lacoste at Wimbledon, 1924.

(*Above, left*) The French actress and singer Yvonne Printemps with the Russian-born French film-maker Sasha Guitry in a Sasha photograph of 1929. (*Above, right*) Heart-throb and music-hall star Maurice Chevalier, 1928. (*Below, right*) The brilliant film director René Clair. (*Opposite, clockwise from top left*) screen beauties Lili Damita, the film actress who (incidentally) married Errol Flynn; Jetta Goudal and Adolphe Menjou in a still from *Open All Night*, 1924; Annabelle, star of the comedy *Le Million*, a very early French talkie; and Renée Adorée staggers under the weight of her fan mail, 1930.

Mlle. MARCHADIER
Mme. JAUME
Mlle. BABELAY
Mme. COLOMB
Mme. CRUCHET
Mme. LABORDE LINE
LANDRU'S
GARDEN
Mme. GUILLIN
Mme. BUISSON.
Mme. PASCAL
BLUÉBEARD.

It was a dark and ugly tale. In 1919 French police arrested Henri Désiré Landru (*opposite* – surrounded by some of his victims), and charged him with a series of murders that had taken place over a period of four years from 1915. Landru was dubbed 'Bluebeard' and his trial in 1921 received huge publicity. (*Above, right*) Police stand guard over the oven in which Bluebeard was said to have disposed of the bodies of his victims. (*Below, right*) Landru in court. He was convicted and executed.

20
WAR AND LIBERATION 1930–1945

On 1 September 1939 Nazi troops entered Poland. The latest in Adolf Hitler's long line of 'final' territorial demands brought Europe face-to-face with the inevitability of war. News of the Nazi–Soviet pact sent shock waves reverberating through the French political scene. The left wing had looked to the USSR for guidance and protection, and felt savagely betrayed. When war came, it was greeted with none of the jingoistic enthusiasm of 1914. Glum resignation was the order of the day. (*Right*) Parisians study news of the outbreak of war, September 1939.

Introduction

As Europe trudged along the well-worn path to war in the 1930s, France stepped out as the best dressed nation in the world. The fashion houses of Chanel, Jean Patou, Jacques Heim, Paquin and Worth produced couture dresses that Hollywood could match but none could rival. Despite the political dramas, the economic crises and the industrial bickerings, France re-established itself as the land where 'style' ruled and life could hardly be bettered.

Henri Cartier-Bresson's camera captured the great and the good, the bizarre and the ludicrous, the rare and everyday images of France. Georges Simenon established the *roman policier* as a major literary form. Jean-Paul Sartre expressed his existentialist doctrines in an autobiographical novel (*La Nausée*) and a book of short stories (*Le Mur*), both published in 1938. In night-clubs and casinos from Biarritz to Boulogne-sur-mer, French singers such as Charles Trenet, Jean Sablon, Maurice Chevalier, Yves Guilbert and Edith Piaf sang of love, romance, coquetry and regret.

Ravel, d'Indy, Roussel and Dukas died. Their places were taken by *Les Six* – Durey, Honegger, Milhaud, Germaine Tailleferre, Auric and Poulenc. During the Nazi occupation, French music was discouraged (to say the least), and at the Opéra French artists had to produce a new German opera and ballet five times a year. The director of the National Conservatoire, Claude Delvincourt, managed to secure an agreement with the Nazis that his students should be excused enforced labour and should instead be formed into an orchestra to play in prison camps in Germany. He then prolonged the process of training and rehearsing to an absurd degree. The device was at last seen through, and Delvincourt and his students went into hiding until Paris was liberated.

The war arrived in 1939. The much-vaunted Maginot Line proved to be not long enough, and the *Blitzkrieg* blasted all before it. One hundred and twenty thousand French and Belgian troops stumbled back to Dunkirk, whence they were rescued and taken to England. The French government fled to Tours. Paris fell. France was divided, the north being occupied by German troops, the south by Marshal Pétain and an older, sadder generation. Alsace and Lorraine were reabsorbed into Germany.

French resistance ranged from the sullen to the heroic. Charles de Gaulle led the Free French government and forces in London. Those still at home prayed for liberation.

From late 1934 French Communists called for a 'Popular Front' – political union with the Socialists. Communists embraced the tricolour, sang the *Marseillaise*, rekindled the memory of Jeanne d'Arc. In the 1936 elections, with the slogan 'Bread, Peace, Freedom', the Popular Front gained a large majority. The increasingly violent right-wing *Action Française* was banned.

(*Opposite, above and below*) Demonstrators at a Popular Front rally following an attack on Léon Blum, 16 February 1936. (*Above*) Léon Blum and his wife arrive at Croydon Aerodrome, 23 July 1936. They were attending a three-power conference with Britain and Belgium. (*Right*) The Elysée Palace, 14 March 1938. Front row, from left to right: Albert Sarraut, Léon Blum and M. Vroltett.

Left-wing governments bring hope to workers, but those hopes often meet with disappointment. In the summer of 1936 a series of agreements promised wage rises of 10 per cent, the introduction of a forty-hour week and two weeks' paid holiday every year for the majority of workers. 'For the first time in history,' declared one trade-union leader, 'an entire class will see its living conditions improved immediately.'

It was not to be. The workers went on strike and took to the streets in peaceful protest. (*Opposite, above*) Strikers march down the Rue Montmartre in Paris, 11 June 1936. (*Opposite, below*) An impromptu dance during a sit-in at the Thomson munitions factory in Paris, 3 June 1936. (*Above, right*) Strikers return to work at the Renault factory, 15 June 1936. (*Below, right*) Whiling away the striking hours during the summer of unrest, 1936.

Serge Stavisky (*opposite, above left*) was a Russian Jew and a highly successful swindler. In 1933 one of his fraudulent schemes was backed by a member of the French government. When news of this broke, there was widespread rioting in Paris (*opposite, below*) and Daladier's government fell. (*Left*) A magazine feature on Stavisky, with a portrait of his wife, who was cleared of complicity. (*Opposite, above right*) Gaston Doumergue arrives at the Elysée Palace to form a new government after Daladier's resignation. Stavisky was found dead near the Swiss frontier in 1934.

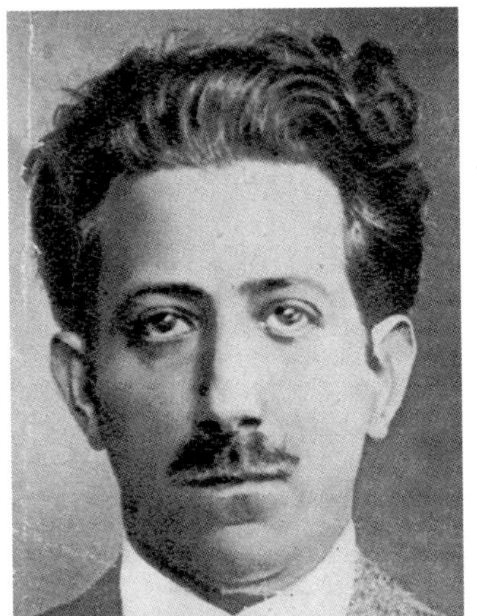

Work began on a new luxury liner in the shipyards of Saint-Nazaire in 1930. The liner was to be called *Le Normandie*, and she was to be the largest and the fastest in the world. (*Above*) *Le Normandie*'s rudder under construction. Five years later, in May 1935, the vessel completed her sea trials (*left*).

The following month *Le Normandie* set up a new record for the fastest transatlantic crossing, with an average speed of 29.7 knots from Southampton to New York. On board were 1,070 passengers and 1,250 crew. (*Above, right*) Lalique columns in the art deco dining-room of *Le Normandie*. (*Below, right*) One of the first-class studio lounges on board.

After the fall of France in 1940, resistance to Nazi rule was strongest in Brittany, in the area administered by the Vichy government, and in the south-east, occupied by Italian forces. Members of the *Maquis* were mostly young, many of them men evading forced labour in the *Service du travail obligatoire.* They learned the skills needed to survive by trial and error, facing the possibility of torture and death with great courage.

(*Above*) A cell of the *Maquis* meets for weapons training in the Haute Loire region of France. The guns were parachuted in by Allied planes. (*Opposite, above left*) Jean Moulin, leader of the National Council of the Resistance, who died under torture at the hands of Klaus Barbie, the Butcher of Lyons. (*Opposite, above right*) Resistance fighters help to drive Nazi troops from Paris, August 1944. (*Opposite, below*) Former collaborators in a French town are taken prisoner by the *Maquis*, 1944.

On 25 August 1944, General de Gaulle, leader of the Free French Forces, entered Paris (*below, left*). The following day, Parisians marched in triumph through the streets (*opposite, below*). Some four hundred German troops in the Chamber of Deputies were among the last to surrender (*above, left*). The Allied liberating troops moved on, eastwards towards the German frontier. Slowly but surely France was becoming free again, to the joy and pride of young and old (*opposite, above, left and right*).

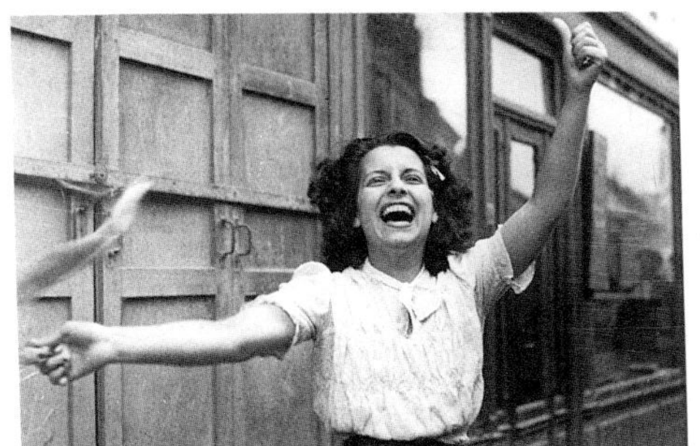

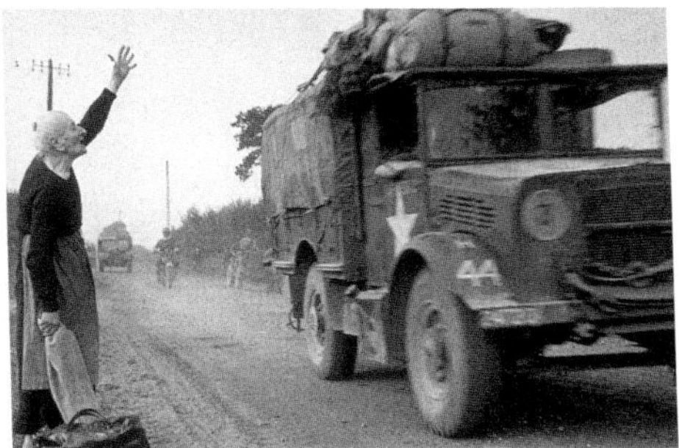

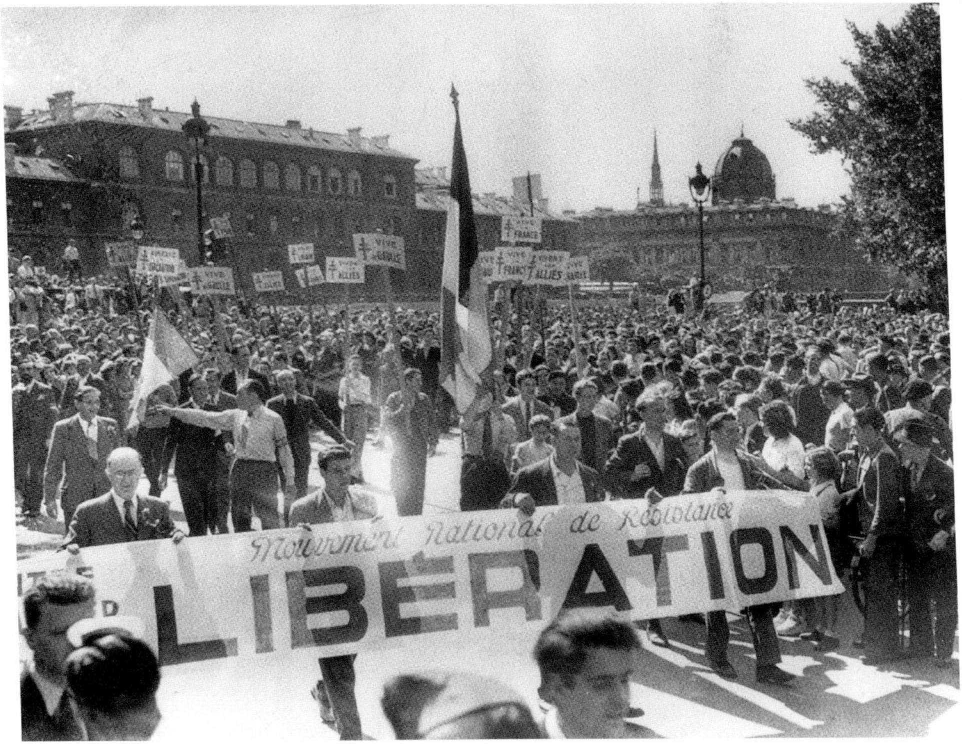
Mouvement National de Résistance
LIBERATION

The French composer Gustave Charpentier (*above, left*), who had made his name with the opera *Louise* in 1900, continued to write music throughout the 1930s and 1940s. Among the new maestros was Darius Milhaud (*below, left*), a leading member of the group of composers known as *Les Six*. The most popular French musician was the jazz violinist Stéphane Grappelli (*below, right*), whose *quintette du Hot Club de France* featured the legendary guitarist Django Reinhardt.

A quartet of writers, exemplifying the vast range of literature produced in France during the 1930s and 1940s. (*Clockwise from top*) Jean-Paul Sartre, existentialist philosopher and novelist; the novelist and dramatist Georges Duhamel, author of *Civilisation*, which won the Prix Goncourt in 1918; André Gide, novelists and founder of *La Nouvelle française*; and Georges Simenon, Belgian-born creator of Inspector Maigret who had arrived in Paris in 1922.

French cinema continued to recruit a legion of talent and produce fine films. (*Above, left*) Pierre Fresnay (real name Pierre Laudenbach) protests his innocence as he is led to the cells in *Chéri-Bibi*, 1934. (*Above, right*) Jean Gabin in *Quai des Brumes*, 1938 – a film which some held responsible for the lack of morale in the French army at the beginning of the war. (*Left*) Charles Boyer and Claudette Colbert in a scene from Gregory la Cava's *Private Worlds*, 1935.

(*Above*) American soldiers pass a Parisian cinema which is showing Marcel Carne's masterpiece, *Les Enfants du Paradis*. The script was by Jacques Prévert, and the film starred Arletty and Jean-Louis Barrault. (*Right*) Madeleine Sologne in *Love Eternal*, a film version of the story of Tristan and Iseult, directed by Jean Delannoy.

As in most European countries during the 1930s, an increasing number of French people sought the countryside. Climbers, ramblers, campers and humble day-trippers flocked to the great outdoors from the increasingly crowded cities. (*Above*) Contestants in the Tour de France burn up their energy as they push high into the Pyrénées during the summer of 1938. (*Right*) Intrepid walkers pit their boots against the rough surface of the Glacier du Géant, 1935.

Paris was the undisputed fashion centre of the world in the 1930s. (*Clockwise, from top left*) The cover of *Marie-Claire* on 23 September 1938; a black evening dress by Worth, 1935; a feathered head-dress by Paquin, photographed by Sasha in 1924; and a three-quarter-length coat with a collar of black lynx, topped by a broad-brimmed felt hat, all by Heim, c. 1935.

(*Clockwise from top left*) The dress designer Jean Patou, photographed in 1925; Gabrielle 'Coco' Chanel, who liberated women's fashion, banishing the corset and introducing the 'little black dress'; a skiing costume of the mid-1940s by Jean Patou; and René Hubert, costume designer and head of wardrobe at the Fox Film Studios in the 1930s.

21
EUROPE UNITED
1945–1965

The bombing, the shelling and the killing stopped. The dust of war settled. Never had there been such a propitious time to build a new Europe. Never had there been such hopes and demands for peace. Yet within a year of hostilities ending, the four major Allied powers were at loggerheads, divided in their aims and ambitions for the new Europe, unable to agree on the future of Germany, and mistrustful of each other. (*Right*) The Committee of Procedure meets at the Paris Conference in the Luxembourg Palace, April 1946.

Introduction

When the dust cleared and the British and American troops departed, France searched through the rubble of victory and began the process of rebuilding a free nation. Old scores were quickly settled against collaborators, and the old arguments between left and right were speedily resumed. Some of the problems of what to do with France's lingering colonial empire were solved by the war of liberation in Indo-China, and the civil war in Algeria, where de Gaulle's volte-face infuriated French settlers and led to attacks on his life.

French cinema glistened in the sun of the Cannes Film Festival while the *enfants terribles* of the *nouvelle vague* played happily nearby. Truffaut, Godard, Chabrol and Rohmer attracted big audiences at home and intellectual attention abroad. Jacques Tati gave the benign Monsieur Hulot to the world. Brigitte Bardot and Jeanne Moreau provided plenty of beauty for the eyes of their beholders. Edith Piaf's powerful voice burst from her tiny frame to fill the concert halls of France. Yves Montand and Simone Signoret married, though they rarely exhibited their considerable artistic talents together.

Christian Dior introduced the New Look and the A-line. The fashion houses of Paris made up for the austerity years of the Occupation and paraded ten metres of material on two metres of model on the catwalk. Le Corbusier spread his architectural genius around the cities of France, along the coastline of the Mediterranean, and in the rainforests of Brazil. Roland Petit and Zizi Jeanmaire put a new spring into French ballet. Marcel Marceau gained international recognition for the noble art of mime – 'walking into the wind' and 'erecting a deck-chair on the beach'.

New hope for European peace came from a Franco-German partnership that forged the Iron and Steel Community, the Common Agricultural Policy and the Treaty of Rome. Citroën's 2CV rattled over the still cobbled streets of many French cities. The elegant new liner *Le France* offered the last word in transatlantic luxury. Jacques Cousteau plumbed new depths to win three Academy Awards for his underwater films: *The Silent World* (1956), *The Golden Fish* (1960) and *World Without Sun* (1964).

By the mid-1960s, 50 per cent of French homes had a refrigerator, a car, a washing-machine and television. Sadly, there were still a large number of French citizens who did not possess a home – the inhabitants of the *bidonvilles* (shanty towns) on the outskirts of the major French conurbations. One step up were those who lived in the *habitations à loyer modéré*, soulless tower blocks, two generations and a thousand years away from the farms of old rural France.

New Europe was only part of a new world. Old colonies sought independence, and were prepared to fight for freedom. The French hold on Indo-China was challenged by the Vietminh. (*Above, left*) French pilots leave their dugout during the siege of Dien Bien Phu and head for their planes, c. 1954. (*Below, left*) A Vietminh insurgent surveys the ruins of his house in the battle for Phuly, 10 July 1954.

Algeria was closer to home and closer to the heart of France. The nation split as to its future. De Gaulle pledged to keep *l'Algérie française*, but changed his mind and his policy. Blood was shed, in Paris and in Africa. (*Clockwise from top left*) Cheering citizens take to the streets of Algiers in support of Ben Khedda, 6 July 1962; a poster urges 'Peace in Algeria – for our children'; victims of police attacks during an anti-OAS demonstration in Paris, December 1961; and Jacques Massu, leader of the French rebels in Algeria.

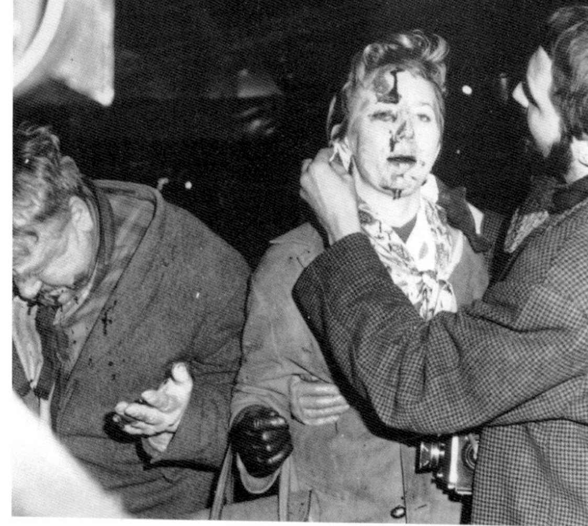

The Catholic Church in France emerged from the Second World War with its shaky reputation under considerable attack. The left-wing governments of the 1930s had shown little respect for the Church, and the Fourth Republic continued to be dominated by Socialists and Communists. Among the mistakes the Church had made during the war was to embrace the Vichy regime in the southern half of France. Vichy was now totally discredited. Pétain, who had shaken hands with Hitler, was charged with treason and imprisoned for life on the Ile d'Yeu.

Gradually, however, the Church began to recover some of the ground it had lost. This was largely thanks to the efforts of the rank-and-file clergy. 'Good works', long the best advertisement for the Church, once again gave strength to the faithful. (*Opposite*) Members of the Sisters of Charity on their way to vespers, c. 1956. (*Above*) Young priests enjoy a game of volleyball, though much encumbered by their robes, in the grounds of the Lazarist Fathers Seminary in Paris.

At a time of bread rationing and food shortages, there was happily little disruption to the production of many of France's most exportable luxuries – among them cognac and liqueurs. (*Top, left*) Farm workers harvest grapes in the Charentes region of France, 1948. (*Top, right*) Maurice Martell, owner of the family firm, raises his hat as he enters the *chais* which contains barrels of fine cognac at the Martell distillery. (*Above, left*) A small-scale bottling plant at a Charentes distillery. (*Above, right*) Michel Martell and his *maître-de-chais* sample cognac produced at the Martell distillery.

Meanwhile, in south-eastern France, the Carthusian monks produce their own *eau de vie.* The Carthusian order has a long history of fine husbandry and agricultural innovation, but one creation stands above all others. The Chartreuse liqueur (in yellow or green form) is flavoured by a blend of some one hundred and thirty herbs. The recipe is a secret known only to the monks. (*Above, left*) Two monks descend from the hills of the Dauphiné with baskets of herbs. (*Right*) A Carthusian monk at work in the distillery at the Monastery of Green Chartreuse, 1953. (*Above, right*) Bert Hardy's photograph of a monk sampling the finished product.

Christian Dior (*left*) founded his own Paris fashion house in 1947. Until his death ten years later, Dior revolutionised the fashion scene with the New Look, the A-line, the H-line trapeze-look, and the sack dress. (*Below, left*) Buyers at the first fashion show by Hubert de Givenchy, Paris, March 1952. (*Below, right*) Pupils at the Collège Feminin de Bouffemont receive fashion advice from Jacques Fath.

After any war, the poor hope for a new world, the rich seek to re-establish the old. But perhaps all are reassured as life returns to normal. All over the world, one sign of recovery was the reappearance of French perfume. (*Above, left*) A magazine advert for Christian Dior perfume, December 1954. (*Above, right*) Michelle Bernardini, a dancer from the Casino de Paris, poses during a beauty contest at the Molitor swimming-pool, 7 July 1946. She is wearing one of the very first 'bikinis', which caused delight and outrage in equal measure.

Whatever demands there were in politics or commerce for a return to the old, in the arts French writers directed the thoughts of their readers towards the new. (*Above, left*) The playwright Jean Anouilh (with the actress Doris Schade); (*left*) Albert Camus, who won the Nobel Prize for Literature in 1958; (*above, right*) the absurdist playwright Eugene Ionesco.

'Writers who stand out, as long as they are not dead,' wrote Simone de Beauvoir (*above, right*) 'are always scandalous' ('*L'écrivain original, tant qu'il n'est pas mort, est toujours scandaleux*'). (*Above, left*) Copies of Beauvoir's *Les Mandarins*, which won the Prix Goncourt in 1954. (*Right*) It took Françoise Quoirez – better known as Françoise Sagan – just four weeks to write *Bonjour Tristesse* at the age of eighteen. The book brought her instant fame.

Le Corbusier was the professional name of one of the greatest architects of the 20th century, the Swiss-born Charles-Edouard Jeanneret (*left*). In 1945 he began work in Marseilles on the first of his Modular projects, buildings which used the proportions of the human figure. (*Opposite, clockwise from top left*) The entrance lobby of Radiant City, Marseilles; Radiant City itself, a development to house 1,500 people; the Chapel of Notre-Dame du-Haut, Ronchamp; and an interior in Chandigarh, the new capital of the Punjab, 1955.

New stars of French cinema: (*clockwise from top left*) Jean Marais as the beast/prince in Jean Cocteau's stunning *La Belle et la Bête*, 1946; Jean-Pierre Aumont, June 1947; Alain Delon (left) in René Clément's *Plein Soleil*, 1960; and Jacques Tatischeff (Tati), actor, comedian, author, film director and creator of Monsieur Hulot.

Four stars who shook the world: (*clockwise from top left*) Anouk Aimée, 1950; Juliette Greco, singer, film actress and early beatnik, 1953; Camille Javal, a ballet student and model until she appeared on the front cover of *Elle* in 1952 and became Brigitte Bardot; and Jeanne Moreau, whose intense screen presence was sought after by directors of the New Wave cinema.

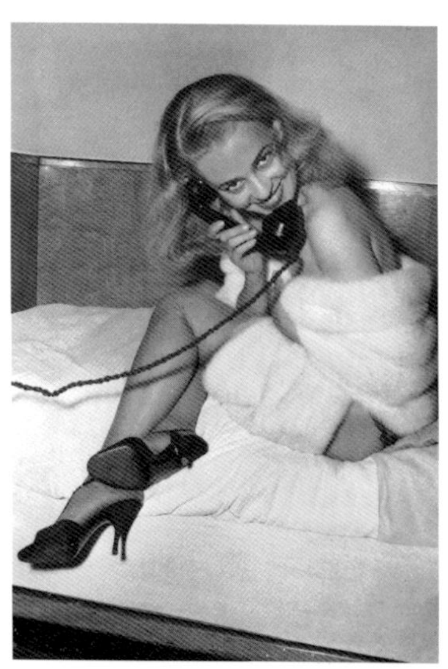

In the late 1950s a new type of film brought fame and success to many young directors within the French film industry. The films were called *nouvelle vague*, and their creators were students of the cinema. (*Above, left*) François Truffaut, 1955. (*Above, right*) Jean Renoir on the set of *Elena et les hommes*, 1956. (*Left*) Jean Cocteau and Jean Marais in a scene from *Le Testament d'Orphée*, 1960.

Two of the finest New Wave directors: (*above, right*) Louis Malle, with Brigitte Bardot on the set of *Viva Maria*, 1965; and Jean-Luc Godard, a contributor to the *Cahiers du Cinéma* from 1952 to 1965, and director of *A Bout de souffle* in 1959.

(*Above*) Simone Signoret and friends in a still from Jacques Becker's *Casque d'or*, 1952. Signoret was the wife of the singer and cabaret performer Yves Montand. (*Far left*) Montand with the legendary *chanteuse* Edith Piaf – 'The Sparrow'. (*Left*) Jean-Paul Belmondo with his co-star Jean Seberg on the set of *Echappement libre*, Boulogne, 11 February 1964.

One of the most successful – and most unusual – French films of the early 1960s was *Les Parapluies de Cherbourg*. The film was directed and written by Jacques Demy. One American critic wrote: 'We are told that in Paris the opening-night audience wept and the critics were ecstatic. It would have made a little more sense the other way round.' (*Right*) Two of the film's stars, Nino Castelnuovo and the more instantly recognisable Catherine Deneuve.

(*Opposite*) Roland Petit and Zizi Jeanmaire photographed by Baron on the set of Petit's ballet *Carmen*. In 1948 Petit founded his own company – Les Ballets de Paris de Roland Petit. (*Below, right*) Jeanmaire and Petit in the ballet *Carmen*, 1949. (*Above, left*) The French ballet dancer and film actress Leslie Caron, who starred in the Hollywood musicals *An American in Paris* and *Gigi*. (*Above, right*) Jean-Louis Bert, a dancer and street performer *extraordinaire*, leaps with the Eiffel Tower as backdrop.

22
THE FIFTH REPUBLIC 1965–1980

It began on a student campus, engineered by a small group of Anarchists, Trotskyists and Maoists. Police brutality and government ineptitude caused it to flare into a nationwide series of strikes, protests and demonstrations. What bound the protesters together was resentment: against government, family, authoritarianism, elitism in education, injustice and insecurity. Ten million workers went on strike – 150 million working days were lost. But the pendulum swung back. By the end of May 1968, de Gaulle had collected his thoughts and his courage, and his supporters, too, were on the march. At the demonstration in the Champs-Elysées (*right*) 50,000 were expected. Nearly 400,000 turned up.

Introduction

The republic tottered, but it did not fall. Students and workers occupied universities and factories, met in cafés, on the street, and even in the Odéon theatre in Paris in the furore of May 1968.

It began on the university campus in Nanterre, where students lived and worked in unacceptable conditions. Initially it was a protest, similar to many across the world, against the American presence in Vietnam. The sons and daughters of the bourgeoisie were rapidly joined by the working class, and matters spun out of control. The government was slow to react, not being quite sure what it was reacting to, and failing at first to grasp how serious a situation it faced. Right and centre-right had shared control of France for ten years, and there were those on the left who believed the entire system had to be overthrown if they were ever to hold legitimate power again. For many of the workers there was resentment that the good times of the consumer society had passed them by. France in 1968 was a country of low wages, poor working conditions, high unemployment and bad management.

Protest turned to riot, riot to near revolution. But de Gaulle produced a masterly performance on national television, and his Prime Minister, Georges Pompidou, offered wage increases of between 7 and 10 per cent. Fifty thousand people were expected to participate in a Gaullist demonstration in the Champs-Elysées on 30 May 1968 – in fact nearly 400,000 arrived. In the election of late June, the UDR (*Union des Démocrates pour la République*) won three hundred and fifty-eight out of a possible four hundred and eighty-five seats – the biggest right-wing victory in the history of the Fifth Republic.

The Republic survived, de Gaulle departed. Less than a year later he resigned and, less than two years later, he was dead. De Gaulle's life had spanned one of the most turbulent and uncomfortable periods in French history.

After his death, France entered a golden age. From 1967 until the 1980s, the French economy grew at an average annual rate of 3.3 per cent, considerably more than that of Germany or Britain. The part played by tourism in the national economy reached an all-time high. On the Mediterranean coast, notably at La Grande Motte, malaria-infested swamps were drained to provide land for new resorts. The Centre Pompidou opened in Paris in 1977. Les Halles were modernised. *Maisons de la culture* were opened throughout France as part of the programme of 'decolonising the provinces'. Skyscrapers appeared on the Paris skyline. The geode rolled into town, as did hundreds of thousands of protesting farmers, for between 1962 and 1975 the percentage of the French population able to find a living on the land had halved.

A new France emerged.

Within a year of the riots of 1968 de Gaulle was no longer President. Within two years, he was dead. At his own request no leaders, presidents or politicians attended his funeral at Colombey-les-Deux-Eglises, but tens of thousands of ordinary French men and women surged into the little village. (*Above, left*) A woman outside the Elysée Palace reads of the death of de Gaulle, 10 November 1970.

And so a new generation of French politicians took centre stage. Georges Pompidou (*opposite, below*) had long been an aide of de Gaulle, though he was sacked after 1968. He became President in 1969. François Mitterand (*right*) had to wait in opposition through the 1970s. From 1974 to 1976 Jacques Chirac (*below, left*) served as Prime Minister to President Valéry Giscard d'Estaing (*below, right*).

It was the age of issue politics – the old ideologies of right and left could no longer count on fervent loyalty. The 'cause', whatever it was, had clear and limited aims – to ban the bomb, save the whale, end a war, stop pollution. (*Left*) Women demonstrate in Paris for the right to abortion, 1976.

Among the most vociferous campaigners were the Gay Rights activists, led by the *Front Homosexual d'Action Révolutionnaire.* Anti-homosexual legislation had been passed by the Vichy government in the 1940s, and was still on the statute books. (*Above*) Lesbians from Nantes take part in a Gay Rights march, Paris 1980. (*Right*) Another section of the 1980 march.

It was an Anglo-French dream that became a reality, and ended as a nightmare. Concorde was the world's first supersonic airliner – beautiful, expensive, luxurious. (*Above, left*) The prototype Concorde 001 under construction at the Sud Aviation factory in Saint-Martin-Toulouse, March 1966. (*Above, right*) A model with Concorde hairstyle and make-up, at the time of Concorde's maiden flight.

(*Above*) The first British-built Concorde rolls out of the British Aircraft Corporation's assembly shed at Filton, Bristol, September 1968. Those passengers that could afford the sky-high fares queued for tickets. (*Opposite, below*) A line of hostesses from the airlines operating Concorde stand in front of a model of the plane, c. 1970. For thirty years the plane roared across the Atlantic. The end came in July 2000. Engine-damage upon take-off culminating in a fatal crash on the outskirts of Paris led to the grounding of Concorde. Beauty had become a beast. It was not a fairy-tale ending.

Technology claimed much for itself. Technologists gave glib reassurances. Nothing was too difficult, too daring, too dangerous. A succession of French governments embraced nuclear power. (*Top, left*) A nuclear power station in Finistère, Brittany, c. 1966. (*Top, right*) Less threatening, and ecologically far more sound, were towers built to conserve water, such as this one at Roissy-en-France, on the site of the new Paris airport. On the Mediterranean coast there were the wonders of La Grande Motte, a new holiday centre designed by Jean Balladuz (*above, left*), and the horrors of the avenues of dead trees in Marseilles – killed by car exhaust (*above, right*).

Others did what they could to protect the world by land and sea. One of the most dedicated was Jacques-Yves Cousteau (*right*), the underwater explorer who invented the aqualung and pioneered underwater television. He won Academy Awards for his films in the 1950s and early 1960s but his most valuable work was in conservation.

elf
Auchan

From the 1970s onwards, a series of brave and ambitious urban projects have reshaped the face of Paris. It began with the Centre Pompidou, followed by the Pyramid at the Louvre, the Opéra Bastille, and then La Défense. The Arche de la Défense was the centrepiece of a massive business and residential development on the western fringes of the city. The Arche itself was opened as part of the bicentennial celebrations of the Revolution of 1789, though work on the project began in the 1960s. (*Left*) An aerial view of La Défense. The cuboid arch leads directly to the Champs-Elysées.

Work began on the Centre Pompidou in the mid-1970s. The complex was designed by the Englishman Richard Rogers and the Italian Renzo Piano, but the concept was French architecture at its most daring. It was one of the first buildings in Europe to have its 'guts' on the outside – pipes, lifts, staircases, ducts and conduits. There were those who believed it would ruin the traditional charm of the city, but it certainly afforded tourists wonderful views (*left*). (*Above*) The Centre Pompidou, also known as Beaubourg, still under construction, though nearing completion, in 1977.

While the Centre Pompidou was being built, another part of Paris was in the throes of redevelopment. Les Halles had been the site of the most famous market in Paris since Roman times, and a place of public penance since the Middle Ages. Now it was to be redeveloped. The market moved and in its place appeared a hole (*above*), which became the most famous hole in France – with the possible exception of the caves at Lascaux. (*Right*) The new commercial development at Les Halles takes shape, 1976.

Markets, arches, centres and holes may come and go – Paris fashion continues to dominate the world's dress-shops and boutiques. New York, Milan and London may issue a sporting challenge from time to time, but the world has only one fashion capital. (*Above, left*) Pierre Cardin, in a photograph of 1965, with some of his creations (*above, right*) of the mid-1960s. The men are wearing winter coats made from fox and lynx fur, and sealskins. The decade of the Sixties was perhaps the last in which designers could use such materials without having either a qualm of conscience or a tin of red paint hurled through their window by animal rights protesters – or both.

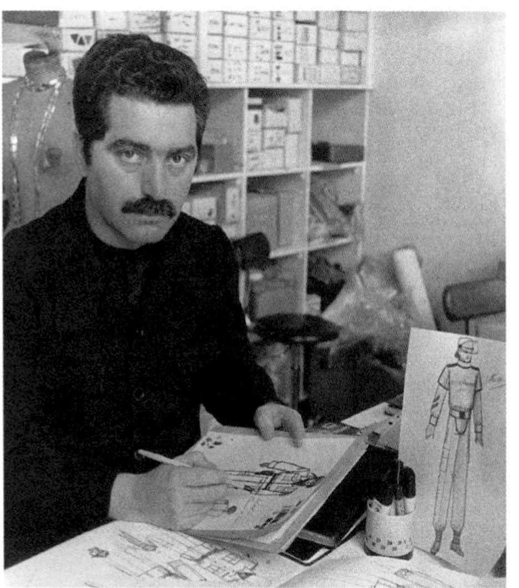

(*Above, left*) The designer Paco Rabanne at work in his studio, sketching new uniforms for the French army. It was a commission that suited him, for among his favourite materials are leather and steel. (*Above, right*) In less military style, a model wears a knitted coat with leather patches designed by Rabanne, 28 July 1966. (*Below, right*) Henri Donat Mathieu, known to the fashion world as Yves Saint Laurent, in his Paris boutique, 26 September 1966.

It is said that every Frenchman dreams of being like Gérard Depardieu (*opposite*) and with Catherine Deneuve. Depardieu made his film début in 1965 in *Le Beatnik et le minet*, though his greatest successes came in the 1980s. Catherine Deneuve and her sister Françoise Dorleac (*above, left*) starred together in *Les Demoiselles de Rochefort* in 1966. (*Left*) Deneuve with her husband, the English photographer David Bailey, 18 August 1965. Deneuve and Bailey were married from 1965 to 1970. In 1963 Deneuve and Roger Vadim (*above, right*) had had a child. In 1972 Deneuve and Marcello Mastroianni had a child. The life of a film star is not easy.

Throughout the 1960s and 1970s Pierre Boulez (*above, left*) was the *enfant terrible* of French classical music, but he established a worldwide reputation as composer and conductor. One of the most respected conductors in the world until his death in 1968 was Charles Munch (*above, right*). Darius Milhaud (*left*) was one of the most prolific and successful of modern composers. His photograph here is by Erich Auerbach.

Mass appeal. (*Clockwise from top left*) The French musician Serge Gainsbourg with the English actress Jane Birkin, Paris, 27 August 1969; French singer Françoise Hardy filming John Frankenheimer's *Grand Prix* at Brands Hatch, 12 July 1966; Charles Aznavour with the fruits of the song *She*, September 1974; and the singer and entertainer Sacha Distel, 22 February 1971.

23
TOWARDS THE MILLENNIUM 1980–2000

The forty years of *grands travaux* in Paris continued through the 1980s and 1990s. One of the most controversial was the Pyramid at the Louvre (*right*). French presidents like to initiate a prestigious work of architecture which will remain after they are gone – a permanent record of their power and influence. The Pyramid, designed by I.M. Pei, was the inspiration of François Mitterrand. It was given a mixed reception. There were those who said it was the right construction, but in the wrong place, and those who said it was the wrong construction in the right place. And there were many who said...

Introduction

François Mitterrand was President of France from 1981 to 1995. No other French politician of modern times has remained so long in power. In 1991 Edith Cresson became France's first woman Prime Minister. There were hopes that the new partnership would breathe new life into French politics and a spirit of optimism ran through France – even the *Marseillaise* was played at a more stirring tempo.

The Géode, centrepiece of the Parc de la Villette on the outskirts of Paris, and the Pyramid facing the Louvre were two geometrical manifestations of the new technology that was to be at the heart of a new France. Futuroscope opened in Poitiers, giving millions of tourists and visitors a glimpse of life to come in the next millennium. The Antigone project in Montpellier gave residents of Languedoc-Roussillon a flashback to an epoch of classical architecture in one of the fastest-growing cities in France.

Sleek *trains à grande vitesse* (TGV) sped through the ex-pat-English-infested French countryside. French politicians and engineers managed to persuade the perfidious English to complete a two-hundred-year-old project and the Channel Tunnel opened in 1994. National electronic communications were revolutionised by the introduction of the Minitel system in 1982, which proved more popular with those seeking romance than those clinching deals. EuroDisney opened shakily, but the fairy-tale land went into fairy-tale profit after a couple of years and all concerned have lived happily ever after.

In sport it was a progress of almost uninterrupted triumph. French footballers won the World Cup in 1998, and were European champions in 2000. French tennis-players won the Davis Cup in 1999. In the same year, French rugby footballers won their World Cup. French masters of bat and ball (cricketers) even managed to beat a visiting English team of flannelled fools.

As the economy grew, France changed. In 1945 two-thirds of the labour force had been engaged in agriculture. By 1995 two-thirds were employed in the service sector. Villages emptied, cities filled. The arrival of many immigrants, including 3 million Arab workers, fuelled much of the race hatred of Jean-Marie Le Pen and the *Front National*. In opposition, Harlem Désir and others created *SOS Racisme* in 1984 and ran American civil rights-style protests against racial injustice in France.

On the way to a new millennium, France celebrated the two-hundredth anniversary of the Revolution of 1789, fought to maintain some of its threatened culture against the encroachments of the English language and the American burger, and sought to promote a new European consciousness. With a fusillade of fireworks, France exploded into the 21st century.

One of the longest-lasting, and most successful, Communist Party leaders in Europe is Georges Marchais (*above*). He became General Secretary of the French Communist Party in 1972, steering its fortunes through the perils of the 1980s and 1990s. He contested the presidential election in 1981. Jacques Delors (*left*) was Mitterrand's Minister for Finance in the 1980s. Few loved his austerity measures, and he was passed over for the post of Prime Minister in 1984. He went on to become President of the European Commission in 1985, thereby gaining further unpopularity.

François Mitterrand (*above, left*) and Jacques Chirac (*above, right*) were forced into a 'co-habitation' when Mitterrand lost his Socialist majority in the National Assembly in 1985. Mitterrand's wiles proved too much for Chirac, and Mitterrand was re-elected President in May 1988. In his second term Mitterrand fell out with Michel Rocard and appointed Edith Cresson (*right*), with whom he had a far better relationship, as France's first woman Prime Minister in May 1991.

Socialists and conservatives jockeyed for power in the market-led years of the 1980s and 1990s, but a sinister figure lurked in the wings of French politics. Jean-Marie Le Pen (*above*) embraced the far right with a series of racist and anti-immigrant policies and promises. (*Left*) Le Pen's three daughters cheer an election victory for their father's *Front National*, 16 March 1986.

The *Front National* polarised French politics, stirring up a great deal of hatred and fear as well as opposition. (*Above*) A group of anti-Fascist protesters at a demonstration in Paris, February 1993. (*Right*) A more personal statement on the same demonstration by visiting members of the British Anti-Nazi League. The effigy of Le Pen hangs from a pretend lamp-post.

On an old industrial site by the banks of the Canal d'Ourcq, to the north-east of Paris, rose another vision – this time initiated by Giscard d'Estaing. This was the Parc de la Villette, a mixture of open space and cathedral to modern science and technology. (*Above*) The footbridge to the Parc de la Villette. (*Right*) The *folie* of the Parc de la Villette by night.

The blossoming of so many public projects in France during the 1980s and 1990s might suggest that there was plenty of money available to fund them. In a way this was true. In 1995 France was still the fourth greatest economic power in the world, and had a record balance of payments surplus of 85 billion francs. France was also one of the highest-taxed nations in the world – 41.1 per cent of GNP at the end of 1994. But at least the money went to good causes. One of the most expensive and most magnificent was the Opéra Bastille (*left*), home of the French National Opera, designed by Carlos Ott and opened in 1989. (*Above*) The grand auditorium of the Opéra Bastille.

Not everything happens in Paris. The European Park of the Moving Image (*above and opposite, above*), known as Futuroscope, was built just north of Poitiers. Its theme is visual communication technology in ultra-modern buildings – a glance into the years to come. The Antigone project in Montpellier (*left and opposite, below*) is more of a backward glance at the past. In 1979 Georges Freche, mayor of Montpellier, commissioned the Catalan architect Ricardo Bofill to design a residential development for Montpellier's fast-growing population.

Not all developments were entirely new. The old Gare d'Orsay, across the river from the Jardin des Tuileries, was gutted (*above*) and became one of the most beautiful (and most richly stocked) art galleries in the world in the 1980s. At much the same time French rail travel was revolutionised by the *trains à grande vitesse*, TGV (*opposite, above and below*) – sleek, supercharged streamliners that connected the major cities of France.

(*Clockwise from top left*) Bernard Hinault takes part in the 1986 World Cycling Championships, Denver, USA; Richard Virenque celebrates his victory in the Courchevel–Morzine stage of the 2000 Tour de France, 18 July; Alain Prost, c. 1985; and Laurent Jalabert shows his relief at gaining the yellow jersey after the second stage of the Tour, 3 July 1995.

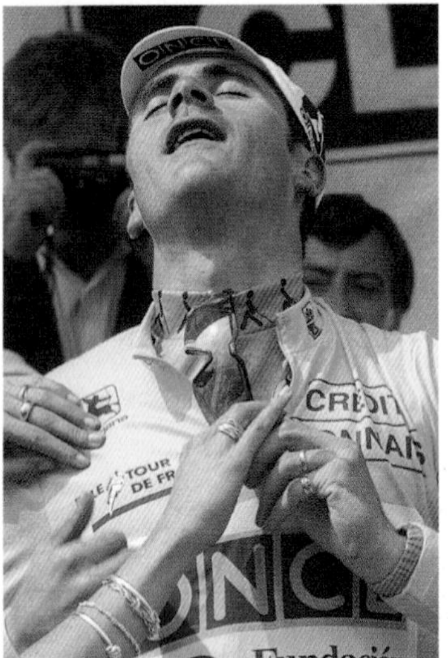

(*Above, left*) Michel Platini holds the European Nations trophy after France defeat Spain 2-0 in the European Nations Cup Final, June 1984. (*Above, right*) French captain Didier Deschamps lifts the Jules Rimet Cup after the World Cup Final, 12 July 1998. France beat Brazil 3-0. (*Right*) Zinedine Zidane, FIFA World Player of the Year 1999.

Index

Acknowledgements

All other images in this book not specifically credited below are from Getty Images.

Hulton|Archive: Ernst Haas Studio: pp 48 and jacket, 613 (l), 777 (bl); John Kobal Foundation Archive: p. 778 (tr); David Newell Smith/The *Observer*: p. 780 (tl); Richard Mildenhall/The *Observer*: p. 791 (br); Steve Eason: p. 815; Eamonn McCabe/The *Observer*: p. 824 (br and jacket).

Stone: George Hailing: p. 250; Pascal Crapet: pp 798-9; Lineka: p. 800 (b); Cosmo Condina: pp 808-9; Simeone Huber: p. 817.

Allsport: Allsport UK: pp 824 (tl), 825 (tl); Tom Able-Green: p. 824 (tr); Pascal Rondeau: p. 824 (bl); Ben Radford: p. 825 (tl); Mark Thompson: p. 825 (b).

© **Könemann Verlagsgesellschaft mbH, Köln/Achim Bednorz:** pp 49, 69, 74-5, 106-7, 112-13, 124-5, 134-5, 165, 265, 267 (r), 332 (tl), 373 and jacket, 375, 376-7, 378, 424-5.

Bayeux Tapestry photographs: pp 50-51 by special permission of the town of Bayeux.

Giraudon: pp 22-3, 84, 86-7, 108, 136, 140-41, 146-7, 156 (b), 158-9, 162, 195, 242, 245, 457, 494-5, 527, 578-9, 601, 604-5 (l), 609, 611, 656, 658 (t), 659.

Sipa Press: Frilet: p. 792 (b); Aral: p. 793 (b); Laski: p. 800 (t); Cinello: p. 801; Chamussy: p. 813 (b); Kessler: p. 814 (t); Baumann Arnaud: p. 816; Moatti/Kleinefenn: p. 818; Moatti: p. 819; Frilet: pp 820 (b), 821 (b); Rossier: pp 820 (t), 821 (t); Frédéric Lert: p. 823 (t), (br); Lacroix: p. 823 (bl).

All jacket images are included in the book. Those not specifically acknowledged above are from Getty Images.

Maps, pp viii-xvii © Studio für Landkartentechnik, Norderstedt.

gettyimages

701 North 34th Street, Seattle, WA 98103

This book was created by Getty Images, Inc, the leading e-commerce provider of imagery and related products. For more information on Getty Images and its market-leading brands, please visit the company's website at ‹http://www.gettyimages.com›. Picture sources for this book include:

Hulton|Archive

Hulton|Archive is widely regarded as one of the finest collections of photography in the world. It contains over 40 million images and more than 300 separate collections, and includes original material from leading press agencies such as Keystone and the *Daily Express.*

stone

Stone creates exceptional contemporary photography for the advertising and design industries. Working with more than 900 leading photographers worldwide, Stone's original conceptual photography identifies and anticipates trends through extensive industry research, representing universal subjects in unusual ways.

ALLSPORT

Allsport was founded in 1968 and has been at the forefront of sports photography for more than 30 years. The Allsport library is now the most comprehensive single collection of sports photography in the world, employing the world's greatest award-winning photographers. Allsport photography is distributed via a network of agents in more than 40 countries worldwide.

Additional sources also include:

Giraudon is one of the oldest and finest collections of art imagery in the world, offering an unsurpassed wealth of subject-matter and depth of content. Available in print or digital form, the images in the Giraudon collection may be easily accessed and are specifically available for commercial use.

How to buy or license a picture from this book

Picture licensing information

For information about licensing any image in this book, please telephone **+ 44 (0)20 7579 5731**, fax: **44 (0)20 7266 3154** or e-mail **chris.barwick@getty-images.com**

Online access

For information about Getty Images and for access to individual collections go to **www.hultongetty.com.**
Go to **www.gettyone.com** for creative and conceptually oriented imagery.

Buying a print

For details on how to purchase exhibition quality prints contact The Hulton Getty Picture Gallery, telephone **+ 44 (0)20 7276 4525** or e-mail **hulton.gallery@getty-images.com**